Designer
UNIVERSE

Designer UNIVERSE

Intelligent Design and the Existence of God

JIMMY H. DAVIS and HARRY L. POE

BROADMAN
&HOLMAN
PUBLISHERS

Nashville, Tennessee

0–8054–2447–4

Published by Broadman & Holman Publishers,
Nashville, Tennessee

Subject Heading: SCIENCE AND FAITH

Unless otherwise noted, Scripture quotations are from the
Holy Bible, New International Version, copyright © 1973,
1978, 1984 by International Bible Society.

1 2 3 4 5 7 8 9 10 07 06 05 04 03 02

For

our students

past, present, and future

who will continue the dialogue

about the Designer Universe

CONTENTS

ILLUSTRATIONS

PREFACE

IN JUNE 2000, two important conferences examined the idea that the universe bears evidence of design. The conference Evidence for Design: Finding New Ground for Dialogue took place June 23–27, 2000, under the auspices of the John Templeton Foundation's Science and Religion Course Award program administered by the Center for Theology and the Natural Sciences at Berkeley. This conference was held in Chicago through the facilitation of the Zygon Center for Religion and Science which is a partnership program of the Lutheran School of Theology at Chicago and the Center for Advanced Study in Religion and Science. Another conference, Design and Its Critics, took place June 22–24, 2000, at Concordia University in Mequon, Wisconsin. This conference sought to bring together both proponents and critics of Intelligent Design to make their best cases.

The two conferences approached the subject from different perspectives. The Concordia conference included critics of Intelligent Design, yet the conference provided a forum for advocates of Intelligent Design. Leading lights of the Intelligent Design Movement took part, including Michael Behe, William Dembski, and Paul Nelson. The Chicago conference did not include any atheists on its program, but it did not advocate an intelligent design position either. Longtime participants in the science and religion dialogue took part, including Ian Barbour, Owen Gingerich, and Philip Hefner. Ironically, the Chicago meeting had no representatives of the intelligent design movement, nor did the Concordia meeting have representatives of the Christian scientific/theological community that criticize this movement. Despite the irony both meetings were quite appropriate for their purposes. The

xiii

Concordia meeting sought to deal with objections to design from the perspective of those who do not believe in a Designer. The Chicago meeting sought to explore other ways of conceiving design than the way suggested by the intelligent design movement.

Due to the limitations imposed on us by the laws of physics, we could only attend one of the meetings. We had explored the views of the leading figures in the Intelligent Design Movement by bringing the mountain to us. Through the Staley lectureship we were able to bring Michael Behe and William Dembski to Union University. Through a generous grant from the American Scientific Affiliation funded by the John Templeton Foundation, we were able to bring Paul Nelson and Jay Budziszewski to Union. These men graciously allowed us time alone to interview them on the question of design. As a result, we chose to attend the Chicago meeting to hear a different voice on design. We experienced the same courtesy in conversation with Barbour, Gingerich, and Hefner.

The two meetings seemed to be striving toward different objectives. The Concordia meeting seemed to strive toward offering compelling evidence that the universe can only be explained in terms of Intelligent Design and the existence of an Intelligent Designer. The Intelligent Design Movement is concerned that people believe in God as the cause of the universe and everything in it. They hope to demonstrate the relationship between God and nature through traditional scientific empiricism. Their argument is with Naturalists, who do not believe such a Being exists.

The Chicago meeting seemed to strive toward identifying alternative ways of reconciling modern scientific understandings of nature with the existence of a Creator. Besides a more traditional theism of Gingerich and an interest in process by Barbour, the Chicago group also heard a feminist perspective from Mary Hunt and an interfaith perspective from Ghulam-Haider Aasi. To a certain degree the Chicago meeting reflected a concern for the implications of design for people of faith. Both Hunt and Hefner spoke in terms of how people will respond to the world in which they live. Hunt voiced a concern for balance in the cosmos while Hefner argued for thinking of one's place in the "project" that makes up the cosmos. Another theme became apparent in the course of the four-day conference. Participants seemed reluctant to think of God as a designer because design suggested a finished product. A finished product suggested a limit to human freedom. The eighteenth-century versions of the design argument sought to explain the design of the universe in determinate terms that corresponded to the determinacy of Newtonian physics. We now see that at least one stream of theologians and scientists wants any view of design to reflect a quantum view of indeterminacy. It is the old problem of tying theology too closely to a replaceable scientific interpretation that may slip out of fashion and take the theology with it.[1]

The two conferences represent a snapshot of the diverse perspectives one encounters when thinking about the universe as a place that bears evidence of design. The two conferences do not even exhaust the major positions found within traditional Christianity, much less the major religions of the world. The Reformed tradition, which has played such a significant role in Western culture and American society in particular, has never regarded "proofs" for the existence of God favorably. The attempt to provide empirical evidence for God meets as much resistance from a good Calvinist as it does from a good Naturalist. Karl Barth, the Swiss neoorthodox theologian who had such an influence on American Protestant theology in the twentieth century, stood squarely in the Reformed tradition. The success of neoorthodoxy explains in part the resistance to the brand of natural theology that the Intelligent Design Movement explores.

This book does not propose to break new ground so much as it hopes to make some established pathways clear. We expect our audience will be primarily drawn from Christians who take an interest in the relationship of modern science to their biblical faith. Agnostics and atheists may read the book. People of other religious faiths or people with a nontraditional view of Christianity may read the book. By and large, however, we expect most of our readers will share a broad though common faith with different denominational and theological expressions. We write from the perspective of faith. Not only do we believe that the universe was designed, but we also know the Designer. How compelling is the evidence, however, for someone who does not know the Designer? Can someone come to know the Designer by observing the design? Does the evidence compel only one conclusion about the origin of the design?

This book explores why the notion of the design of the universe should suddenly reappear at the end of the twentieth century after its supposed demise at the hands of Darwinian naturalism. The first three chapters of the book explore the different ways in which people have considered design over the last three thousand years or so. While the brief study is not exhaustive, it does provide a condensed overview of many of the major positions that have influenced the course of thought in the West. We mention briefly how different religions and philosophies have thought about design. We then explore how philosophical views have influenced both the theology and the science of the West.

Chapters 4 through 6 explore three major realms of scientific study in which major breakthroughs have provided renewed speculation on design. The chapters explore cosmology, math and physics, and chemistry and biology. In the course of this survey we introduce the new terminology of the design discussions: anthropic principles, irreducible complexity, and specified complexity. The discussion suggests that science has been quite successful at describing processes but has failed at explaining origins.

We have attempted to keep the technical discussions to a minimum. Unfortunately, it is impossible to discuss this subject without some basic knowledge of the scientific, philosophical, and theological issues at stake. By writing at a basic level, we have failed to give adequate depth to our subject for the well-informed professional. We hope we have succeeded in making the material accessible, however, to those who lack training in these fields. While the molecular biologist may consider our biology section thin, we hope they will benefit from an equally thin treatment of the philosophy.

ACKNOWLEDGMENTS

WE WISH TO EXPRESS our appreciation to Len Goss, our acquisitions editor at Broadman & Holman, who asked us to consider writing this book as a sequel to our last book, *Science and Faith: An Evangelical Dialogue.* John Landers, our project editor, worked tirelessly to make the final product clean and readable. This topic is one we would have enjoyed pursuing in length in the last book, but space did not permit; therefore, we appreciate the opportunity that Broadman & Holman has given us with the present project. It has been a pleasure to work again with Jonathan Gillette, who illustrated the book, and Melissa Mann, who burned the CD of our illustrations. Our research could not have been completed without the conscientious aid of Paul Sorrell in the Emma Waters Summar Library of Union University who secured many rare volumes for us through interlibrary loan. We also appreciate the cheerful work of our student research assistant, Tammy Meyers.

One of the great pleasures of writing this book has been the many conversations about this subject that we have had with guests at Union University and at meetings elsewhere. In particular we wish to express our appreciation to Arthur Holmes, Michael Behe, Ian Barbour, William Dembski, Owen Gingerich, Paul Nelson, Robert Russell, John Brooke, Jay Budziszewski, Gayle Woloschak, Alesia Maltz, Mark Noll, John Albright, Richard Randolph, Harold McKone, and Mil Thompson. We also have relied upon the continuing conversation and insights of our colleagues with whom we teach and work at Union University; notably, Brad Greene, Greg Thornbury, Randall Bush, Wayne Wofford, Michael McMahon, James Huggins, and David Ward. It would be difficult to carry on a writing project of this nature without the support and encouragement of David Dockery, our president, Carla Sanderson, our provost, and Barbara McMillin, our dean. Finally, we express our gratitude to Pam Dennis who also read the manuscript and offered many stylistic suggestions.

A project of this sort could never be completed in the course of normal business hours. We have taken our work home to our families, who have given us more than support and encouragement. Our wives, Christine Menzel and Mary Anne Poe, have read the manuscript thoroughly and made numerous suggestions for its improvement in addition to correcting earlier drafts. We could not have completed this project without their presence and interest. We proudly acknowledge their contribution to the book.

Jimmy H. Davis
Harry L. Poe

Jackson, Tennessee

CHAPTER ONE

LOOKING FOR THE LABEL

Designer labels have made their mark in popular culture and the consumer economy. The youth culture in particular pays attention to brand names. The designer label often determines which pair of blue jeans or tennis shoes a young person buys. Clothes that seem indistinguishable to the casual older adult observer bear no resemblance at all for the person who is only concerned with the label. At any point in time, one designer name brand is more popular than another for no particular reason.

Indulgent parents go along with this pop fad approach to buying clothes and other goods, often paying outrageous sums for items that have nothing to commend them above the competition except for the designer label. In an age of media hype and image building, the price a person pays for goods may have no significant relationship to the quality of goods. This trend represents a radical departure from the historic reason for placing the name of the manufacturer on its goods.

My grandparents went through the Depression. Even though they survived with their home intact and lived until 1980, they never got over the challenge of living with so little disposable income. They managed their money carefully and saved a little each month. They took care of the things they had and knew how to make things last. If something was broken, they fixed it. With what has come to be called a "Depression mind-set," however, they always bought the best-quality goods they could find. In the long run it paid to buy the best quality because in those days quality meant that something was made to last. Quality meant both excellence of design and manufacture. In those days people went by the slogan "You get what you pay for!"

When craftsmanship and price had a direct relationship, the label on a product meant a great deal. The label did not appear on the front of a shirt for the neighbors to see. Instead, it was discreetly sewn into the fabric where only the wearer of the shirt could see it. The neighbors saw only the quality.

DURING THE LAST DECADE of the twentieth century, scientists and theologians began to use the word *design* when speaking of the universe. People had used this word or at least this idea to speak of the universe for thousands of years in different parts of the world. Most scientists and theologians in the West, however, rarely used this idea after the mid-1800s. Why, after all this time, has the idea of design of the universe and everything in it once again come into the conversation of scientists and theologians?

The idea of design provides a way of coming to the idea of God from the back door. The idea of design suggests the existence of a designer. If the universe actually was designed, how did it come to be designed? More importantly for personal beings, if the universe actually was designed, who designed it?

It does not take a philosopher, scientist, or theologian to discuss the idea of design. People around the world do it every day. In fact, even after the academic community of scientists and theologians had discarded the idea of design, the overwhelming number of laypeople in the West clung to it. The great philosophers of the last twenty-five hundred years, going back to Plato and Aristotle, developed elaborate logical arguments to prove the existence of God by appealing to the idea of design. The average person, however, discusses the same idea without the need of such a carefully thought-out argument.

Plato often used dialogues to present his philosophical arguments. He set the philosophical conversation in the context of a conversation between two people so that he could present both sides of the question and systematically answer the objections to his argument. When most people first encounter the design idea, they hear it in the form of a dialogue. I do not recall how old I was when I first heard the idea of design explained to me, but I clearly recall the terms of the explanation.

"Momma," I asked, "where did the sky come from?"

"God made the sky," my mother replied.

"Momma," I continued, "where did the sun come from?"

"God made the sun," my mother replied.

"Momma," I persisted, "where did the trees come from?"

"God made the trees," my mother patiently answered. "God made everything."

In its simplest and most common form, the idea of design is not an argument to prove the existence of God. It is an explanation of who God *is*. It assumes the existence of God and proceeds to explain how God relates to everything else. But people talk about the idea in more sophisticated terms in the everyday as well.

Before taking the path that would eventually lead me to writing books that deal with theological themes, I had intended to pursue a career in law. In the early 1970s I served as law clerk for a year to Fletcher Mann, a brilliant trial lawyer in South Carolina. Mr. Mann was involved in what was then the largest antitrust suit ever tried in the United States. It involved many textile mills primarily in the South and in Europe. In the midst of the suit which dragged on for years with hundreds of millions of dollars at stake, Mr. Mann turned to me and mused:

I remember the most peaceful, serene day I ever spent. It was an early fall day, and I was with your parents at your grandmother's mountain house. I was stretched out in that big Pawley Island rope hammock they had on the front porch. The sound of the river rushing over the rocks around three sides of the house was like music. From there I could look straight up the Jones Gap with those mountains in full color on both sides. The temperature was just perfect, and the air smelled so sweet and fresh. I remember thinking, *On a day like this, how can anyone doubt the existence of a great and good Supreme Being?*

The discussion suggests that it is easy to believe in a great, good creator when everything looks beautiful. The discussion seems almost glib because it ignores those days when the storms rage and everything lies in darkness. What happens to the discussion on those days? The problem of evil, pain, and suffering inevitably raises its head when scientists, theologians and philosophers discuss the question of design. Note the context in which Mr. Mann raised the question of design. Everything was not beautiful and sweet smelling. He was living out of a suitcase in Rock Hill, South Carolina, eating a steady diet of motel food, enduring an endless contest of wits with a stable of high-priced lawyers from New York. The litigation had gone on for years and would go on for years more. It was in the midst of the strife and the darkness that he remembered an experience that became as real again as the moment it had occurred.

Mr. Mann did not raise the question of design to prove the existence of God to me. At that point the question of design did not involve the theoretical idea of what kind of God exists. Instead, he was reliving the experience of having met the Designer on a balmy fall day in the mountains. It did not matter what might happen on any other day. The Designer penetrated his soul and gave him a peace that he could draw upon for the rest of his life. He had experienced the personal implications of the existence of a Designer who relates personally to what he has designed. To that extent, what he had to say was not intended to persuade me or change me. On the other hand, on a lousy fall day in Rock Hill, the observation did persuade him and change him. The idea of design sometimes has a purely personal quality to it.

When scientists, philosophers, and theologians speak of design, they usually think in terms of a formal proof for the existence of God. They may digress and discuss the possibility of ever proving anything. Then they explain they mean to show a preponderance of evidence that would demonstrate the strongest possible probability that something may be so. The first time I ever heard such a formal proof for the existence of God, it did not come from a Christian theologian, philosopher, or scientist. In fact, it did not come from a Christian at all.

I first heard the design argument for the existence of God from Swami Chinmayananda. He had formerly had a successful law practice in India before his experience of enlightenment during a mountain retreat. The year was 1972 on the campus of the University of South Carolina. I chaired the Lectures Series Committee of the University Union, and my committee had agreed to help the Indian students by providing travel expenses to allow the Hindu teacher to visit Carolina and give a lecture. As the chair of the committee, I was invited to eat with Swami Chinmayananda and the Indian students. He was a charming and engaging man who spoke with me for several hours. He agreed to give one public lecture for the student body but devoted the rest of his time to the students from India.

He chose as his topic the theme "Why God?" The provocative title was intended to stir interest. The large lecture hall in Currell College was almost full to hear Swami Chinmayananda explain what he meant by "Why God?" He proceeded to give what I now know to be three of the classical proofs for the existence of God: the argument from first cause, the argument from necessary being, and the argument from design. We will explore these proofs later.

He presented the arguments quite clearly with wit and contemporary illustrations, but I learned several years later that they were the same arguments Thomas Aquinas had elaborated seven hundred years earlier. These arguments of Thomas Aquinas were the same ones Aristotle had elaborated sixteen hundred years before that. Aristotle, Thomas Aquinas, and Swami Chinmayananda had radically different understandings of God. Aristotle and Swami Chinmayananda did not share the biblical concept of creation held by Thomas Aquinas. Yet all three found the idea of design compelling.

They lived, thought, worked, taught, and wrote in quite different cultures, times, and places. Nonetheless, design stood inescapably obvious to them and helped them make sense of their world. In spite of many varied understandings of the nature of the universe and the nature of God, some understanding of design forms an aspect of most of the world's great cultures past and present.

A WORLD OF VIEWS

People do not always mean the same thing when they speak of design, just as they do not always mean the same thing when they use the word *God*. Before exploring why the design argument would reappear after so many thinkers assumed it had been stone cold dead for one hundred years, it may prove helpful to understand how other people in different times and places have viewed design.

People living in the West tend to make enormous assumptions about what "everyone knows" or what "other people think." In terms of design, people with quite different views of reality have recognized design in nature, yet they have given different accounts of it. Judaism, Islam, and Christianty share a common understanding of why nature might appear to have characteristics of design. The people of these faiths believe that a personal being created all of physical reality with a purpose for all things from beginning to end. The Bible and the Qur'an relate God's relationship to the physical order as its Creator. These three religions have different perspectives on the person of Jesus Christ and the way to salvation, but they agree about God as Creator. Even people in the West who do not have personal faith in God have tended to have at least a general awareness of the view of God and creation held by these three great monotheistic religions. While the Christian perspective will be discussed in more detail later, several other religious perspectives will help to illustrate that the idea of design is not simply a culturally derived concept of the West.

Hinduism

As I mentioned earlier, the first person to explain to me the design argument for the existence of God was a Hindu teacher. I did not know much about Hinduism when I heard him speak, but his lecture seems all the more fascinating now that I have studied a little about Hinduism. Unlike the three monotheistic religions, Hinduism does not conceive of God as a personal self-conscious being. Westerners often think of Hinduism as a polytheistic religion, but this view is not quite accurate. Hindus do believe in many gods as they conceive of gods. They do not believe in many gods in the way Christians conceive of God. Instead of the word *god* it may be more helpful to use the Hindu word *Brahman*. Brahman is Absolute Reality. Brahman is everything physical and everything spiritual, because ultimately there is no difference between the physical and the spiritual. These are merely two different expressions of Brahman. Whereas Christians, Jews, and Muslims believe that people are made in the image of God, Hindus believe that people are God or an expression of Brahman.

Behind what we think of as the objective, physical reality of a person or a tree or a solar system or a pebble lies the Absolute Reality of Brahman. The person, the solar system, the pebble, and the tree have the same ultimate nature as expressions of Brahman. They have no separate and individual identity distinct from one another. The great Jewish philosopher Martin Buber made a significant contribution to Western thought in his discussion of the "I-it" relationship. These distinctions are ultimately meaningless in Hindu thought. Hindu thought has a different expression to describe the unity of all things as expressions of Brahman: "That thou art."

Walk barefoot along a sandy beach on a summer afternoon with the sun beating hot upon your face, the waves of the ocean crashing on the shore, a gentle breeze breaking the heat, and a seagull screeching overhead. Feel the sand between your toes. That thou art. See the glare of the sun millions of miles away. That thou art. Hear the waves as they scatter their spray. That thou art. Feel the coolness of the breeze. That thou art. Watch the gull as it darts and dives for a fish. Thou art both the gull and the fish! All is One. All is Brahman.

Though all is One, not every expression of Brahman has experienced the enlightenment necessary to realize their own unity with Brahman. Every form of life, whether human, animal, or plant, undergoes an endless series of rebirths or reincarnations as other forms of life unless the series of births is broken by enlightenment. The law of Karma determines the future destiny. According to the law of Karma the form of one's next birth is determined by one's behavior in the present life. Whatever one experiences in the present, whether good or evil, pleasure or suffering, is the consequence of actions in a previous existence.

The ultimate goal of Hindu faith comes in freedom from the endless series of death and reincarnation. Three principal "schools" or systems of thought have developed through the centuries to help people experience the bliss that comes from knowing one's identity with Brahman: *Karma Marga* (Path of Duties), *Jnana Marga* (Path of Knowledge), and *Bhakti Marga* (Path of Devotion).[1] The *Karma Marga* involves keeping the rituals and ceremonies, dietary laws, and ethical values of the Hindu tradition. The *Jnana Marga* provides an intellectual approach to breaking the series of reincarnation through attaining the bliss that comes through realizing the illusion of physical reality. By far the most popular of the three ways to liberation, however, is the *Bhakti Marga*. This path follows personal devotion to one of the thousands of gods or deities known to Hinduism.

If all is One, then how do Hindus think of the deities whom they worship and adore? The philosophical understanding of the unity of all things as the Absolute Reality is a fairly recent aspect of Hinduism, perhaps no more than two thousand years old. By comparison one might think of the incarnation of God in Christ as a fairly recent aspect of

Abrahamic faith. The ancient stories of the deities continued as an aspect of Hinduism after the understanding of deity changed. Rather than an earlier understanding of separate or independent beings, later Hinduism tends to see the deities as the expression of Brahman in purist form, not subject to the Karma of reincarnation.

Although Hindus may show devotion to as many as 330 million household deities, three great deities receive the greatest honor and attention: Brahma, Shiva, and Vishnu. Veneration of these gods predates the Arayan invasion of northern India thirty-five hundred years ago that resulted in one of the earliest periods of development in Hindu thought. Shiva is known as the Destroyer, Vishnu is known as the Preserver, and Brahma is known as the Creator. Of the three, Brahma receives the least attention, though he is probably the most ancient of the deities.[2]

As Creator, Brahma might be thought of as the most obsolete or unnecessary of the deities in modern Hindu thought. Ancient epics and other sacred writings described the creation of the physical world in varied ways. Deities of the Vedic or early Hindu period included Varuna, the sky god who created the universe and maintains it by ritual order. Agni, the god of fire, produced humanity and sustains creation as mediator between humanity and the universe. As Hinduism embraced the idea of the One, the universe came to be viewed as the result of a human sacrifice by Purusha, from whom all the gods came.[3] In time the view developed that all reality emanates from the One. The view that all reality consists of a single unity is referred to as *monism*.

From this brief and superficial overview, we can see that Hinduism as a whole and individual Hindus may tolerate a wide-ranging understanding of deity. Within this wide tradition, what did Swami Chinmayananda mean when he used the design argument to prove the existence of God within a Hindu understanding of God? In a sense he argued for design without an actual creation! Here we should distinguish between the universe as the creation of God and the expression of

Brahman. Creation implies an object separate from the Creator. Creation is an artistic idea that takes different forms. We may think of the artistic expression of the potter who fashions a lump of clay into a beautiful vessel in which the mind of the artist skillfully takes shape in physical form. We may also think of the creative expression of the dancer whose body moves gracefully into a thousand different shapes before the dance is done. The monotheism of Judaism, Islam, and Christianity involves faith in the potter, while the monism of Hinduism involves faith in the dancer. The pot and the potter are separate, but the dance and the dancer are inseparable.

Observation: In the discussion about evidence of intelligent design of the universe, we do well to recognize that different groups in the conversation mean different things when they say "design." Just as *God* means different things to people of different religions, *design* means different things to different groups. This is not merely a matter of different religious perspectives. An engineer will understand design in a way different from a biologist. Design may have a more mechanical quality or a more artistic quality. It may mean a sense of order or purpose. It may mean a recognizable pattern. As we explore the question, we will begin to see that design itself may be as elusive as God.

A-theistic Religions
Two great religions have come out of Hinduism that take one step beyond the monism of Hinduism. Buddhism and Jainism both deny the existence of a creator God and Absolute Being. While Hinduism allows for the continuing adoration of and devotion to individual gods, most forms of Buddhism and Jainism deny the existence of these beings. Worship and prayer to such deities serves no purpose. The path to liberation from the endless cycle of birth, death, and rebirth comes through the denial of the individual self, usually through an ascetic regimen. More important, however, is the ethical approach to life, known as the eightfold path in Buddhism and the twelve vows of Jainism.

Like Hinduism, Buddhism and Jainism have a major concern for how one escapes the law of Karma and the otherwise
endless repetition of death and reincarnation. While
Buddhism and Jainism both deny the existence of a God in
the sense of a self-conscious, self-expressive, personal
supreme being, they have different views of the nature of reality. Jainism acknowledges a dualism of matter and mind (or
soul).[4] Buddhism, on the other hand, acknowledges only soul
and denies the validity of differentiation between anything.
While the Hindu would acknowledge the underlying unity of
all things with the statement, "That thou art," Buddhism
would deny the distinction of anything. Buddhism might say,
"That isn't and neither are you!"

Observation: In such a religious context, what implications for design appear? Without a Creator, does it make
sense to speak of design? Though we usually think of design
as relating to how things began, it also concerns how things
operate and where they are going. The concern of Jainism,
Buddhism, and Hinduism with the law of Karma is a concern
for how moral life operates and what will be the ultimate end
of people. These religions assume the operation of Karma as
a fundamental principle of reality.

Mahavira, the founder of Jainism, believed in both the
material and spiritual realms. He believed that the way to
escape the cycles of birth and death lay in mortification of the
flesh, or extreme asceticism. Gautama, the founder of
Buddhism, denied the existence of the material world. He further denied the existence of individual souls. Escape from the
cycle of birth and death came intellectually because no flesh
actually exists that one may mortify. In both cases these religions believe that a moral law operates throughout all reality.
This moral law or order represents design, though it is interpreted within these theologies as design without a Designer.

One also should note that Jainism and Buddhism have
multiple groups with variations of these beliefs. These religions also have popular forms that differ from the traditional
formulations. In both communities, popular religion provides

for prayer and the recognition of deities! One must consider whether this situation suggests a projection of the personal on the universe as Freud suggested or a recognition of the personal at the heart of the universe.

Religions of Harmony

Taoism of China and Shinto of Japan both strive for harmony in this life. This goal contrasts with the ultimate concern for escape from life implied by the religions of Karma. Both religions comingle freely with Ch'an or Zen Buddhism. In antiquity both China and Japan had accounts for the divine origins of things, but these religions have a greater concern for the state of the cosmos than for the origin of the cosmos. The pragmatism of Confucian philosophy also influenced how these two religions developed to stress the national character of their religions.

The ancient religion of China understood that deities filled the whole cosmos. Shang Ti ruled as the supreme deity, but many other deities were associated with natural forces and physical locations. These deities required propitiation in order to ensure prosperity, success, wealth, health, and all that might imply harmony within all dimensions of life and the cosmos. Deities included both helpful and harmful spirits. Around 1000 B.C. Chinese thinkers developed a new way of conceiving the relationship between these two opposite groups of spirits known as *yin* and *yang*. The *yin* represents the dark forces and the *yang* represents the light forces. Tao came to involve the complex interrelationship of opposite forces at all levels of nature throughout the cosmos. By extension the *yin* represents the dark, evil, negative, wet, cold, passive, and feminine principle of the cosmos. By extension the *yang* represents the light, good, positive, dry, warm, active, and male principle of the cosmos.

People at all levels of society had relative degrees of status or spiritual power. The emperor had the greatest *te,* or inherent power; therefore, he played a crucial role in maintaining the balance or harmony of the opposite forces by offering sacrifice to the deities. Because the ancestors of the emperor dwelt with Shang Ti, their influence in heaven was considered critical to maintaining harmony. The practice of ancestor worship developed with the emperors, who sacrificed to their ancestors and consulted them for advice. By 1000 B.C. ancestor worship had become a common feature of Chinese religion for people at all levels of society.

Tao, or "Way," involves a way of behaving as well as an understanding of the forces behind all phenomena. Tao has a more philosophical side that approximates Western ideas of naturalism and relativism. Yet the religious side of Tao makes it quite different. The religious side of Tao strives for communication between people and the supernatural powers. Unlike the religions of Karma, Tao describes a universe of ceaseless mutation and development in which people experience an infinite process of transformation.

Like the ancient Chinese, the ancient Japanese conceived a cosmos filled with deities. Japanese culture also regarded many other things as possessing a superior power called *kami*. *Kami* is a quality found throughout the cosmos that elicits awe and wonder, fear and dread, and attraction. (Rudolf Otto commented on these same qualities in *The Idea of the Holy*, which we will examine later.) The *kami* account for the origin of heaven and earth but more importantly for the origin of Japan. Originally one mass, heaven and earth were separated by something like a reed-shoot that grew up between them and caused them to split. This reed-shoot was transformed into one of the first *kami*. The first man and woman came about by spontaneous generation. The Japanese islands formed from the coagulation of drops of water that fell from the spear of the *kami* Izanagi after he had dipped it in the ocean of chaos.

Izanagi and his consort Izanami descended to Japan and had many *kami* offspring, who continue to be worshiped in Japan. In addition, Izanagi and Izanami produced the sun goddess Amaterasu. Because of the disorder present in the islands of Japan, Amaterasu sent her grandson Ninigi to rule

Japan. His great-grandson succeeded him as the first human emperor of Japan from whom the present emperor is descended in unbroken line. Other *kami* produced the *samurai* class within Japanese society as well as all other Japanese people.

This concern for harmony and balance that *kami* ancestors might help assure provided a logical connection for the introduction of ancestor worship from China along with Confucianism. With the introduction of Buddhism from China, the *kami* were recognized as manifestations of Buddha.

Observation: The concept of harmony, balance, and order (as opposed to chaos) which Taoism and Shintoism stress would correspond to the concept of design. In this sense the two religions recognize a fundamental pattern of order despite the presence of competing forces. The occurrence of disequilibrium does not negate the concept of harmony. Instead, it heightens the recognition of the presence of that harmony. Disaster does not mean that the world does not operate according to a prescribed Tao.

Eclipsed Religions

Some religions that thrived for a thousand years or more have since died out. The three great religious systems of the West faded as their adherents adopted the monotheism of Christianity. To the south of the Mediterranean Sea, ancient Egypt had a flourishing civilization for thousands of years with an elaborate religion that faded after the conquest of Egypt by Alexander and later Rome. Long before Christianity became a legal religion in the empire, Egypt became a center of Christian faith. To the east of the Mediterranean Sea, ancient Greece enjoyed a rich civilization and religion for a thousand years before its conquest by Rome. The hellenistic world also became an early center for Christianity in spite of periodic persecution by the Romans. To the north the Celtic religion of Gaul, Germany, and the British Isles faded back into prehistory. Yet these fierce tribes abandoned their ancient religion and embraced the preaching of poor, wandering monks. Each of these ancient religions viewed the world as having an intentional, divine origin.

The Egyptians believed that Ptah ordered the world to arise from the mud after first conceiving it in his heart. Egyptian religion, however, involved a collection of deities from two kingdoms. Thus, the Egyptians had other stories of creation. Atum, the hill god emerged from the primordial waters that appear in other ancient stories of creation. To Ptah was attributed the creation of air, sky, earth, and dew. From him descended the gods and goddesses of these domains. His son Shu became the air god, and his daughter Tefnut became the dew goddess. Their son Geb became god of the earth, and their daughter Nut became goddess of the sky. From this brother and sister came Osiris and Isis.

The ancient Greeks believed that all of creation came from one shapeless mass known as Chaos, within which the seeds of future things slept. What would become earth, sea, and sky mingled in Chaos until separated by one of the ancient gods.[5] By another account, Earth (Gaea), Erebus (Darkness), and Love (Eros) were the first beings to emerge from Chaos. Love came from the egg of Night, which floated on Chaos.[6] Love produced life by using his torch and arrows. Reus, the grandson of Earth (Gaea), fashioned people from the ashes of the Titans whom he destroyed with thunderbolts.[7] By another account, the Titans Prometheus and Epimetheus were assigned the responsibility for making man. It was left to Zeus to make woman, who was intended as a curse for man or a blessing, according to two different stories.

The Celtic accounts of the origin of the world and all living things are best known by the Norse version of the tales. The brothers Odin (Woten), Vili, and Be made the earth from the body of the giant Ymir, whom they slew. With his blood they made the seas, with his bones they made the mountains; with his hair they made trees; with his skull they made the heavens; and with his brains they made storm clouds. Midgard (middle earth) was made with Ymir's eyebrows, and this realm became the dwelling place of people. Before heaven and earth were made there was a bottomless pit and a world of mist in which flowed a fountain that fed twelve rivers. These rivers froze not far from the fountain and filled the pit with ice. South òf the world of mist lay the world of light, from which blew a warm wind to melt the ice. The vapors from the melting ice formed a cloud from which the Frost giant Ymir, his children, and his cow sprang. The great cow Audhumbla licked the ice for nourishment. As the cow licked the ice one day, the head of a man appeared. She kept licking until the whole man appeared, who was actually a god. He took to wife one of the giants, and from them came Odin and his brothers. The gods made man from an ash tree and woman from an elder tree.[8]

While Midgard was home to people, Asgard was home to the gods, Jotunheim was home to the giants, and Niffleheim was home to the dwarves. The Celtic peoples believed that the day would come when all of the world would be destroyed together with the gods. After that, however, the hidden and remote Alfadur (the Almighty) would make a new heaven and earth free of misery.[9]

Observation: These ancient and geographically isolated religions have remarkably similar styles in spite of the differences in content. They all contain a close identification between deities and natural phenomena. One may wonder if the ancients actually thought of the deities as the natural phenomenon itself (the sun, the sea, the earth, the storms) or the being that exercised control over that aspect of nature. All three religions have views of nature that suppose design, but not necessarily creation. Sometimes the present world is fashioned out of something that already exists.

Monotheistic Religions

The three great monotheistic religions of Judaism, Christianity, and Islam share a common understanding of the origin of the world with respect to design. Followers of these faiths believe in one eternal Supreme Being who created all things. Western culture uses the generic term *God* to refer to the Creator, but the holy books of these three faiths use many names to speak of God. God spoke the cosmos into existence which began in a chaotic state. God ordered the chaos, however, by dividing it into the fundamental elements of light, heaven, earth, and water. He then ordered these to bring forth the various forms of life. Finally, God made humans in his own image.

The problem of pain, suffering, or disharmony that concerns all of the religions we have examined arose because of the human dissatisfaction with its place in the order of the cosmos. The knowledge of God came to Christians and Muslims from Judaism and the Law and Prophets of ancient Israel. From oral tradition as well as final written form stretching over a thousand years, the Bible makes clear that God not only planned and created the universe but that he also remains intimately involved and concerned with the affairs of people. As such, God has a moral expectation of the behavior of people that conforms to a plan for humanity.

Christians, Jews, and Muslims believe that people have one life to live, then they face the judgment of God. People are judged according to their conformity to the moral standards of God. For Jews, people attain eternal life with God by keeping the Law as given to Moses and interpreted by the rabbis. For Muslims, people attain eternal life with God by keeping the Law as given to Mohammed. For Christians, people attain eternal life through receiving the Holy Spirit of God into their lives by faith in Jesus Christ. By receiving God's Spirit in this life, they avoid the judgment of God and are counted righteous on account of the righteousness of Christ which the Holy Spirit applies to them.

Observation: The monotheistic religions make a sharp distinction between God and nature, of which people are a part. They also distinguish between God and all other spiritual beings, of which there are many. God made all spirits, life, and the material world originally from nothing, not from himself. Besides an intentional creation of the material world,

God also has a moral plan for the world and a purpose for people. Thus, nature is an expression of the creative mind of God, but it is not God.

PHILOSOPHICAL PERSPECTIVES

In addition to the religious perspectives on the concept of design, many important philosophical perspectives have addressed this issue. In most cultures the areas of philosophy, science, and religion are indistinguishable. They represent interrelated aspects of a unitary outlook and approach to life. This can sometimes cause confusion for the modern Western observer who may confuse the science of another culture for an aspect of their religion. Philosophy also may be confused for religion. For instance, statements in the Bible about the movement of the heavenly bodies represent ancient Hebrew science rather than the faith of the Hebrew people.

The fragmentation of science, philosophy, and religion began in ancient Greece with Plato and Aristotle. These two philosophers had a profound influence on the development of Christian theology and modern science, even though they were not Christians. What they had to say about design had a direct relation to how Christians would talk about design for centuries. They had perspectives on reality entirely different from each other, yet both had a concept of the design of the universe.

Plato
Plato's teacher, Socrates, believed in only one God, and this put him at odds with the traditional polytheism of his fellow Atheneans. During a trial at the court of the Areopagus, or Mars Hill, they condemned him to death for corrupting the morals of the youth with his perceived atheism. Plato followed Socrates in his attitude toward the ancient gods, though he was more careful in how he articulated his views. He was an idealist, which meant that he believed ideas took priority over the physical. Ideas were more real to him than actual physical counterparts. He believed that all actual physical things

correspond to an ultimate and absolute ideal upon which all examples of that thing are based. For instance, for all the many chairs in the world he believed that only one perfect, ideal chair existed in the realm of the ideal for which all the actual chairs are vague corruptions.

Plato's concept of ideals or universals relates directly to his conception of the design of the world of experience. He explored this issue in *Timaeus,* which he wrote in the form of a dialogue between Socrates and his student Timaeus. In the course of the dialogue Plato introduces the argument of first cause as a means to discuss the issue of design. He acknowledges several questions that need an answer. Was the universe created? If not, how could it exist? Has the universe always existed, or did it have a beginning? In this regard he distinguishes between "that which always is and has no becoming; and . . . that which is always becoming and never is."[10] Put more simply, he distinguished between what never changes (that which always is and has no becoming) and what does change (that which is always becoming and never is).

The visible, tangible, material world corresponds to Plato's world of becoming. The physical world is in a constant state of change. For this reason it is always *becoming* something different from what it was. Because it always changes, it never *is* or it never reaches a stopping point at which it is complete. The world of ideals, however, is a world that the senses cannot apprehend. It is not tangible, nor does it change. The ideals are perfect and complete. Things that change or *become* require a cause. Things that do not change are eternal; therefore, they do not require a cause. Plato argued on the basis of the first cause that set change and becoming in motion, that the physical world of change had been created. On the same basis, however, he argued that the changeless world of ideals had eternal existence and had not been created.

Plato's understanding of design proceeds from his understanding of the changing and the unchanging. He argued that in creating a world, God looked to a pattern that was eternal and perfect because it did not change. In this sense, the physical world of change is the *image* of the eternal, unchanging world of *ideal*. The ideal provided the pattern or design by which God created the physical world.

In other places Plato discussed ideas such as goodness. For purposes of this dialogue, he assumes the values he has argued for elsewhere. Because God is good, he would create only the most perfect possible world. Because intelligence is better than unintelligence and because intelligence is only present in soul, God created the universe with an intelligent soul. To be the fairest of all possible worlds (for God would not create less than the fairest), there can only be one universe. Plato spoke of the universe in relation to God the same way the New Testament speaks of Christ in relation to God: the "only-begotten."[11] Keep in mind that Plato's concept of "God" is quite different from that found in the Bible, just as his concept of "design" is quite different from the watchmaker philosophers of the eighteenth century we shall see.

Plato argued that the universe, a *living* creature, came about by design.[12] All of its features are intentionally so for specific reasons, the logic of which he spelled out. For instance, the world was made in the form of a globe with a smooth surface. It is a globe since that shape represents the most perfect of figures, and it is smooth because it has no need of eyes, ears, arms, feet, or other appendages.

Because the world he created experiences change, God designed a way for it to bear the image of eternity. This moving image of eternity is called *time*. Time does not exist in eternity, for time relates to motion and change. In eternity the ideals are all at complete rest; therefore, they do not experience time. They have no previous state (past) or any subsequent state (future).

Most of what Plato had to say represents classical philosophy, but it also includes the necessary intersection with theology and science. Plato dealt with the most current science of the day, which involved astronomy and geometry to describe the motions of the heavenly bodies in relation to the great globe of the universe (which to him was little more than the inner solar system and the patterns of the constellations). His description of the relationship of God to the universe, which he conceived of as possessing a soul, represents Plato's speculative theology.

By Plato's account God created the gods of ancient Greece just as he created their physical counterparts in the heavens. Plato's understanding of the Greek gods would correspond more to the biblical idea of angels in that they stand on a different plane between God and humans and in that they are created while God is eternal. God also created a star for each man he created. First he separated the soul of each man from the soul of the universe. Then he implanted each male soul into a physical body. By the *laws of destiny* each man who lived well would return to dwell in his appointed star at death. Those who failed in life would be born a second time as a woman. Failing in the form of a woman, the soul would continue rebirth as lower and lower forms of animals until they overcame by reason their failure and ascended by further rebirth.

Observation: Plato did not write his argument to prove the existence of God or design. He and his audience would have assumed these in some form. He used the assumption of design to argue for the priority of mind over matter, ideal over image. In so doing, he argued that God did not create out of nothing. Rather, God created an ordered (designed) universe out of the chaotic, preexistent elements.

Aristotle

Aristotle studied under Plato, but he developed an entirely different approach to philosophy. Plato placed his stress on the world of eternal, unchanging, perfect ideals, on the mind as the point of contact with the ideals, and on reason as the most reliable form of knowledge. Aristotle, on the other hand, placed his emphasis on the physical world that people know through their senses. This is a remarkable shift because Plato had taught that our senses only give us imperfect knowledge of an imperfect world that he regarded as opinion.

The question of design arises in Aristotle's book on *Metaphysics* in his discussion of substance. Because of his interest in the physical world and the reliability of sensory knowledge, he explored what made up the physical world and where it came from. *Substance* is the term Aristotle used to describe what makes up the world of experience. An apple has substance, but my idea of an apple does not. Substance is subject to change. As we have seen with Plato, accounting for change was a major philosophical problem for the ancient world.

Change involves two contrary states and a third thing. The contrary states are of four kinds: (1) "thisness" or existence, which consists of beginning and destruction; (2) quantity, which consists of increase and decrease; (3) affection, which consists of alteration from this to that; and (4) motion, which consists of movement from here to there. Aristotle argues that the contraries do not change but represent the criteria for recognizing the change. The change occurs in the third thing, which Aristotle calls *matter*. The contrary state of beginning never changes to destruction. Furthermore, beginning does not continue. It eventually becomes destruction. The apple, on the other hand experiences both contrary states, changing all the time. All things that change have matter.

The philosophical question behind all of this discussion relates to the origin of things. Where did the matter come from? What causes it to change? Aristotle believed that the elements present in things are causes, but he also believed some external cause was involved. He identified different elements and different kinds of moving causes for different things, but this only moved the question back further. What was the original cause that set all things in motion? Aristotle believed with Plato that an unmoved mover set things in motion. The unmoved mover is Aristotle's conception of God.

The unmoved mover, however, is not a creator. Aristotle believed the substance of the universe to be eternal. The unmoved mover merely set the universe in motion. The unmoved mover, as the greatest good and most beautiful thing, thinks only of itself. The unmoved mover acts upon the cosmos in bringing about the first motion in the same way that the object of thought acts upon the thinker. Because God is in such a state of goodness and beauty, he compels the motion of the universe in response to him in the same way that something or someone beautiful might attract a person's attention. In responding to the excellence of God, the universe moves with a circular motion because the circle is the closest that substance can come to emulating the goodness of God. Aristotle's God might be said to set things in motion quite unintentionally. Though profoundly self-conscious while spending eternity thinking of himself, he or it has no awareness of anything else.

Observation: Other than getting the ball rolling, Aristotle's God serves little function. Once substance was set in motion, God could retire to think about himself while the eternal universe took over. In this view, design appears as the eternal ordered patterns of motion and principles that govern substance.

CONCLUSION

The concept of design with respect to nature has appeared around the world in past and present cultures. This chapter surveys the concept of design among a few cultures, chosen because of their contact or interaction with other cultures. This study could have included perspectives from sub-Saharan Africa or from the indigenous cultures of the Americas. What these all have in common with the views briefly discussed here is the perception of design within nature.

We also have seen that different cultures have recognized different things about design. For some, design has to do with the ordered movement of the heavenly bodies, the cycle of the seasons, and the passage of time. For some, design has to do with the presence of underlying principles for living or moral law. For some, design is understood as purpose, where the end goal rather than the beginning of the process takes priority.

For some, design means that the appearance of things suggests they result from intentional craftsmanship. For some, design involves the harmony and balance of nature.

We have seen that however design is conceived by different cultures, it appears as a basic assumption of the worldview from which it comes. People assume it as self-evident truth. Furthermore, it does not serve as proof for the existence of God. Where it is discussed in relation to God, it tends to be used to explore the question of what kind of God and what kind of universe exists.

In the religions concerned with Karma and in the monotheistic religions, design has great implications for the ultimate goal of things. The law of Karma is seen to operate with rules of morality designed to move humanity toward an ultimate goal of union with Brahman. Christianity, Judaism, and Islam recognize the law of God as the standard by which people are judged. These three religions view history as moving toward an ultimate end when those judged righteous will dwell with God forever while those judged unrighteous will be expelled to outer darkness forever.

This survey provides a picture of how things stood a thousand years ago. Since then the development of modern science and the secularization of Western society have witnessed the separation of science, philosophy, and theology in the West. This fragmentation of knowledge has led to a general view that these disciplines have nothing to say to each other. Their different methods and theories of knowledge certainly reinforce the idea that they have nothing to contribute to each other's understanding of the world.

Despite the perception all over the world of the presence of design in nature, the idea of design has been viewed with profound skepticism by the intellectual community in the West since the time of Charles Darwin. Design has generally been regarded as a code word for Christianity, though, as we have seen, it is one of those rare features of faith common to virtually all religions. At the close of the twentieth century, however, a group of scientists, philosophers, and theologians once again began exploring the relevance of the idea of design when speaking of the cosmos. This time the discussion is not merely about design but about *intelligent design*. This time the discussion involves a serious examination of the complex structures of life, the cosmic context in which life has emerged, and probability theory. Before exploring the new developments in the intelligent design argument, however, we will examine how the idea of design changed from the assumption of faith to an intellectual argument for faith and the role this argument played in the secularization of the West.

CHAPTER TWO

THE CUSTOM-DESIGNED HOME

THE HEBREW WORLDVIEW of revelation and the Greek world-view of philosopy first began to mingle in the Egyptian intel-lectual center of Alexandria. Philo of Alexandria (20 B.C.–A.D. 40) attempted to reconcile Plato's understanding of God and creation found in *Timaeus* with the biblical understand-ing of God and creation found in the Hebrew Scriptures.

Philo found the concept of an eternal God who existed alone and then brought the world into existence compatible with biblical teaching. He also found the nonphysical exis-tence of this God compatible with biblical teaching. But Plato taught that eternal ideas existed in addition to this God. Philo could not accept eternal ideas that existed alongside and inde-pendently of God. He reconciled the problem by making the eternal ideas the thoughts of God, thus eliminating their inde-pendent existence but retaining their eternal existence.

This Alexandrian philosophical tradition entered Christian theology through Clement of Alexandria (d. 215?) and his pupil Origen (c. 182–c. 251). Clement sought to interpret Christianity through the Hellenistic philosophies, as Philo had done for Judaism. He considered philosophy for the Greeks as the corollary to the Law for the Jews. Strongly influenced by Platonic and Stoic philosophy, Clement had less interest in the physical earthly life of Christ than in the eternal Logos. Origen followed Clement's approach and developed a complete system that interpreted the Bible allegorically in order to harmonize it with philosophy. His work gave theology scientific standing by the standards of the day as he sought to demonstrate that philosophy could serve Christianity.

Origen's scheme relied heavily on Platonic concepts. He considered the spiritual world as the "real" world because the physical world merely provided a context for punishment and salvation. This scheme necessarily made the physical world of less interest to Origen, who conceived of the major events as taking place in the spiritual realm. Following Plato, he believed that all people preexisted in the spiritual world, where sin originally occurred, and that they took on physical form in proportion to their sin. The least sinful are the angels whose bodies are the stars. The most sinful are the demons who inhabit depraved bodies. While this scheme worked well with Platonic philosophy, it departed from the Jewish and Christian understanding of creation and the worth of the physical world.

Not all Christian theologians embraced philosophy as eagerly as Clement and Origen. Tertullian of Carthage (c. 150–c. 225) took quite a different view. He refused to bend Scripture in order to conform it to a philosophical understanding of reality. He stressed the irreconcilable differences between philosophy and revealed faith in several of his writings. In his *Apology* he remarked, "So, then, where is there any likeness between the Christian and the philosopher? between the disciple of Greece and of heaven? between the man whose object is fame, and whose object is life?"[1] In *The Prescription Against Heretics* he asked, "What indeed has Athens to do with Jerusalem? What concord is there between the Academy and the church? What between heretics and Christians?"[2]

As time passed, however, theologians found that they could not leave philosophy alone. They lived in a world in which people thought about the world. Because the Christian faith was concerned with the world, theologians had to think about the world as well. Especially in a world where few people were Christians and Greek philosophy provided the foundation for knowledge and understanding, Christian theologians had to discuss faith in dialogue with philosophy. People who converted to Christianity brought their old philosophical thought patterns and categories with them when they converted. Even Tertullian brought Stoic ideas with him when he became a Christian.

SCIENCE AND CREATION

Perhaps the most famous convert from paganism and Hellenistic philosophy was Augustine of Hippo (354–430). The question of the origin of the physical world formed the critical question in Augustine's conversion. His answer to that question would form the central element of his theology and the theology of the Christian West for the next thousand years. Before becoming a Christian, Augustine had embraced the religious teachings of Manichaeism as well as the philosophical teachings of Platonism and Stoicism as filtered through Neoplatonism. In his pre-Christian quest for meaning, Augustine encountered the struggle between science and faith in the contest between philosophy and Manichaeism.

Though raised by a Christian mother, Augustine embraced the dualistic religion of Manichaeism as a youth. For Augustine the problem of evil clouded his view of a designed universe. As he looked about, he saw evil scattered throughout the beauty and goodness and truth he desired. He asked himself, *How could a good God be responsible for evil?* Manichaeism allowed him to believe in God, goodness, beauty, and truth, while attributing the evil he saw to another God. Light, goodness, beauty, truth, and spirit belonged to the God he loved. Darkness, evil, ugliness, error, and matter belonged to the God he despised.

Manichaeans taught that the present universe resulted from an intrusion of evil into the bounds of goodness. People represent a comingling of good and evil. The comingling began when Darkness attacked Light. The five powers of darkness defeated the five powers of light and devoured part of their light. This episode began the comingling. The Father of Greatness sent the Living Spirit to overcome the powers of darkness, whose carcasses became the heavens and the earth. The purest part of the Light, which the powers of darkness had devoured, became the sun and the moon. The appearance of another messenger of Light induced the Darkness to produce Adam and Eve in the form of the Father of Greatness. Adam and Eve enclosed the remaining Light that the Darkness had available to it. Each subsequent birth further dilutes the Light and advances the power of Darkness. Buddha, Jesus, and Zoroaster were all sent as messengers to bring the knowledge to people that would allow them to escape the bondage of the material world. The final messenger was Mani, who established the Manichaean religion.[3]

The Manichaean religion allowed Augustine to make sense of the existence of evil and good by allowing for two independent, eternal "forces." The Manichaeans had an explanation for the relationship between the spiritual and the physical, yet they taught that both had "material" substance. The Manichaeans provided an explanation for the origin of the cosmos and for the behavior of the heavenly bodies.

Study of Cicero had produced in Augustine a thirst for wisdom. This thirst, coupled with his training as a rhetorician, led Augustine to ask the critical question about his own religion.[4] After reading how the Greek philosophers could accurately calculate the phases of the moon, the eclipses of the sun and moon, the equinoxes, and other movements of the heavenly bodies, Augustine began to doubt the Manichaean fables about the nature of the cosmos.

The Manichaeans taught that Christ dwelt in the sun, his wisdom dwelt in the moon, and the Holy Spirit dwelt in the air. The Father dwelt in a secret light. The part of the divine Light entrapped in the material world is released by "the elect," those faithful of the Manichaean religion who have attained enlightenment and live the ascetic life. All that passes from the elect in the course of their bodily functions rises upward as vapor through the air (Holy Spirit) to the sun and moon. The waxing and waning of the moon results from the moon's receiving souls from matter (waxing) and transporting

Fig. 2.1. The All-Seeing Eye. Manichaeism taught
that the sun is a triangular window in heaven
through which God observes the world.

them like a ship to the sun (waning). The sun serves as the final ship to transport souls on to their final destination with the Light. Besides being a ship to transport souls, the sun also forms a triangular window in heaven through which the light of Christ shines (no matter that the sun appears to be round). This feature of Manichaeism survives graphically on the reverse side of the Great Seal of the United States, where the all-seeing eye peers through the triangular window with light emanating around it (see fig. 2.1).

From the philosophers, Augustine learned that the heavenly bodies move in ordered patterns according to predictable "laws." The philosophers recorded their rules and calculations so that anyone who took the time to learn them could use them with the same results.[5] Mani, the founder of Manichaeism, wrote extensively on this subject, but his teachings seemed to Augustine to be at odds with the scientific calculations of the secular philosophers. He raised his questions with Faustus, a leading bishop of the Manichaeans, but found that he was generally ignorant of the liberal arts and unable to give a satisfactory response. Guided by the best science of his day, the earth-centered cosmos of Ptolemy, Augustine rejected his religion because it could not reconcile its teachings about the cosmos with the teachings of the philosophers (see figs. 2.2 and 2.3).[6]

While philosophy helped Augustine reject the Manichaean religion, it did not provide him with a religion that satisfied his spiritual awareness. The problem of evil continued to be his gnawing concern about the nature of the cosmos. A great obstacle for him consisted in his inability to conceive of "spiritual" substance.[7] As a Manichee, Augustine believed that nothing existed unless it had "material" substance. He also believed that evil existed as a material substance that intruded upon the good.[8] His own evil deeds resulted from the evil intrusion or invasion upon him. Though many of the philosophers, and Platonic philosophers in particular, had a negative view of the physical world, Augustine learned from them a different way of conceptualizing reality.

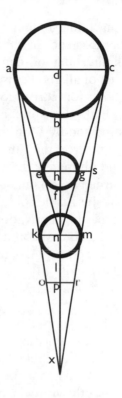

Fig. 2.2. Ptolemy's Scheme for Understanding the Relationship of the Earth, Moon, and Sun. Adapted from Ptolemy, *The Almagest*, Great Books of the Western World, ed. Robert Maynard Hutchins, vol. 16 (Chicago: Encyclopaedia Britannica, 1952), 173.

Until he began to explore Platonic thought, Augustine conceived of God as a great corporeal mass, yet a "vain phantom."[9] He also conceived of evil as another great corporeal mass, equally infinite with God, though on a smaller scale.[10] Through the philosophers Augustine came to reject his lingering understanding of evil as a substance with an independent existence of its own. He came to regard corruption as the diminishing or deprivation of something good; things deprived of all good cease to exist. As long as things exist, they are good, for corruption involves damaging that which is good. Evil, therefore, cannot be a substance; otherwise it would be good.[11] With this insight, Augustine revised his view of the universe, the value of physical substance, the nature of evil, and ultimately the nature of God. He now saw that what he regarded as evil might be present yet uncreated and not self-existent. Just as he could now envision evil as not existing but describing the deprivation or twisting of God's good creation, he could also envision how God could be spiritual substance. From a corporeal mass that filled part of infinite space not relegated to evil, to a god who filled all of infinite space, Augustine finally arrived at a God who transcends all of time and space.[12]

Until this point in his pilgrimage, Augustine paid little attention to Christianity as a viable alternative to Manichaeism. His reading of the Bible had led Augustine to think that the Christian God had a body like humans with arms, hands, eyes, and a mouth with which he spoke. At least the Manichaeans conceived of God as a corporeal mass rather than as a human! Augustine also rejected the idea of an incarnation of God in the flesh as Jesus because the flesh would have defiled the Savior according to his Manichaean views of the body.[13] The cross had no attraction because, as a Manichee, Augustine believed the crucifixion had no objective reality. Instead, it served him merely as a metaphor of human suffering.

Science and faith coincided for Augustine through the preaching of Ambrose of Milan. As a teacher of rhetoric, Augustine went to hear Ambrose because of his reputation as a public speaker. When he heard Ambrose expound the Bible, he came to understand the figurative meaning of the biblical references to God in human terms.[14] The allegorical interpretations of Old Testament texts in particular helped Augustine see that the Christian faith had a legitimate position, if not a conclusive position.

In the end, Augustine found that the science of his day helped him clarify his thinking but that it could not take him to God. It could help him think about God, but it could not provide a way to God. He gladly accepted the rules that govern the order of the heavenly bodies, and this overwhelming evidence of order forced him to reconsider his concept of God. Philosophy brought Augustine just so far, however, before it could help no more. Finally, drawn by his attraction to the source of the good, the true, and the beautiful, Augustine went beyond the logic of philosophy. From his consideration of evil, he felt drawn to consider the beautiful: "I was caught up to you by your beauty and quickly torn away by my weight."[15]

Years after his conversion Augustine reflected on how much the philosophers had achieved in understanding the operation of creation, yet how little they knew about the Creator. He marveled at what seemed evident to him after his conversion but what eluded the great philosophers. When Augustine finally became a Christian, his conversion did not come as an intellectual accomplishment, though his mind had been active throughout the process. His mind could take him just so far, but in the end he felt God reaching out to him. He felt as though he were being told to cast himself upon God, who would catch him.[16]

Augustine considered creation a self-evident truth, yet a truth that people choose not to know. He believed that the heavens and the earth and all of creation cry out that they were created, but people do not necessarily receive what is evident.[17] The beauty and goodness of creation that should draw people toward God becomes corrupted by the human mind, which settles for the lesser good and the lower beauty when it could gain access to God.[18] He perceived that the human mind, so drawn by the beauty of creation, tends to love the creature more than the Creator.[19] Once turned away from the Creator, the soul deprived of the greatest good

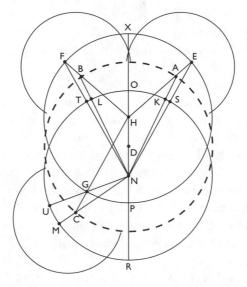

Fig. 2.3. Ptolemy's Scheme for Understanding the Eccentric Motion of Mars in Relation to Earth. Adapted from Ptolemy, *The Almagest,* Great Books of the Western World, ed. Robert Maynard Hutchins, vol. 16 (Chicago: Encyclopaedia Britannica, 1952), 325.

expresses the corruption that the word *evil* describes.[20] The failure of creation to point to God came not from the inadequacy of God's handiwork to proclaim him as the Creator but from the failure of the human soul to accept the truth.

Observations: Design played an important part in Augustine's grasp of God, but for him the focus came in order and beauty. The design he experienced came as the work of an artist. He always accepted the reality of God, but he struggled with the nature of the real God. At one point as he pursued Manichaeism, he embraced a theology that accepted a form of design that accounted the physical world as the product of evil infringing on goodness. This approach made sense to him because he struggled with the problem of evil. How could a good God create a world where evil appeared at every step?

In his Manichaean solution, Augustine reasoned that God could not have intimate contact with the physical world without suffering pollution. In his Christian conclusion, Augustine believed that God must have intimate contact with the world to account for the very presence of the goodness and beauty that suffer from corruption.

Though Augustine expressed a lofty understanding of Scripture as revelation from God, he embraced the learning of the philosophers as legitimate knowledge and truth despite its limitations. While the science of the philosophers could not carry one to God, it could offer insights that aided in the interpretation of Scripture. In the end, however, knowledge of God comes through the spirit because God is Spirit. Perception of the handiwork of God provides evidence that cannot be understood fully until faith enlivens the heart to perceive what was always clearly evident. Knowledge of God, however, only comes from God. Augustine's theological perspective of the knowledge of God, with its strong Platonic undertones, would become the dominant and normative understanding of Western Christianity for eight hundred years.

PROVING THE EXISTENCE OF GOD

In the late Middle Ages the understanding of design came to have a new function related to matters of science and faith. Instead of a declaration about God and the universe, design came to form the critical aspect of an elaborate argument for the existence of God that built upon the ancient Greek philosophy of Aristotle. In the first part of his magnum opus *Summa Theologica,* Thomas Aquinas explored five proofs for the existence of God. These five proofs, however, do not stand alone. They compose elements of a single, unified argument on the unity of creation.[21]

1. *The argument from motion.* The first argument relates to motion and change, which was a serious problem for the ancient Greeks. This argument refers to a Prime Mover and is based on the idea that objects remain at rest unless set in motion. An object cannot move itself; therefore, whatever moves must be moved by something else. An infinite regression

of movers would not be possible, because such a situation would never account for the act of motion that set the potentiality of motion into motion. "Therefore it is necessary to arrive at a first mover which is moved by no other. And this everyone understands to be God."

2. *The argument from cause.* The second argument relates to efficient cause. Thomas identified four kinds of cause. Formal cause referred to the form or nature of a thing and involved defining what something is; such as a water molecule. Material cause referred to the processes and constituents that cause a thing to be; such as the chemical elements that combine to form water molecules. Final cause referred to the goal or purpose for which something existed; such as the purpose of water to sustain life. Thomas distinguished between these three understandings of causality and efficient cause. By efficient cause he meant the agent that caused a phenomenon to be; such as heat that causes water to evaporate.[22] Thomas argued that every effect must have an efficient cause other than itself. As in the argument related to the Prime Mover, Thomas contended that an infinite regress of causes would not be possible. "Therefore it is necessary to admit a first efficient cause, to which everyone gives the name of God."

3. *The argument from possibility and necessity.* This argument is also known as the argument from Necessary Being. Thomas argued that everything in nature has the possibility "to be or not to be" as Hamlet would muse. The paper on which these words are printed illustrates how something can be, but because there was a time not too long ago when the page did not exist, it also illustrates how something in nature can not be. Since everything can not be, then there could have been a time when nothing existed. If such a situation existed, it would be impossible for anything ever to exist since things only begin to exist because of something that already exists. Thomas then argued for two types of beings: the possible and the necessary. A necessary being, however, would not be necessary if it had its cause in another. This would repeat the problem of an infinite regress of beings who have their

necessity caused by another. "Therefore we must admit the existence of some being having of itself its own necessity, and not receiving it from another, but rather causing in others their necessity. This all men speak of as God."

4. *The argument from gradation or relative value ascribed to things.* Things are referred to as "more" or "less" in relation to some other thing, ultimately to that which is "most" and "least." Something is called "hotter" as it more resembles that which is "hottest." This situation leads us to believe that there must be those superlatives that perfectly exhibit their being. Thomas argued that "the maximum in any genus is the cause of all in that genus; as fire, which is the maximum of heat, is the cause of all hot things. . . . Therefore there must also be something which is to all beings the cause of their being, goodness, and every other perfection. And this we call God."

5. *The argument from governance.* Not until the fifth and final argument does Thomas introduce design in terms of "the governance of all things." Thomas argued from the assumption that all nonintelligent things act toward an end or goal that is evident from their acting to obtain the best result. From this assumption he concludes that things achieve their end "not by chance, but by design." Thomas further argued that things lacking knowledge could not move toward a goal or purpose unless directed by an intelligent being. "Therefore some intelligent being exists by whom all natural things are ordered to their end; and this being we call God."

Thomas offered these five proofs in response to what he considered the two strongest objections to the question of the existence of God. The first objection related to the presence of evil in the world. If God is infinite goodness, then no evil should be found in the world. The presence of evil, however, serves as proof to the argument that God does not exist. The second objection related to natural causes. This objection states that the supposition of God is unnecessary because all natural phenomena can be reduced to one principle called "nature" and all voluntary phenomena can be reduced to one principle called human reason or will. The five proofs of Thomas are intended to be understood in reference to these two objections to the existence of God rather than as free-standing proofs. The argument has a context related to the problems of evil and naturalism.

After stating his proofs, Thomas drew two conclusions that represent the force of his argument. His first conclusion restates the teaching of Augustine nearly eight hundred years earlier: "As Augustine says (*Enchiridion* 9): 'Since God is the highest good, He would not allow any evil to exist in His works, unless His omnipotence and goodness were such as to bring good even out of evil.' This is part of the infinite goodness of God, that He should allow evil to exist, and out of it produce good."[23]

The second conclusion demonstrates the relationship between the five proofs:

> Since nature works for a determinate end under the direction of a higher agent, whatever is done by nature must be traced back to God, as to its first cause. So also whatever is done voluntarily must also be traced back to some higher cause other than human reason or will, since these can change and fail. For all things that are changeable and capable of defect must be traced back to an immovable and self-necessary first principle, as was shown in the body of the Article [argument].[24]

A critical, if *not* the critical, element of the combined argument of Thomas rests in this rejection of an infinite regress. This argument depends upon a beginning. If an infinite regress is possible, then the argument fails. Thomas is noted as the theologian who introduced Aristotle's philosophy into Christian theology, but an essential aspect of Aristotle's understanding of the order of the universe lay in his concept of the eternity of the universe. Though Thomas borrowed heavily from Aristotle, especially from his theory of knowledge, Thomas departed from him at important points. He used Aristotle's method and system to a large extent, but he drew some different conclusions.

Thomas accepted the doctrine of a temporal beginning to the universe by faith based on the traditional understanding of the Genesis creation account. He did not, however, believe in the philosophical necessity of a temporal beginning for God to be the one who created out of nothing. On philosophical grounds, he could argue that God eternally created the world out of nothing, which would result in an eternal universe which had a first cause! First cause speaks to origins rather than to time from a philosophical point of view.[25]

This point has significant implications in today's debate over the meaning of time in cosmogony. The Big Bang Theory suggests a beginning to the universe, though it does not necessarily require a beginning of matter. The theological implications of a beginning along the lines suggested by Thomas Aquinas have not escaped Stephen Hawking, who is now exploring a way to account for a finite universe without boundary! Hawking explains the significance of such a view:

> The idea that space and time may form a closed surface without boundary also has profound implications for the role of God in the affairs of the universe. With the success of scientific theories in describing events, most people have come to believe that God allows the universe to evolve according to a set of laws and does not intervene in the universe to break these laws. However, the laws do not tell us what the universe should have looked like when it started—it would still be up to God to wind up the clockwork and choose how to start it off. So long as the universe had a beginning, we could suppose it had a creator. But if the universe is really completely self-contained, having no boundary or edge, it would have neither beginning nor end: it would simply be. What place, then, for a creator?[26]

Observations: Thomas had confidence in the senses to perceive the real world and communicate that reality to the mind. What people know, they know through their bodily senses. This confidence resulted in numerous assumptions about nature. Thomas assumed the existence of the physical world; thus, he argued from a position that not all people share. Beyond this assumption, he assumed the order and purpose of the universe. Living in the ordered society of Christendom with its strict hierarchy, order, and purpose seemed a self-evident truth. In a different society, however, the existence of order and purpose may seem a larger question than the existence of God.

THE REJECTION OF ARISTOTLE

The philosophy of Aristotle came to dominate the scientific and theological thought of the late Middle Ages after Thomas Aquinas used Aristotle to provide the intellectual foundation for his system. Augustine and his preference for Plato fell from his once preeminent position. Thomism and the Thomists who followed Thomas Aquinas soon captured the universities and through those powerful institutions gave shape to the intellectual revival that would blossom as the Renaissance.

John Calvin

In many ways the Protestant Reformation of the sixteenth century represented a return to Augustinian theology after several centuries of the triumph of Thomism. Far too many dynamics were involved to reduce the Reformation to a simple return to Augustine, but Augustine clearly had a strong influence on the leading reformers. Perhaps the most prominent expositor and popularizer of Augustine was John Calvin. Calvin had many other significant influences on his theology besides Augustine. A great deal had happened in the eleven hundred years between the two theologians, but in the matter of design, Calvin took his cue from Augustine.

Calvin's *Institutes of the Christian Religion* opens with a discussion of our knowledge of God. Calvin believed all people are born with a knowledge of God. This prior knowledge of God leaves all people without excuse when they fail to worship God or give their lives to his service. This knowledge exists more as a memory than as a clear vision, but it is sufficient to provide some concept of God.[27] This *a priori* knowledge is not the only knowledge people have of God. Calvin also taught that the whole structure of the universe manifests God's perfections and that "on each of his works his glory is engraven in characters so bright, so distinct, and so illustrious, that none, however dull and illiterate, can plead ignorance as their excuse."[28]

In opening his discussion of the knowledge of God, Calvin employs a variety of evocative phrases and terms that support the idea of God as the great Designer: "the elegant structure of the universe," "divine skill manifested so conspicuously," "well-ordered array," "ingenious contrivance," "architect."[29] He does not hesitate to say that nature presents "innumerable proofs" of God that may be understood technically through the sciences or casually by the most illiterate observer. Calvin acknowledged that the study of astronomy, medicine, and the natural sciences provided insight into the wisdom of God. He also argued that anyone could observe the underlying order of the universe reflected in the motion of the heavenly bodies.

In addition to the knowledge of God that comes through the technical or casual pursuit of the sciences, Calvin also argued that knowledge of God comes to a person by "descending into himself." There people will find "in their own persons a factory where innumerable operations of God are carried on. . . ."[30] Augustine had illustrated this descent within through his *Confessions,* but he took that insightful journey within after his conversion. Here lies the problem. While knowledge of God may be possible by inward examination, people suppress the knowledge they may find there. People not only suppress the knowledge of God they might find within, but they also ignore the majesty of the evidence of God's power in nature. In spite of the "mirror of his works, so great is our stupidity, so dull are we in regard to these bright manifestations, that we derive no benefit from them. For in regard to the fabric and admirable arrangement of the universe, how few of us are there who, in lifting our eyes to the heavens, or looking abroad on the various regions of the earth, ever think of the Creator?"[31]

The culprit in undermining the very fabric of the universe is none other than the human imagination. Calvin illustrates his critique of the human imagination by referring to Plato, the Stoics, the Epicureans, Socrates, and Xenophon, all of whom speculated upon God. The knowledge of God available to people by science and spiritual introspection inevitably ends in a perversion of the truth of God by the human imagination. Thus, the patterns and arrangement of the universe prove futile in demonstrating true knowledge of God to the one who will not know the truth. Appealing to Scripture, Calvin argues, "Wherefore, the apostle, in the very place where he says that the worlds are images of invisible things, adds that it is *by faith* we understand that they were framed by the word of God (Heb. 11:3); thereby intimating that the invisible Godhead is indeed represented by such displays, but that we have no eyes to perceive it until they are enlightened through faith by internal revelation from God."[32]

Observations: Calvin affirmed that nature bears the imprint of God's handiwork, but he denied that this proof actually proved the existence of God to someone who did not already have faith in God. Despite the ever present evidence of God's creative activity, the mind that lacks faith cannot recognize the evidence.

René Descartes
While Protestants like Calvin distanced themselves from the philosophical approach of Thomas Aquinas that relied upon Aristotle's understanding of knowledge, a growing number of Catholics began to challenge the Aristotelian-dominated realm of science. Galileo ran afoul of academic authorities,

not because his science contradicted the Bible but because it contradicted Aristotle! René Descartes (1596–1650) also rejected the philosophy of Aristotle that stressed the reliability of sensory knowledge.[33]

Like Calvin, Descartes felt drawn toward Augustine's Platonic philosophical foundation. Unlike Calvin, Descartes went in quite an unorthodox direction with his emphasis on the mind. He was consumed with the idea of absolute certainty as the only valid basis for human knowledge. Descartes hoped to develop a unified science of nature based on mathematics. He proposed a method based on four rules that began with doubting: (1) accept nothing as true that the mind cannot accept clearly, distinctly, and without doubt; (2) divide the difficulties of a question into the smallest number of parts to allow for the most adequate examination; (3) examine the parts of the question beginning with the most simple and moving toward the most complex; (4) make such thorough observations and recordings of data as to allow for no omissions.

Descartes's method depends upon doubting everything except what is so clearly and distinctly true that it will not allow for doubt. By identifying what cannot be doubted, he then expected to build on that foundation of certainty to develop a unified theory of knowledge that included physics, metaphysics, and the other sciences. In applying the method, Descartes had to doubt the existence of the physical universe, of God, and even of himself. In analyzing the extent of his doubt, Descartes concluded that he could not doubt his own existence. He found his own existence to be that clear and distinct certainty for which he searched as a starting place for knowledge. As he thought about what he doubted, he realized that he was the something that was thinking. To think, he had to exist. The Latin version of this conclusion, *cogito ergo sum* (I think; therefore I am) stands out as one of the greatest philosophical maxims of all time. He held to this conclusion with absolute certainty.

While his method provided Descartes with certainty that he existed, it did not provide certainty that his body existed. He demonstrated to his satisfaction the existence of the mind as a substance, but he also concluded that the body must be a distinct substance from the mind. With this line of thought, Descartes developed a dualism of mind and body, the spiritual and the physical. This dualism depended upon Descartes's assumption that all things involve only two essential attributes: thought and extension. This means that all properties of thinking things may be described in terms of ways of thinking. All properties of extended things may be described in terms of ways they are extended.

Descartes proceeded to prove the existence of God from his own existence because his own thinking existence was the only clear and distinct certainty he had. Not until he had proved God's existence could he move on to prove the existence of a physical universe. Here Descartes turned upside down the arguments of Thomas Aquinas. Thomas had sought to prove God's existence based on the existence of a physical universe, but Descartes would not allow the presupposition that the universe actually exists!

Descartes's argument for the existence of God begins with the idea in his mind of God. While Thomas argued that the physical universe must have a first cause, Descartes applied the same logic to his thoughts. His idea of God represented an effect that must have a cause. Every idea is an idea of something, whether it actually exists or not. The degree of reality of an idea depends upon the reality of the object of thought. Because the idea of God is an idea of infinite perfection, its cause must lie outside Descartes's whose doubts betray his imperfection. Since imperfection could not be the cause of perfection, then a perfect Being independent of Descartes must exist. This Being is God.

From the existence of God, Descartes argued for the existence of a physical or external world beyond the mind. As part of the perfection of God, Descartes stated that God cannot deceive his creatures, nor would he want to deceive them.

Because ideas of a physical world do not have perfection as one of their attributes, such ideas do not necessarily have an objective reality. Nonetheless, creatures tend to believe that an external physical world exists. This tendency to believe in a physical world would be misleading if such a world did not exist. In such a case, God would be guilty of creating creatures who are easily misled.

As a result of his approach, Descartes concluded that knowledge of the physical world does not come through the senses. Knowledge of matter is an intellectual concept constructed in the mind. While he believed in the existence of many minds, Descartes believed that the physical world existed as a single, continuous material extension. He could not accept the idea of a void, so he concluded that all physical substance represents a unified extension that operates mechanically.

Observations: Descartes's method proceeded from a basic skepticism that doubted the existence of nature and the physical world. Such skepticism did not allow for the assumptions from which Thomas developed his arguments. For Thomas, a world that did not exist would have neither motion, nor cause, nor order, nor purpose. By making a radical distinction between mind and body, Descartes laid the intellectual foundation for the separation of science and faith. Rather than proving the existence of God from nature, Descartes proved the existence of nature from his belief in God.

Blaise Pascal

Perhaps the brightest star in the intellectual galaxy in the generation after Descartes was Blaise Pascal. Like Descartes, Pascal (1623–1662) made significant contributions to mathematics, philosophy, and theology. Like Descartes, Pascal challenged the old Aristotelian system.

In the area of experimental physics, Pascal demonstrated the probability that a vacuum could and did exist in nature. Aristotle had taught that nature abhors a vacuum. Pascal's work on the vacuum began when he heard of Torricelli's experiment with the barometer. When Torricelli placed a tube of mercury upside down in a bowl of mercury, some of the mercury remained in the bottom of the tube while a space remained above the mercury (see fig. 2.4). Pascal simply asked (1) why the mercury would remain in the tube above the bowl while its open end was submerged in the mercury, and (2) what filled the space in the tube above the mercury? Because of Aristotle's view of the impossibility of a vacuum, the prevailing wisdom of the day concluded that some invisible substance filled the space.

In *Experiences nouvelles touchant le vide* published in 1647, Pascal described the series of experiments he had performed with tubes of different sizes and shapes filled with various liquids. His experiments led to the formulation of basic laws related to air pressure including his conclusion that vacuums can and do exist. When his conclusions were challenged on Aristotelian grounds, Pascal distinguished between observable facts of an experiment that follow from the hypothesis or that contradict the hypothesis. If the facts follow from the hypothesis, they merely demonstrate the possibility or probability of the hypothesis. If a single fact contradicts the hypothesis, however, then the hypothesis has been falsified. The facts of the experiment can never lead to absolute proof of a hypothesis because other possible experiments that might lead to falsification might be performed if

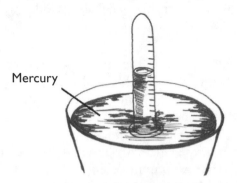

Mercury

Fig. 2.4. Torricelli's Barometer Experiment.

they could be conceived. In his experiments, Pascal demonstrated the falsification of Aristotle's hypothesis about vacuums, but he only demonstrated the *probability* of his own hypothesis about the existence of vacuums. Pascal's statement on scientific method further shook the old Aristotelian consensus.

His experiment with vacuums led Pascal to several important insights about theology and science. His work contributed to the emerging mechanical view of nature that replaced the mysterious, invisible substance that had filled the empty spaces of Aristotle's universe. Pascal's contributions to science virtually eliminated the place for traditional authority (as opposed to experimentation) in science. Old understandings of the working of nature would fall away as experimentation led to new understandings. The Greek philosophers should no longer hold a special place in presupposing the nature of the universe when the study of nature could be expected to lead to new understandings. His emphasis on probability in scientific experimentation also would appear in his understanding of religious knowledge.

Pascal's theory of knowledge owes a great deal to a religious conversion he underwent on November 23, 1654. Pascal became an active participant in Jansenism, a movement within the Roman Catholic Church that shared many features with Protestantism. Pascal wrote a series of eighteen letters, published as the *Lettres provinciales* during 1656–1657, in which he defended one of the leading Jansenist philosophers and theologians against attack within the academy. Despite Pascal's efforts, Antoine Arnauld was condemned by the faculty of the Sorbonne, Jansenism was condemned by the pope, and *Lettres provinciales* was placed on the Index of forbidden books.

Pascal the mathematician considered the method of geometry to offer the most perfect procedure for knowing truth. The discovery of the truths of geometry depends upon using axioms that everyone accepts as true. These axioms are principles so clear that nothing clearer can aid in proving them.

From these first principles it is possible to derive the propositions of geometry through a logical system of thought. Axioms cannot be proven by appeal to more basic fundamental principles; therefore, people can never know with absolute certainty the truth of the geometric principles. Nonetheless, this method allows the greatest certainty that people may obtain through their mental capabilities.

Because of the inability to arrive at the truth of first principles, skepticism constantly hovers at the edge of Pascal's method, but he does not attempt to minimize the skepticism. Instead, Pascal argues that the skepticism occurs because people refuse to recognize that first principles (axioms) come through instinct and revelation rather than through the same processes of thought and experimentation that lead to knowledge derived from first principles. Pascal argued that "feelings" play a crucial role in understanding the fundamental truths upon which all other knowledge depends.

Descartes made a radical distinction between the physical and the spiritual, between mind and body. Pascal, on the other hand, insisted that knowledge of the physical world ultimately depends upon intuition and revelation as much as religious knowledge does. He explored this theme in his unfinished work that was later published simply as *Pensées* (Thoughts). In a world where one's mental faculties always lead to skepticism, Pascal had little regard for the attempt to prove the existence of God from nature. One either knows intuitively through revelation that God made all of nature, or one does not. On this subject Pascal deserves to be quoted at length:

> I admire the boldness with which these persons undertake to speak of God. In addressing their argument to infidels, their first chapter is to prove Divinity from the works of nature. I should not be astonished at their enterprise, if they were addressing their argument to the faithful; for it is certain that those who have the living faith in their hearts see at once that all existence is none other than the work of the God

whom they adore. But for those in whom this light is extinguished, and in whom we purpose to rekindle it, persons destitute of faith and grace, who, seeking with all their light whatever they see in nature that can bring them to this knowledge, find only obscurity and darkness; to tell them that they have only to look at the smallest things which surround them, and they will see God openly, to give them, as a complete proof of this great and important matter, the course of the moon and planets, and to claim to have concluded the proof with such an argument, is to give them ground for believing that the proofs of our religion are very weak. And I see by reason and experience that nothing is more calculated to arouse their contempt.

It is not after this manner that Scripture speaks, which has a better knowledge of the things that are of God. It says, on the contrary, that God is a hidden God, and that, since the corruption of nature, He has left men in darkness from which they can escape only through Jesus Christ, without whom all communion with God is cut off. *Nemo novit Patrem, nisi Filius, et cui voluerit Filius revelare.*[34]

This is what Scripture points out to us, when it says in so many places that those who seek God find him. It is not of that light, "like the noonday sun," that this is said. We do not say that those who seek the noonday sun, or water in the sea, shall find them; and hence the evidence of God must not be of this nature. So it tells us elsewhere: *Vere tu es Deus absconditus.*[35]

Everyone has the same evidence. Some believe and some do not. Those who believe do not do so because the evidence is more compelling for them but because they believe. Once they believe, the evidence becomes compelling.

Order, purpose, and design do not prove the existence of God. Instead, faith in God allows one to grasp the order, purpose, and design of nature. Ultimately, Pascal considered all knowledge to be religious knowledge. From his description of the method of geometry, Pascal considered reliance upon intuition and revelation to be a most reasonable course. In his famous wager argument, Pascal challenges skeptics to consider what they might gain by faith in God as opposed to what they might lose. If they choose God and God exists, they have gained eternity. If they choose God and God does not exist, they have lost nothing. If they do not choose God but God does exist, they have lost everything.

In this argument, Pascal's mathematical and methodological stress on probability played a great part. He did not intend his wager argument as the grounds for faith so much as a demonstration of the reasonableness of faith, for he went on to discuss the person who, even though recognizing the reasonableness of faith and the desirability of faith, yet lacks faith. Pascal offered the example of others who struggled with faith: "Follow the way by which they began; by acting as if they believed, taking the holy water, having masses said, etc."[36] In short, faith will come to those who seek it.

Observations: Pascal regarded faith in God as the basic axiom from which all certain knowledge proceeds. Skepticism performed a useful function by demonstrating the limits of human reason and the need people have for God. Pascal had little confidence in formal proofs for God. Having experienced a conversion, he believed that knowledge of God does not come through the reason of philosophy but through the reason of the heart.

CHAPTER THREE

INDUSTRIAL DESIGN

THE SEVENTEENTH CENTURY BEGAN with English monarchs who claimed to rule by divine right. It ended with monarchs who reigned at the pleasure of Parliament. The century began with Englishmen living in a New World. It ended with Englishmen living in a "new universe" created by Isaac Newton. Newton did not create his universe *ex nihilo* but glued together all the pieces that scientists of the previous few centuries had been constructing. He glued it together with his genius. When he finished, he had a great machine. The universe was truly a great machine to symbolize the progress of the exploding industrial age.

With his laws of gravity, Newton drew a picture of the universe as a great machine with interconnecting parts. Seventeenth-century theological and political thought had been dominated by advocacy and reaction to Reformed thought, which pictured the universe as a vast kingdom presided over by a sovereign king who had absolute power over everything. With the triumph of Puritans and Parliament over King Charles I in the 1640s, Reformed thinkers had the opportunity to put into practice their theory of government. The experiment took place not only in England but also in New England and the city of Geneva where John Calvin had developed his understanding of Reformed theology. When the experiment failed, the influence of Reformed thought declined not only in politics and theology but also in the universities. When the commonwealth government collapsed and King Charles II was restored in 1660, the former Puritans were expelled from their posts in the universities.

As the Great Fire of London swept the city clean to make way for the new pattern of architecture devised by Christopher Wren and others, so the Restoration with its democratized monarchy swept church, state, and academy clean of old ideas. Isaac Newton (1643–1727) was born during the Commonwealth, but he came to intellectual flower during the reign of the "merry monarch," Charles II. The reign of Charles II allowed broad latitude in the matter of morals, in keeping with the king's own sexual exploits. Though John Bunyan wrote *The Pilgrim's Progress* during this period, he did so from a jail cell, where he sat imprisoned for the crime of preaching. *The Pilgrim's Progress* looked back to the earlier literary tradition for its home. The Restoration gave birth to a new intellectual tradition whose literature would flow well into the eighteenth century with bawdy classics such as *Moll Flanders, Fanny Hill,* and *Tom Jones.* As Shakespeare had captured the climate of his day, so these early novels captured their times as well.

Until Newton, all professors of mathematics at Cambridge were required to come from the clergy since mathematics was considered a philosophical discipline. Like astronomy and chemistry, mathematics fell within the category of natural philosophy. Science as we know it today did not exist as a discipline distinct from philosophy. The word *science,* when it was used, simply meant knowledge. The medieval assertion that theology was the queen of the sciences referred to theology as the fountain of knowledge in general. With Isaac Newton, however, the academy took the bold step to make a clean division between mind and body, between spirit and matter, as Descartes had advocated only a few decades earlier. Cambridge University granted Newton the chair of mathematics, though he lacked the requisite theological qualification and the orthodox faith of a theist.

The climate for the constructive engagement of theology and natural philosophy was far worse on the Continent. While England had been engaged in its own Civil War for several years in the 1640s, Europe had been inflamed with a major war that devastated most of Germany and sapped the energies of France and the Lowlands. The Thirty Years War destroyed the earlier enthusiasm the Europeans had for matters theological. The pious motives of theological conviction with which the war began dissolved into cynical power plays and establishment of nation states by the war's close. In the earlier phases of the war, lines were drawn along religious distinctions—Catholic, Calvinist, Lutheran. As the war dragged on, participants made treaties and chose sides in the conflict without regard to religion. With the growth of cynicism, religion as seen in traditional Christian faith played a smaller and smaller part in the intellectual discussions of the day. During the Enlightenment in France, discussions of natural philosophy and moral philosophy continued, but without the need for reference to God.

Gottfried Wilhelm Leibniz (1646–1716), Newton's great rival in Germany, also made his own contribution to the design discussion, even though he did not take part in it himself. His work would have implications for others several generations later. He prepared the way for evolutionary thought with his *principle of continuity:* things pass from one state of being to another state through an infinite number of intermediate states. All of reality, whether consciousness or motion, exists as a continuum. He had rejected Aristotle's notion of a finite universe and replaced it with the notion of infinity expressed symbolically through differential calculus, which he invented in 1676. He attempted to apply the function of an infinitesimal algorithm within infinitesimal calculus to all realms of discourse, whether theology, philosophy, mathematics, physics, metaphysics, or moral philosophy.

Leibniz embraced a mechanical understanding of the universe within the infinite continuum of change. He believed that all matter was composed of yet smaller matter in an infinite regression, just as he believed that all lines were composed of an infinite number of points. Furthermore, each subpart of matter has within it a degree of *force* in constant agitation. This internal force interacts with external forces in the phenomenon of motion. Upon analysis, the ball that strikes a wall and bounces back does not suddenly stop moving and then start moving again in another direction. Instead, it goes through a continuous process of change very quickly. The change in motion involves the elasticity of the ball (or any other matter) as its internal force interacts with the external force. The loss of motion occurs gradually but quickly.

Leibniz's ideas of infinity and force in the seventeenth century would have a profound impact on the intellectual environment. He removed the intellectual stigma of an infinite regress that insisted upon a first cause. His concept of force internal to matter made it possible to conceive of a motion without a prime mover. Leibniz himself was not a naturalist, but his ideas made it possible to conceive of naturalism. In the next generation David Hume would demonstrate how devastating these simple ideas could be to the design argument.

LOCKE AND THE KEY TO DESIGN

All of the people we have examined so far have approached design from the perspective of faith. All believed that God designed the world, though they disagreed as to what they meant when they used the word *God*. They also disagreed about what one may know of God from the physical evidence of the world. Those who shared a common Christian faith did not reach the same conclusions about what the physical world can tell us of God. They subscribed to differing philosophical perspectives through which they interpreted the physical world and through which they interpreted the Bible. Even in their disagreements, however, they assumed that God designed the world.

In the seventeenth century tremors began that would lead to a collapse in the eighteenth. Thomas Hobbes, who had gone into exile in France with the Stuarts during the time of the Puritan dominance in England and the Thirty Years War on the Continent, began to discuss political and moral philosophy in ways that did not reflect the traditional role of God. The same latitude allowed in moral behavior gained acceptance in discussions of theology. The old precision of the Puritans seemed out of place. Amos Funkenstein has argued that a change in the theological perspective of the intellectual tradition occurred beginning in the seventeenth century with men like Galileo, Descartes, Leibniz, Newton, Hobbes, and Vico. Funkenstein refers to this development as a "secular theology."[1] These important thinkers either had no theological training or their training was minimal. Yet they persisted in discussing the theology of their work. Their theology, however, focused on the world as they understood it from their work.

John Locke (1632–1704) also contributed to the intellectual climate in which people considered the evidence of design in the universe. Raised in a Puritan family, Locke remained a committed Christian all his life, though he insisted upon testing even the truth of faith by reason. He set the stage for the English love of empiricism with his "Essay Concerning Human Understanding," arguing that people acquire all of their ideas from experience. Experience involves both sensation through the body and reflection through the mind. Locke rejected the Platonic notion of innate ideas that people bring into life. The ability of the mind to organize sensations into ideas comes from its ability to make associations or analogies between things and build upon these. Many have regarded his views on knowledge as an answer to Descartes because Locke also contended for the unity of body and mind. Furthermore, Locke assumed the existence of the physical world. A variety of internal inconsistencies in Locke's thought made it possible for later thinkers to accept his priority of knowledge through the senses without accepting his understanding of the unity of mind and body. As we shall see, committed Christians like Bishop Butler would use Locke's empiricism to ground Christian faith in physical evidence while Hume would use the same approach to discredit the claims of Butler.

Deism came to prominence during this same period. It spread through British intellectual circles after the Restoration but lacked a systematic approach or unified program. The most prominent early advocate of Deism, Lord Herbert of Cherbury (1583–1648), had no clear followers except Charles Blount (1654–1693), who took up Deism after Herbert's death. Deism took many forms, though it generally involved belief in a Supreme Being who established the natural and moral order of the universe. Most Deists regarded the Scriptures of all religions as human inventions and unnecessary to true religion. They rejected miracles and all forms of the supernatural as contrary to reason. What can be known of God is known by reason. Most of the Deists also would have denied the incarnation of God as Jesus Christ. The title of the most famous work by John Toland (1670–1722) sums up the attitude of many Deists: *Christianity not Mysterious: Or a treatise Shewing That there is nothing in the Gospel Contrary to Reason, Nor above it: And that no Christian Doctrine can be properly call'd a Mystery* (1696).

While Deists believed in a God who could be known by reason, they had a strong revulsion for the church and its priests. In a sense the Deists represented the same revolutionary spirit in the theological/philosophical area that had been shown in the Glorious Revolution of 1688, when the British Parliament deposed their king. Deism represented an individualistic approach to religion. This revolutionary spirit appeared most clearly among the French Deists, Voltaire (1694–1778) and Rousseau (1712–1778), and the American Deists Benjamin Franklin (1706–1790) and Thomas Jefferson (1743–1826). While the Deists had no common creed, they all shared a strong confidence in human reason.

RELIGION BOYLES DOWN TO DESIGN, OR THE BUTLER DID IT

Robert Boyle (1627–1691) promoted the design argument, but he also advanced the mechanical view of the universe. He inherited a great fortune from his father, the first Earl of

Cork, with which he pursued a career that would contribute to the development of experimental science. He improved the air pump and demonstrated that air has both weight and elasticity. His mechanical view of the universe provided the Deists with philosophical ground on which to stand, but his fortune provided an endowment to support a lectureship for the defense of Christianity. The Boyle Lectures produced many a hard-crafted argument over the years. They did not always produce their intended result, however, for Benjamin Franklin claimed that he became a Deist as a result of reading some of the Boyle Lectures! Despite important lectures based on design by figures such as Richard Bentley and William Derham, the lectures tended toward the highly rationalistic, like the Deists they tended to combat. Anthony Collins, a prominent Deist, joked that no one doubted the existence of God until Samuel Clark's lecture proposed to demonstrate it.[2]

Perhaps the most influential work by a Deist was *Christianity as Old as the Creation: Or, The Gospel a Republication of the Religion of Nature* (1730) written by Matthew Tindal (1657–1733). This book drew over 150 responses, among which was *The Analogy of Religion* (1736) by Bishop Joseph Butler. Butler (1692–1752) was every bit the rationalist that the Deists were, but he wanted to make a case for revelation. He based his argument on the design of the universe evident in nature.

Butler adopted the empiricism of Locke and set about to make religion a matter of sober reason. In this regard he accepted Descartes's dichotomy of mind and body in an interesting way. He rejected "religious affections" in his approach to religion, and he strongly distinguished between reason and emotion. He believed that emotion and enthusiasm had no place in religion since they relate to the body. He ordered John Wesley out of his diocese in 1739 to protect his people from the Awakening. Though Butler developed his argument in a highly rationalistic way, he rejected rationalism as the final judge of knowledge and gave that dignity to empiricism. What can be known must ultimately be demonstrated by the sensory experience of empiricism. The data for science and religion must be the same! Our knowledge of God does not come from ideas of God implanted into us before birth but from observing the physical world God has made. Once supplied by data through the senses, human reason has the capacity to analyze and draw reliable conclusions from the data. Butler considered the mind entirely trustworthy.

Butler's argument from design assumes that if the evidence so analyzed measures up to the standards of reason, the prudent person must assent.[3] This approach relies upon probability as assessed by a prudent person rather than upon absolute proof, since Butler would argue that we do not have absolute proof for anything. The prudent person would not require more than reasonable evidence. While attempting to construct an argument for revelation within a design scheme, Butler also insisted that revelation falls under the judgment of reason both in terms of the meaning of revelation and the morality of revelation. Though he worked in a design context, Butler did not have as his aim an argument to demonstrate the existence of God on the basis of design. He and his opponents assumed the existence of God and the orderly design of nature. He wrote primarily against the Deists within their philosophical frame of reference to make a case for specific revelation and redemption through the incarnate Christ.

Butler stressed that God has established universal laws of nature that people may recognize through sensory observation and understand through reason. As governor of the universe, however, God has established laws that govern every other aspect of human experience as religion or moral law. Laws in one realm have their counterpart in the other realm because they form part of a single universal scheme of God's governance. Through experience we have developed *probabilities* of the course of nature so that we know how to dress in January and July. We may experience a warm day in January and a cold day in July, but we have probability as a guide that serves us well if not absolutely. We may discern the laws of nature and draw applications that guide our lives based on probabilities. If we conduct our everyday life according to probability, then we behave prudently. We would be imprudent if we did not also conduct our religious life by probability. If the evidence for Christianity is only probable, rather than absolute, the prudent person has a moral obligation to follow its dictates.

By *analogy* Butler makes the transfer from everyday life to the religious life. The combination of the probabilities of nature and the cumulative history of the experience of the human race provide the data from which analogies may be drawn. Because God governs both the natural and the moral realm, we may derive analogies of one from the other. Pain serves a function in nature to warn animals of potential danger. It serves as a means of guidance through the avoidance of pain. By analogy, we may see that God has provided the same principle of pain through punishment in society to give guidance to society. Butler's use of analogy depends upon the acceptance of the idea that God governs all realms of reality by the same universal laws. Probability reveals the law in one realm and analogy provides the basis for recognizing it in another realm. The laws of nature and of religion (morality) may be understood as representing the same basic principles. Butler's discussion of immortality will illustrate how analogy provides evidence for immortality.

In nature we may observe that many creatures undergo dramatic changes in the course of their lives: the maggot that becomes a fly or the egg that hatches into a bird. The embryonic changes of humans further illustrate this point. The evidence suggests by analogy that people will live on in some altered state beyond death. Nature's laws of motion and momentum demonstrate that a body persists in its course. We know that people also have powers of momentum related to human capacities—powers such as action, love, and suffering. The evidence suggests by analogy that some dimension of the human personality will persist after death. Furthermore, Butler argued that we lack any evidence to indicate what happens at death other than the observable physical results.

He stresses that the body is merely the medium of the self and not the self per se. While we have no empirical evidence that life ends at death, we have no empirical evidence that it does not. In the absence of data one way or the other, then analogy provides the most reliable evidence that life persists.

Special revelation represents the third area in which analogy provides access. The first area of *nature* led to the second area of *natural theology*. These led to the third area of *revealed religion*. Butler illustrated the application of analogy to special revelation through the concept of mediation, a notion that Deists had little use for. Butler observed that people experience mediation all the time in everyday life whenever one person helps another person. To object to mediation by Christ is to object to all mediation as such. In social experience we observe judges who grant leniency and creditors who extend credit. God's extension of mercy to provide spiritual help to those in trouble is analogous to this common experience. In nature we observe that medicine provides remedy and healing for different illnesses and afflictions. By analogy, Jesus Christ provides the remedy for the sickness of sin. Having established analogy as a principle in the area of natural theology, Butler demonstrated the reasonableness of extending it to special revelation.

Observations: Butler's approach builds upon the assumptions of the best science and philosophy of his day. As such, his theology is bound to the intellectual context of the mid-eighteenth century. He has adapted empiricism to the formulation of theology within a rationalistic framework hostile to emotion. Religion was primarily for him a matter of morality. His argument from analogy assumes the order of nature and society in a way that Deists would approve. He assumed the existence of God and God's design of the universe. Eliminating any of his assumptions collapses his whole system. We shall see that David Hume attacks his concept of analogy without allowing him to assume either the existence of God or the order of the universe.

FORM FOLLOWS FUNCTION, OR
THE DESIGNERLESS HOME

Newton could look at the vast engine of the universe and conclude, "He must be blind who from the most wise and excellent contrivances of things cannot see the Infinite Wisdom and Goodness of their Almighty Creator, and he must be mad and senseless who refuses to acknowledge them."[4] The same data by itself, however, left room for other interpretations. In *Dialogues Concerning Natural Religion* (1779) David Hume (1711–1776) took quite a different position.[5] Hume inherited the skepticism of Calvin, Descartes, and Pascsal, but he inherited none of their faith. Once the Cartesian dichotomy between mind and body had entered the intellectual environment, the skeptic could only appeal to common experience. Transferring experience of the physical world by analogy to the spiritual world created particular logical problems. Hume pressed this issue particularly with the standard argument of natural theology that the universe gives evidence of mind or intelligence behind its order and purpose.

Hume suggested the analogy of the design of the universe with reference to human creativity as it had developed:

> Throw several pieces of steel together, without shape or form; they will never arrange themselves so as to compose a watch: Stone, and mortar, and wood, without an architect, never erect a house. But the ideas in a human mind, we see, by an unknown, inexplicable economy, arrange themselves so as to form the plan of a watch or house. Experience, therefore, proves, that there is an original principle of order in mind, not in matter. From similar effects we infer similar causes. The adjustment of means to ends is alike in the universe, as a machine of human contrivance. The causes, therefore, must be resembling.[6]

Having stated the conventional analogy of mind behind the universe, Hume points out that experimental facts depend upon similar causes that produce similar effects. Any alteration in circumstances raises doubts about the event. Such changes will require renewed experimentation to determine what effect the changes have had on the event. It is one thing to compare the universe to houses, ships, furniture, and machines but quite another to infer a similarity in cause. Hume challenged the traditional attribution of mind to the underlying cause of the universe. People have many examples of house, ship, furniture, and machine by which to infer that they result from the action of a mind. Since we have but one universe, we do not have an adequate experimental basis to draw a similar conclusion. By experiment we have knowledge of the place of mind in the construction of a house, but in that experiment we have access both to the house and to the builder. With the case of the universe, it is the existence of the mind of the builder that lies in doubt. Furthermore, Hume disallows the argument that the mind behind the universe represents self-evident truth. If it can be doubted, as Hume has done, then it is not self-evident. If any other explanation comes to mind, then it is not self-evident.

By pressing the analogy of the mind, Hume suggests that people have made themselves the model for the universe. This anthropomorphic approach amounts to little more than what Freud would call over a century later a "projection" upon the universe. Hume argued that the existence of intelligent mind behind the material universe represents an unnecessary intrusion into the natural order. In describing God as the first cause or the prime mover, one must next explain why God does not have a cause other than himself. Hume argued that one may just as easily argue that the universe has no cause other than itself. It is not necessary to go so far as to posit a God when one may stop with the physical world.[7] It is not necessary to look for some ordering principle outside of matter when the principle of order may just as easily be seen as an aspect of matter itself. In this line of discussion, Hume began to build a case for looking no further than the tangible evidence in arriving at an explanation: "An ideal system, arranged of itself, without a precedent design, is not a whit more explicable than a material one, which attains its order in a like manner; nor is there any more difficulty in the latter supposition than in the former."[8]

Even if one were to allow as self-evident the existence of God, the evidence of the material world does not necessarily lead to the God of the Bible.[9] Using the analogy of the house, ship, or city, many people are involved in constructing these human artifices. If the universe is like a human artifice, then why would we not suppose the existence of many gods? Even if the universe arose by the design of some single deity, one is left to creative imagination to determine what kind of deity designed it. It might have been an infant deity who made this universe as a first, inferior attempt, and that universe construction was soon abandoned. It might have been an inferior deity who made this universe that is considered with contempt for its shoddy workmanship by superior deities. It might have been an old, retired deity who made this universe in senility and who has since died. Without a basis for comparison and experimentation, it would be impossible to say what kind of God might have made a universe like ours.

Instead of granting that the universe resembles a machine or other human artifice, Hume argued that the universe seems more to resemble some life form, either animal or vegetable.[10] While the ancient philosophers spoke of design, they also seem to have had a preference for understanding the world as a great body whose mind was God. Hume allows the reasonableness of this inference since people expect to find a mind where they find a body, but the experience of humans does not reasonably transfer by analogy as evidence to support the existence of God. The sense of order that some attribute to design, Hume attributes to the "inviolable laws" inherent in matter itself. If the universe bears a greater resemblance to life than to machines, then its origin would more probably come from generation than from design.[11] Referring to his earlier example, Hume declared that the world resembles an animal or vegetable much more than a watch. The internal organization of life that causes a tree to have the same order as the tree from which it sprang would explain why the universe would have a sense of order. It is the order of its nature. Hume allows that order in human experience does arise from reason as well as from generation, but without more data the explanation for order in the universe is simply a matter of arbitrary choice.

In a universe of finite matter but infinite duration, Hume argued that every possible order and position would occur an infinite number of times. People currently experience just one of those infinite possibilities that the universe has undergone. Whenever the universe reaches a state of order, it would have the appearance of design. Hume assumed that motion and force belonged to matter as an aspect of its nature; thus, the universe required no prime mover to set the universe in motion. Hume reasoned that "thought has no influence upon matter, except where that matter is so conjoined with it, as to have an equal reciprocal influence upon it. No animal can move immediately any thing but the members of its own body; and indeed, the equality of action and re-action seems to be a universal law of nature. . . ."[12]

Hume next moves on to the necessary existence of God and the problem of evil. As for the necessary being upon whose existence the universe depends, Hume reasoned that any being who can be conceived of as not existing could hardly be called necessary.[13] The problem of evil involves more discussion. After a general survey of human misery and the natural order of the strong preying upon the weak, Hume questions the validity of attributing to God such moral qualities as justice, benevolence, and mercy: "His power we allow infinite: Whatever he wills is executed: But neither man nor any other animal are happy: Therefore he does not will their happiness. His wisdom is infinite: He is never mistaken in choosing the means to any end: But the course of nature tends not to human or animal felicity: Therefore it is not established for that purpose."[14]

Hume argues that the only purpose of nature with respect to life is the preservation of individuals and the propagation of species. Hume would not allow the appeal to a final judgment and heavenly reward to resolve the problem of divine benevolence because these would be unprovable hypotheses. He insisted that "the only method of supporting divine benevolence . . . is to deny absolutely the misery and wickedness of man."[15] No one can deny this misery because pain is "infinitely more violent and durable" than pleasure.[16] Any resolution to these difficulties must come from faith, not from experience of the material world.

Observations: Hume laid the intellectual foundations for naturalism that would blossom through the work of Charles Darwin. He suggested that all of nature could be explained by nature itself. It need not have had a cause any more than God would have had a cause. What appears to be design could be nothing more than the natural state of nature that could produce life to observe it. Rather than supporting the Christian understanding of God, Hume suggested that an argument from nature could more strongly support a Hindu understanding of God in which nature represents the body and God the mind.

PALEY'S WATCH

William Paley (1743–1805) developed perhaps the most famous argument from design in his *Natural Theology: or Evidences of the Existence and Attributes of the Deity, Collected from the Appearances of Nature* (1802). As we have observed, several others before Paley had used the watch as an analogy of the mechanical nature of the universe. Paley built upon this well-known analogy and began his book without any other introduction than the analogy itself:

> In crossing a heath, suppose I pitched my foot
> against a stone, and were asked how the *stone* came
> to be there; I might possibly answer, that, for any
> thing I knew to the contrary, it had lain there for ever:
> nor would it perhaps be very easy to show the
> absurdity of the answer. But suppose I had found a
> *watch* upon the ground, and it should be inquired

how the watch happened to be in that place; I should
hardly think of the answer which I had before given,
that for any thing I knew, the watch might have
always been there. Yet why should not this answer
serve for the watch as well as for the stone? Why is it
not as admissible in the second case, as in the first?
For this reason, and for no other, viz. that, when we
come to inspect the watch, we perceive (what we
could not discover in the stone) that its several parts
are framed and put together for a purpose, e.g. that
they are so formed and adjusted as to produce
motion, and that motion so regulated as to point out
the hour of the day: that if the different parts had
been differently shaped from what they are, of a
different size from what they are, or placed after any
other manner, or in any other order, than that in
which they are placed, either no motion at all would
have been carried on in the machine, or none which
would have answered the use that is now served by it.
To reckon up a few of the plainest of these parts, and
of their offices, all tending to one result:—we see a
cylindrical box containing a coiled elastic spring,
which, by its endeavour to relax itself, turns round
the box. We next observe a flexible chain (artificially
wrought for the sake of flexure) communicating the
action of the spring from the box to the fusee. We
then find a series of wheels, the teeth of which catch
in, and apply to, each other, conducting the motion
from the fusee to the balance, and from the balance to
the pointer; and at the same time, by the size and
shape of those wheels, so regulating that motion, as
to terminate in causing an index, by an equable and
measured progression, to pass over the given space in
a given time. We take notice that the wheels are made
of brass in order to keep them from rust: the springs
of steel, no other metal being so elastic; that over the
face of the watch there is placed a glass, a material

employed in no other part of the work, but in the room of which, if there had been any other than a transparent substance, the hour could not be seen without opening the case. This mechanism being observed (it requires indeed an examination of the instrument, and perhaps some previous knowledge of the subject, to perceive and understand it; but being once, as we have said, observed and understood), the inference, we think, is inevitable, that the watch must have had a maker: that there must have existed, at some time, and at some place or other, an artificer or artificers, who formed it for the purpose which we find it actually to answer; who comprehended its construction, and designed its use.[17]

Paley's argument operates by analogy, like Butler's argument. One can anticipate where he is going with his argument. The universe and everything in it is even more complex than a watch and bears even more evidence of contrivance than a mere watch; therefore, we conclude that the universe must have had a maker. By analogy, his argument also involves a first cause and a prime mover who set it all in motion. The argument hinges on design rather than existence. He does not question the origin of the existence of the material world. Rather, he questions how a world with the appearance of *design* came to be. Infinite regress becomes a much thornier problem when exploring the explanation for something with the appearance of design.

Having established the basic principle of his argument, Paley applies the analogy to case after case in the natural world beginning with the comparison of the eye to a telescope. He then discusses how the eyes of different animals differ yet are perfectly suited to that animal's way of life. From the eye he moves to the ear and from ears to reproduction which duplicates the organization of design. The presence of flaws or imperfections in nature does not offer counter-evidence against a designer any more than the failure of a watch to keep good time offers evidence that the watch had no designer. Because of the frailty of the parts, the watch-maker will regularly clean the watch and make repairs.

Most modern treatments of the development of the design argument discuss Hume after Paley to show how Hume destroyed Paley's argument, even though these discussions acknowledge that Hume wrote before Paley. John Hick states that Paley did not deal with any of Hume's criticisms of the design argument, and Hugh Ross writes as though Hume actually wrote after Paley.[18] Paley actually addressed the issues raised by Hume. Hume's argument would not gain its real force until joined with Darwin's theory, as we shall see. Hume had argued that any universe would have to have some form that might be mistaken for design. Paley countered with his litany of specific examples from biology to show that such features as eyes are not simply some random form that fills an empty cavity in the head. Paley also responded to Hume's suggestion that in an infinite amount of time, all the possible configurations could occur that might account for the kind of universe in which we live. Paley simply replied that no exper-imental evidence existed to support such a conjecture. Paley speculated on what we might say of the person who explained the existence of mills and engines by arguing: "That a mass of metals and other materials having run when melted into all possible figures, and combined themselves in all possible forms and shapes, and proportions, these things which we see, are what were left from the accident, as best worth pre-serving. . . . I cannot distinguish the hypothesis as applied to the works of nature, from this solution, which no one would accept, as applied to a collection of machines."[19]

BRIDGING THE GAP

The picture of God as a designer and watchmaker has an inter-esting influence on how some people view God's relationship to nature. The Deists had followed that line to conclude that God had established laws for the physical and moral governance of the universe but that he remained removed from the day-to-day operations. This view, known as *uniformitarianism,* gained growing acceptance in scientific circles by the early 1800s. It did not represent the exclusive view, but it represented a growing perspective. In this climate, Francis Henry Egerton, eighth Earl of Bridgewater, commissioned a series of eight essays known as the *Bridgewater Treatises* that appeared in the 1830s to refute uniformitarianism.

Not all of the *Bridgewater* contributors took a design approach to their argument, but several did.[20] Perhaps the most significant of these was geologist William Buckland (1784–1856) of Oxford University. Buckland began by establishing a link with the earlier Boyle Lectures through his quotation from William Derham's *Physico-Theology* as an opening epigram. In his preface he further made clear that he hoped to do through geology what William Paley had accomplished through biology: the "demonstration, of the continuous Being, and of many of the highest Attributes of the One Living and True God" through an "examination of the evidences of Design" found in the fossil record.[21] Geology itself was in its infancy as a science when Buckland wrote.

Buckland had the added difficulty of fashioning his argument around the fossils of extinct animals. The fossils suggested that the earth was much older than the six thousand years commonly held by the religious community when Buckland wrote. To resolve this difficulty, he suggested a gap of time between the creation of the universe in Genesis 1:1 and the fitting out of the earth in Genesis 1:2.

In answer to Hume's complaint about the universal presence of pain and death, Buckland argued that the sudden death of animals, either by falling prey to a carnivore or by some natural disaster, represents an act of kindness by God. Rather than subjecting creatures to the slow process of sickness and decay, God provided a way to experience sudden and unexpected death.[22]

Paley, Buckland, and others did answer Hume's views, and they did so in the way most attractive to the English of their day. They compiled case after case of empirical evidence to support the position of design. Hume had a theory, but he lacked empirical evidence. Butler, standing in the tradition of Locke, had held the day on the priority of empirical evidence over rationalism as the final determination of knowledge. Hume had only offered a theory that nature had within itself the power to produce the marvels that appear to be designed. Paley and Buckland, on the other hand, produced specific cases involving the structure of living things to demonstrate the necessity of design. As John Hadley Brooke and Geoffrey Cantor have observed, "David Hume's critique of natural theology was not only indecisive but ingeniously contested."[23] Hume's views could not have standing unless someone produced the missing empirical evidence to support a natural explanation for the structures of biology.

LEAVING EVERYTHING TO CHANCE

Between 1831 and 1836, Charles Darwin (1809–1882) took an extended voyage to the Southern Hemisphere aboard the *H.M.S. Beagle*. In the course of his journey as the ship's naturalist, Darwin collected the empirical data he would use as evidence to support a natural explanation for the adaptation of life forms to their environments as well as an explanation for the complex organs that have special functions for a species. The theory of evolution did not originate with Charles Darwin, but he did succeed in providing it with an experimental basis that captured the imagination of the scientific community.

As far as Darwin's theory relates to design, its most significant feature lies in the concept of *natural selection* as an alternative to design. The variety of forms of life relates to the urge for survival. Each generation of life produces variety in its offspring, however subtle the variation may be. Those variations that are more conducive to their environment have the greater chance of survival and produce offspring that build on these variations while adding new ones. Over a period of thousands of generations, the varieties that are less conducive to their environment die out while the successful varieties thrive until they eventually become a new species. The changes that occur take place by chance, rather than by design. The successful changes lead to ever advancing forms of life, while the unsuccessful changes lead to extinction.

While many criticisms of Darwin's theory arose at the time of the publication of his book *The Origin of the Species* (1859), the criticism that has the most direct application to the question of design concerns the presence of complex organs. The eye is perhaps the most obvious of such organs. The eye had been the first organ to which Paley had pointed to demonstrate design within life forms. Darwin's critics asked how the eye could evolve as a slight variation between generations. It would have to appear in its completed form or else serve no function at all for untold generations until all the pieces necessary to make an eye work had come about through variation between generations. Darwin admitted that the eye gave him "a cold shudder."[24] As we shall see, the problem of the eye and the explanation of complex organs by appeal to natural selection alone would reappear in the closing days of the twentieth century.

Darwin defended natural selection with the theory that the earliest stages of the development of the eye must have been useful in some way in the struggle for survival. He suggested a possible sequence of development that would have involved "functional eyes" that could be illustrated from several forms of life. In other words, Darwin appealed to Butler's old analogical approach in the absence of clear evidence! While this approach did not prove his case in the matter of complex organs, it satisfied his supporters. Those dissatisfied with his case would have to wait for new evidence. In the meantime, Darwin provided Hume's theory of naturalism with an empirical base. Hume had not destroyed Paley's argument, but Darwin's evidence for Hume's theory took the punch out of Paley's argument so that it fell into disfavor.

Darwin did not have the only interpretation of the data about evolution. Alfred Russel Wallace was working on the same idea at the same time as Darwin. Wallace, in fact, wrote a paper on the subject that compelled Darwin to go public with his views quickly or be left at the starting gate by Wallace. The two men issued a joint paper on evolution for the Linnaean Society in 1858. Wallace had quite a different perspective on what conclusions could be drawn from the data of evolution. He believed that God guided the process of evolution as his instrument for creation. Wallace pointed to such *orthogenetic trends* as the increasing size of the human brain over a period of thousands of years during which the functions of such a brain were not utilized. Natural selection would suggest that the development of an ability over such a long period of time could not occur if it did not give people an advantage in survival. That humans would use the brain for speculative thought only after thousands of years suggested to Wallace both purpose and design. He interpreted this data as evidence of a superior intelligence that guided the development of people "in a definite direction, and for a special purpose."[25] The agreement of Wallace and Darwin on the data and their disagreement on the question of mechanism behind the data suggests that evolution involves both scientific and philosophical implications.

Observations: By the time Darwin wrote *The Origin of the Species,* science had come into its own as a field of thought distinct from philosophy. Until the middle of the nineteenth century, those disciplines grouped under the umbrella of *science* had a different umbrella over them known as *natural philosophy.* When science ceased to be called natural philosophy, it appeared that a formal break had occurred that separated science from the philosophical discussions that had accompanied it since the time of the Greek philosophers. Descartes's dichotomy between body and mind had suggested this separation between empirical data and rationalistic thought.

The change of name, however, merely veiled a relationship that continues to this day. Much of what passes for empirical science is actually rationalistic philosophy. *The Encyclopedia of Philosophy* acknowledges this situation in the way it attends to Darwin. It treats Darwin in two articles. One article discusses Darwin and his contributions as a scientist. A second article discusses the philosophical view known as *Darwinism*. Today the philosophical views embodied in Darwinism form a major aspect of the worldview assumptions of modern life. Darwin's *science* describes the change in life forms that has taken place over time. Yet the issue of change and accounting for why change should occur is as old a question as the Greek philosophers, as we have seen. Darwin's *philosophy*, or Darwinism, gives a naturalistic explanation for his observations. Just as the Aristotelian philosophical assumptions of the academy provided a framework for science to develop in the late Middle Ages, the philosophical assumptions of Darwinism have provided a framework for science to develop in the twentieth century. Just as the philosophy of Aristotle became enmeshed in the science of the Renaissance, the philosophy of Darwinism has become enmeshed in the science of the twentieth century so that the philosophical assumptions are regarded as scientific dogma.

LANDSCAPE DESIGN

By and large, philosophy in Britain had conceded the playing field to empiricism by the early 1930s. C. S. Lewis studied philosophy at Oxford just before and after World War I. By the time he had done additional study in literature and become a tutor at Oxford, the entire conception of philosophy had changed. Under the influence of *Logical Positivism* in Vienna after World War I, philosophy took a new direction that focused on "cognitive meaning" or empirically verifiable experiences. For a word to have meaning, it must have a physical object to which it refers. Many of the things about which people talk may be satisfying to them, but the positivists would argue that they had no cognitive meaning. They applied this principle to religious issues such as the existence of God. In a famous parable, John Wisdom illustrated the religious problem:

Two people return to their long-neglected garden and find among the weeds a few of the old plants surprisingly vigorous. One says to the other "It must be that a gardener has been coming and doing something about these plants." Upon inquiry they find that no neighbor has ever seen anyone at work in their garden. The first man says to the other "He must have worked while people slept." The other says, "No, someone would have heard him and besides, anybody who cared about the plants would have kept down these weeds." The first man says, "Look at the way these are arranged. There is purpose and a feeling for beauty here. I believe that someone comes, someone invisible to mortal eyes. I believe that the more carefully we look the more we shall find confirmation of this." They examine the garden ever so carefully and sometimes they come on new things suggesting that a gardener comes and sometimes they come on new things suggesting the contrary and even that a malicious person has been at work. Besides examining the garden carefully they also study what happens to gardens left without attention. Each learns all the other learns about this and about the garden. Consequently, when after all this, one says "I still believe a gardener comes" while the other says "I don't" their different words now reflect no difference as to what they have found in the garden, no difference as to what they would find in the garden if they looked further and no difference about how fast untended gardens fall into disorder. At this stage, in this context, the gardener hypothesis has ceased to be experimental, the difference between one who accepts and one who rejects it is not now a matter of the one expecting something the other does not expect. What is the difference between them? The one says, "A gardener comes unseen and unheard. He is manifested only in his works with which we are all familiar," the

other says "There is no gardener" and with this difference in what they say about the gardener goes a
difference in how they feel towards the garden, in
spite of the fact that neither expects anything of it
which the other does not expect.[26]

The parable suggests that when people have the same
empirical data available, they may disagree over the interpretation of the data. Wisdom argued that the interpretation of
the data in this situation has to do with the feelings of the
observers rather than the data they observe. This line of
thought represents the development in philosophy from
Logical Positivism, which looked for the empirically verifiable
fact about which language could speak with meaning, to
Linguistic Analysis, which came to regard language as a game
by which people express their feelings. This philosophical
stream would blossom at the end of the twentieth century as
a full-blown cultural trend known as Postmodernism.

Observations: Notice that the parable allows the existence
of the garden but questions the existence of the gardener. The
parable acknowledges the *appearance* of design. The objection to design does not lie within the data itself. The objection
lies within the philosophical assumptions of the interpreter of
the data.

UPDATING THE DESIGN

Though interest in the design argument faded significantly in
the new theological/philosophical/scientific climate of the
early twentieth century, a major revision of the design argument appeared in Britain at Cambridge at the same time the
philosophers of Oxford were capitulating to naturalism. F. R.
Tennant (1866–1957) revived not only the design argument
but also the ancient tradition of education. He was trained in
chemistry, biology, psychology, theology, philosophy, and
logic.

A rabid empiricist in the British tradition, Tennant refuted
the rationalism of Plato, Augustine, and Calvin that would
attribute reason and knowledge of universals to people at

birth. He insisted that knowledge requires sensory data. He further rejected other classical modes for establishing the existence of God. He gave no ground to mysticism with its claim to ineffable experience of the divine. He denied the existence of any "religious organ" or biological structure that accounted for human knowledge of God. (It is interesting to note that people involved in genetic research at the end of the twentieth century again began to postulate the existence of a "religion gene.") Tennant rejected Rudolf Otto's concept of the universal religious experience. He argued that Otto's *numinous* (Otto's term for religious experience) was too vague and nebulous to serve as valid data for resolving so weighty a matter as the existence of God. He was also averse to admitting data so open to alternative explanations by abnormal psychology! Finally, Tennant would not admit revelation as knowledge of God for apologetic purposes because so much of the Bible involves moralization that might be accounted for in the natural development of cultures. We should note that whereas Tennant strove to demonstrate the existence of God and ascribed to Christ the reverence due the one who had the keenest insight into God's purpose, he belonged to the liberal wing of the church. As such, he accepted many of the higher critical ideas then in fashion about the nature of the Bible.

Tennant believed that empirical evidence provided the only legitimate basis for establishing theistic religion. His argument rested on two points: the existence of the soul and of God. He reasoned that without a soul, it makes little difference whether God exists! He based his argument for the existence of the soul on the experience of consciousness and self-consciousness. Consciousness involves being aware, but self-consciousness involves being aware of being aware. Because of this reflexive awareness, the memory of the awareness builds a collection of data upon which the self-conscious person may draw. Awareness remains even after the object of awareness has gone! At this point Tennant makes a bit of a logical stretch by assigning this ability to bring order and continuity to life experience as residing in the soul. He has the advantage of defining soul as an observable trait of people that involves the qualities related to the awareness of experience.

Tennant's argument for the existence of God does not depend upon his argument for the existence of the soul except in his own mind. His position involves a revival of the design argument in terms of *cosmic teleology*. The term *teleology* has an ancient origin from the Greek word *telos* which means end, goal, or final outcome. Cosmic teleology implies that the entire universe seems designed to lead to a certain goal. In this case, Tennant argued that the universe was designed in such a way as to make life in general, and intelligent life in particular, come to pass. He builds on the tradition of Paley and the authors of the *Bridgewater Treatises,* but he relies heavily on the work of L. J. Henderson. In the same way that Darwin gave empirical evidence to support Hume's idea for the natural explanation of life, Tennant presented an empirical case for the divine origin of life.

L. J. Henderson published a book in 1913 entitled *The Fitness of the Environment* in which he explored for page after page the adaptations of inorganic aspects of nature that made life possible. Tennant took up Henderson's data in constructing his own argument that too many variables had to be exactly right in order for life to appear, and the likelihood of these happening by chance is too improbable to consider. On this basis, he argued that some Designer must have arranged the conditions necessary to make life possible. While evolution may describe how changes occur in life forms, it does not account for how life emerged in the first place. One thing the fossil record does not allow is an infinite regress.

This argument is susceptible to the criticism that Tennant does not have a large enough experimental model to predict whether life may emerge by chance. With only one universe, he cannot make comparative analysis. Hume had made this criticism of the design argument 150 years earlier. Tennant responded to this critique by distinguishing between pure mathematical probability and probability as experienced in the world of fact. This second kind of probability Tennant identified with the induction method of scientific inquiry that cannot be fully explained by reason. At this point Tennant's rigid empiricism lies on the slippery slope of openness to "hunches" for which successful scientists are famous and to the intuitive domain of religious knowledge.

Observations: The commitment to natural theology with its most cherished child, the design argument, has carried with it an increasing commitment to empiricism as the principal and most reliable form of knowledge. In the seventeenth century, advocates of design saw specific revelation as the highest form of knowledge, but by the time of Tennant we see that the leading natural theologians did not even consider specific revelation a possibility.

We have also seen that the design argument depends to a great degree on the probability of whether the structures of the universe can best be accounted for by chance or by design. Opponents of design have argued since the eighteenth century that we do not have a large enough experimental basis for study because we have only one universe. We are restricted to what actually happened and cannot consider what might have happened. As we shall see later, the development of the computer has created the possibility of experimenting with innumerable models of the universe. This possibility for research has contributed to a renewed interest in the design argument.

We also have seen that the design argument has developed over the centuries from a general statement about what the casual observer might notice about the universe and its structures to what the trained specialist in precise fields of science might investigate under the most rigorous of circumstances. As we shall see, the new examination of design focuses on scientific research and its implications.

As philosophy capitulated to empiricism in Britain, as we saw briefly, it focused almost exclusively on the meaning of language. In this discussion, philosophy moved from considering questions of verification (how to prove something true) to questions of falsification (how to prove something false). In the new conversation about design, we will see that William Dembski focuses a great deal of attention on how one might establish the criteria for determining if the evidence for design makes a convincing case. We now turn to an examination of those areas of science in which the new design movement has developed.

CHAPTER FOUR

THE UNIVERSE: DESIGNER SHOWCASE

"Do you feel lucky? Well do ya?"
—Clint Eastwood, *Dirty Harry*

Do PEOPLE FEEL LUCKY when they look into the night sky and see the Milky Way, the Big Dipper, and the North Star? Do they feel lucky when photographs from the Hubble Space Telescope reveal how vast the universe is? Do they feel lucky when they turn their gaze to the earth and see its blue sky, green land, and emerald oceans? Do they feel lucky that there is a place (the earth) in the vastness of space that has life—not only life but also intelligent life?

A VERY BRIEF HISTORY OF THE UNIVERSE

Before we answer Dirty Harry's question about how lucky we should feel about the universe, we need to review the current scientific thinking on the origin (cosmogony) and structure (cosmology) of the universe. The current scientific understanding is called the Big Bang theory.[1] According to this theory, the universe began about 13 to 15 billion years ago, extremely small, very hot, and very dense. Since that beginning, the universe has been expanding and cooling. Within this tiny universe were contained the four fundamental forces that regulate the structures of the nucleus (strong and weak nuclear forces), atoms (electromagnetic force), and clumps of matter (gravity). The theory predicts that atomic nuclei began to form about three minutes after the Big Bang, atoms began to appear about 500,000 years later, and galaxies began to emerge about one billion years after the Big Bang. Since first-generation stars are thought to contain only hydrogen and helium, no rocky planets existed in the first galaxies. Throughout the different star life cycles, elements such as carbon and iron were synthesized by nuclear fusion. Upon the death of the first stars through supernova explosions, elements beyond iron were synthesized. About 10 billion years after the Big Bang, second-generation stars and their planets condensed from the dust clouds that resulted from the death of the first generation stars. Life appeared about 12 billion years after the Big Bang.

Observations: The scientists who proposed the Big Bang Model did not start with a religious belief in creation and then look for scientific evidence to support it. Rather, the scientists were following a naturalistic or materialistic path of discovering what happens to matter under the influence of the four forces over long periods of time. Thus, many scientists were surprised and disturbed to discover that the Big Bang Model pointed toward Christian themes: a beginning for the universe (creation) and a creator who planned (designed) a universe perfect for human life. The more information scientists collected within the materialistic framework, the more data they had that was consonant with Christianity. Let us review four facets of these findings: a created universe, a fine-tuned universe, an extradimensional universe, and an uncommon earth.

A Created Universe

From the ancient Greeks until the early 1900s, the prevailing scientific view was of a static, eternal universe. This view posed a major challenge to the Christian view of a created universe. In fact, Thomas Aquinas (1224–1274) had to conclude that knowledge of creation did not come by science but by faith when he harmonized the Greek thought of Aristotle (384–322 B.C.) with Christian thought. In spite of the conclusion of Thomas, by the early 1900s several observations were beginning to challenge the model of a static, eternal universe:

- *Radioactivity.* With the discovery of radioactivity in 1896 by the French physicist Antoine Henri Becquerel (1852–1908), scientists realized that some of the elements of which the universe is composed do not last forever. Since these elements are still present, can the universe be eternal?

- *Relativity.* In 1916 the German physicist Albert Einstein (1879–1955) published in the prestigious German physics monthly, *Annalen der Physik,* the article "Die Grundlagen der allegemeinen Relativitätstheorie" ("The Foundation of the General Theory of Relativity"). Einstein realized that his proposed understanding of the universe led to the idea of an expanding universe with a beginning. Einstein believed in a static universe, and he modified his equations (adding the cosmological constant) to remove the expansion of the universe and its beginning. Einstein later said that this modified proposal was the greatest mistake of his life.

- *Red Shift of Galaxies.* As the elements within the sun are heated, they emit light. Each element emits light at characteristic wavelengths. The wavelengths of the light emitted by the same element in other stars was discovered to be shifted toward longer wavelengths. Since the color red has the longest wavelength of the visible colors, the observed shift is called a red shift. In 1929, the American astronomer Edwin Hubble (1889–1953) interpreted the observed red shifts as evidence of an expanding universe.

Using the relativity calculations and the red shift data, the Belgian priest and astronomer Georges Lemaître (1894–1966) proposed that the universe began as a "primeval atom" that exploded to cause an expanding universe. Lemaître's model was refined by the Russian-American physicist George Gamow (1904–1968) into what is today called the Big Bang

Model. Thus, scientists using just the concepts of matter and forces stumbled upon a beginning for the universe.

Observations: A beginning implies a cause and a cause implies a creator. Having a creator does not imply a personal caring God. As we have seen in chapter 1, since ancient times other accounts for creation have been given besides the one that credits the universe to God. For example, Plato's creation account attributed the creation not to God but to a Demiurge, a subordinate deity who did the manual labor of heaven. But as scientists continued to examine the universe, they found that the universe is not just any old universe but one designed for human life.

A Fine-Tuned Universe

We live in an exciting time, a time when scientists are able to measure many of the parameters that determine the characteristics of the universe. Also, at this time, scientists can use computers to examine how changes in these parameters affect the universe's characteristics. Scientists knew that the Big Bang Model implied certain broad constraints on the occurrence of life: the universe must exist long enough for life to occur; certain stars must be stable long enough for life to occur; heavy elements must be present for the formation of planets and the chemicals of life. At the same time, because scientists were considering only matter and force, they assumed that there could be large leeways in the values of the parameters without affecting the occurrence of life. From a materialistic point of view, they did not expect to find fine tuning.

Getting the right atomic parts. Atoms are made of nucleons (protons and neutrons) surrounded by orbiting electrons. The neutron outweighs the proton by 0.138 percent. This mass difference is surprising as both neutrons and protons are composed of three smaller particles called *quarks.* Yet the implication is significant: "There seems no fundamental reason why the neutron should be the more massive of the two. Furthermore, the mass difference is quite small, a mere tenth of a percent. One might think it would make no difference. But it does make a difference. Indeed it is crucial."[2] It is crucial because neutrons decay while protons do not. Beta decay results when a neutron in the nucleus decays to a proton and an electron. The electron is emitted from the atom as a type of radioactivity called the beta particle. If the proton were more massive than the neutron, then the proton would be the particle that underwent decay; in this case, hydrogen, which is composed of an electron and proton, would not exist. (Hydrogen is a necessary element for life as we know it.) Also, if protons decayed rather than neutrons, stars would exhaust their fuel within a century, which is a lifetime too short for life to form.

Atoms are composed of two charged particles. The electron has a negative charge, while the proton has a positive charge. Static cling in clothes from a dryer shows that like charges repel and unlike charges attract. That the charge of the electron is equal to the charge of the proton is surprising since the electron and proton appear so different. The proton belongs to the family of elemental particles called *hadrons,* which are made of three quarks, while electrons are in the *lepton* family and are not made of quarks. The proton is also about 1,836 times more massive than the electron. What if the charges of the electron and proton were not equal in magnitude? Depending upon the difference, objects could be torn apart by electrostatic repulsion. For an object the size of a person, a charge difference of one part in a billion would cause the object to fly apart. A difference in electrical charge of one part in a billion billion would cause an object as large as the earth to fly apart. Thus, the electron-proton charge equality must be finely tuned for the universe to exist.

Getting the right atoms. Having the correct subatomic particles is not enough. To have life, these subatomic particles need to combine to form the atoms of life. The atoms needed for life are shown in figure 4.1 with the most abundant elements being oxygen, carbon, and hydrogen. To obtain the right atoms, there must be a balance among the strong

Element	Percent by by Mass in Human Body	Significance
Oxygen	65%	
Carbon	18%	Components
Hydrogen	10%	of major
Nitrogen	3%	biological systems
Phosphorus	1.2%	
Sulfur	0.2%	Produce electrolytes
Potassium	0.2%	responsible for fluid
Sodium	0.1%	balance and nerve
Chlorine	0.2%	transmission
Calcium	1.5%	Bones, nerve function
Magnesium	0.05%	
Zinc	< 0.05%	Essential trace metals in human metabolism

Fig. 4.1. Most Important Elements in Living Organisms.

nuclear force, the weak nuclear force, and gravity. Another factor in obtaining the right atoms is the relationship among the nuclear energy states of different atoms.

The *strong nuclear force,* which is the strongest of the four fundamental forces, governs the degree to which protons and neutrons stick together in the nucleus. If the strong nuclear force were 2 percent weaker than it currently is, protons and neutrons would not stick together, and the only atom that could form would be hydrogen; hydrogen has only one proton and no neutrons in its nucleus. With this slightly weaker strong nuclear force, the heavier elements needed for life would not form. If the strong nuclear force were just 0.3 percent stronger than it currently is, the affinity of protons and neutrons for each other would be so great that none of them would occur alone. In this case the atom hydrogen could not exist, eliminating a vital component of biological systems.

The *weak nuclear force* is active among subatomic particles and governs the rates of radioactive decay. If the weak nuclear force were stronger than it currently is, all the atoms would be converted to heavier elements, and life-essential elements such as carbon, oxygen, nitrogen, and phosphorus would not exist. If the weak nuclear force were weaker than it currently is, the universe would contain only the lightest elements. In the latter case, the concentrations of carbon, oxygen, nitrogen, and phosphorus would be too small to build biological molecules. Finally, if the weak nuclear force were weaker than it currently is, not enough neutrinos would be produced to cause supernova explosions. Supernova explosions scatter heavy elements into space. Heavy elements are needed to form rocky planets like Earth.

Gravity is the weakest of the four fundamental forces, but it operates over long distances. According to current cosmological theory, a star begins as a cloud of hydrogen gas held together by gravity. The force of gravity gradually pulls the hydrogen gas toward the center of the cloud causing the gas temperature to rise. As the contraction continues, the hydrogen gas reaches a temperature high enough for hydrogen atoms to fuse into helium atoms. The star "ignites" and expands outward because of the forces released by the fusion. Calculations reveal that if the force of gravity were slightly less, the friction from the collapse of the hydrogen cloud would never reach a temperature high enough to cause fusion to occur. According to current theory, stars are needed for life to exist. Conversely, if the force of gravity were slightly larger, the resulting hydrogen clouds would be so large that only very large stars would form. The larger a star, the faster it "burns" its nuclear fuel and the shorter its life span. Thus, in a universe with a stronger gravity, the life span of stars would be too short for life to develop.

According to the Big Bang Model, the nuclei of all the elements above hydrogen are synthesized by nuclear fusion within the stars. Nuclear fusion occurs when two nuclei collide and stick together to form a larger nucleus. For the two smaller nuclei to stick, the energy of the two nuclei plus their energy of motion must be equal to or slightly smaller than a stable *energy level* for the new atom. One can model the

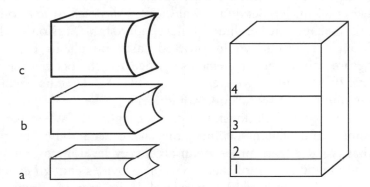

Fig. 4.2. Nuclear Energy Levels. The books a, b, and c represent nuclei that can possibly fuse. The four-shelved bookcase represents the nuclear energy levels of a nucleus that could possibly be formed by fusion. The energy of the fused atom is modeled by stacking the books on their sides. Books a and c or b and c could not fit on any of the shelves. These combinations will not result in fusion. Books a and b could fit on shelf 4. Fusion will occur with this combination.

nuclear energy levels by using books and a bookshelf (see fig. 4.2). The widths of the books represent the energy of one of the small nuclei. The shelves of the bookcase represent possible allowed energy states of an atom that could result from the fusion. If the combined height of the two books (their combined energy) is greater than the height of the shelf (energy level of new nucleus), then fusion will not occur. If the stacked books can fit on a shelf, fusion will occur, and a new atom will be formed.

In the nuclear reactions of stars, there is fine-tuning among the nuclei of helium, beryllium, carbon, and oxygen. The relationships among these nuclei[3] are helium-4 plus helium-4 equals beryllium-8; beryllium-8 plus helium-4 equals carbon-12; and carbon-12 plus helium-4 equals oxygen-16.

In the first relationship beryllium-8 is formed from two helium-4 nuclei. Beryllium-8 has a very short half-life of only 10^{-15} seconds. If beryllium-8 were more stable, fusion to the heavier elements would proceed fast enough to explode before enough heavy elements formed for the occurrence of life. If beryllium-8 were even less stable, no elements beyond beryllium, such as carbon, would form.

The second relationship involves carbon-12. When beryllium-8 and helium-4 collide, they have a combined energy that is just 4 percent less than an energy level in carbon-12. The kinetic energy of their collision provides enough energy to match the carbon-12 energy level. If the combined energies of beryllium-8 and helium-4 were anything other than this precise fit, not enough carbon would be synthesized for life to occur.

The third relationship involves oxygen-16. When carbon-12 and helium-4 collide, they have a combined energy that is 1 percent greater than the energy level of oxygen-16. This energy level mismatch prevents all the carbon from being converted to oxygen. The helium-4, beryllium-8, carbon-12, and oxygen-16 relationships were predicted by the British astronomer Fred Hoyle (b. 1915) in 1954. Hoyle, though an atheist, wrote, "A common sense interpretation of the facts suggests that a superintellect has monkeyed with physics, as well as with chemistry and biology, and that there are no blind forces worth speaking about in nature. The numbers one calculates from the facts seem to me so overwhelming as to put this conclusion almost beyond question."[4]

Getting the right molecules. For life to be possible, atoms must combine to form molecules. Figure 4.3 shows some common molecules found in living organisms. Molecules form when atoms share electrons. Two atoms can share electrons if their outermost electrons have similar energies. The ability of atoms to bind together to form molecules depends upon two factors: the strength of the electromagnetic force and the ratio of the mass of the electron to the mass of the proton. Daily we experience electromagnetic force through magnetism and electrical interactions such as static cling. If the electromagnetic force were smaller, the atomic nucleus could not hold onto the electrons, and there would be no sharing of electrons to make molecules. If the electromagnetic force were larger, elements above boron, such as carbon, would be unstable. In either case the molecules needed for life would not exist.

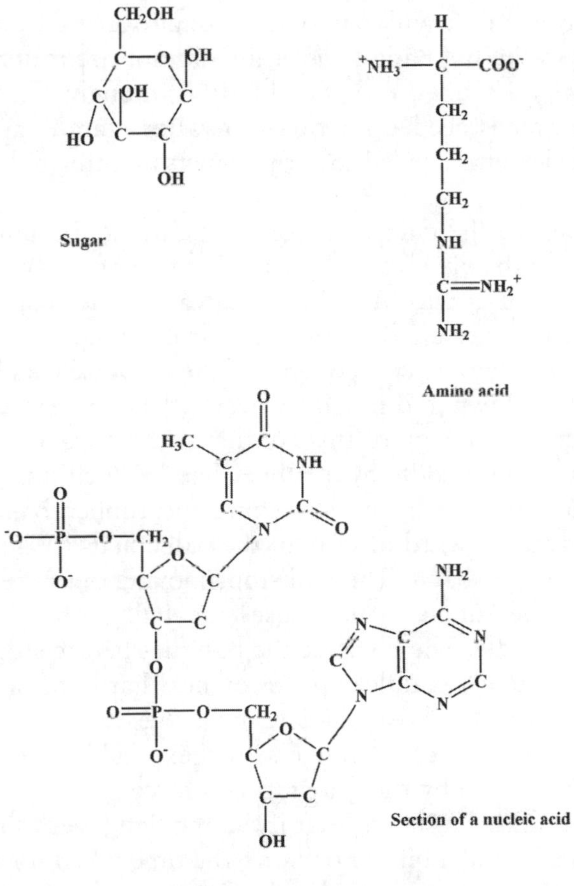

Fig. 4.3. Molecules of Life. In the molecules, carbon = C,□ hydrogen = H, oxygen = O, nitrogen = N, and phosphorus □ = P. The lines represent bonds between the atoms.

The proton is 1,836 times more massive than the electron. The ratio between the mass of the proton and electron determines the paths that the electrons travel as they orbit the nucleus. If the ratio between the proton and electron were slightly larger or smaller, no molecules could form, and life would be impossible.

Having enough time. Even if we fine tune all the previously discussed variables to produce the molecules of life, we still need a universe that will exist long enough for life to occur. According to the Big Bang Model, life did not occur until the universe was 12 billion years old. It is thought that this amount of time is needed for first-generation stars to synthesize all the elements needed to form planets and the molecules of life.

According to the current theory, the fate of the universe depends upon the interaction between the size of the Big Bang and the force of gravity. The Big Bang causes the space-time fabric of the universe to expand outward. The gravitational attraction between the components of the universe acts like a brake to slow down and possibly reverse the expansion.

An everyday analogy of this conflict is the attraction of a ball attached to a paddle by a rubber band. When hit by the paddle, the ball flies away, stretching the rubber band. At some point the outward motion of the ball equals the inward pull of the rubber band. The ball stops moving outward, and the pull of the rubber band causes the ball to fly inward toward the paddle. The distance the ball flies before stopping and returning to the paddle depends on how hard the ball was originally struck. Likewise, the larger the Big Bang the longer the space-time fabric of the universe will expand before it can possibly be stopped by the gravitational force.

Calculations have shown that if the Big Bang were slightly smaller (one part in a billion trillion), the time taken for gravity to stop the expansion of the universe and recompact the universe (the *Big Crunch*) would be less time than it took for life to develop in the current universe. If the Big Bang were slightly larger (one part in a million), the expansion would be too fast for gravity to collect matter into stars and planets which, according to the current model, are needed for life to form. In either case the "birth" of the universe (the force of expansion) had to be finely tuned for life to develop.

Another factor is the amount of time it took for life to occur on the earth. The current model estimates the time between the formation of the earth and the appearance of life on the earth as about 2 billion years with man appearing about 3 billion years later. Thus, life needs stars with stable energy-outputs over billions of years. The ratio of the electro-magnetic force constant to the gravitational force constant determines the type of star that forms. If this ratio were decreased by just one part in 10^{40}, only stars larger than the sun could form. These large stars rapidly burn their fuel and have lifetimes too short for life to develop. For a further discussion see the section entitled "Uncommon Earth" (p. 97).

Having enough space. In the movie *Contact,* a character remarks that if the universe did not have life scattered throughout the galaxies, it would be a waste of space. But is it really a waste of space? In 1900, astronomers believed that the universe consisted of only the Milky Way Galaxy. If life is found only on the earth, then this would seem to be a much more economical universe than a universe with countless galaxies void of life. The Milky Way contains about 100 billion stars. A universe of this size and mass would have expanded only for about a month before the Big Crunch. Such a small universe might be more economical but would be lifeless.

Another version of the "waste of space" argument involves reasonings about why the universe contains so much empty space—why the stars are so far apart. If the stars were closer to one another, the stellar gravitational interactions would disrupt planets from their orbits around the stars, flinging the planets into interstellar space to freeze.

Observations: Working within a materialistic worldview, many scientists were very surprised to discover that the existence of life requires a fine tuning of the universe. Everywhere

Hedrons	Leptons	Elemental Bosons
Protons	Electron	Photon (Electromagnetic force)
Neutrons	Neutrinos	Gravitons (gravity)
Pions	Nuons	Gluon (strong nuclear force)
Kaons	Positron	w and z particles (weak nuclear force)

Fig. 4.4. Families of Elementary Particles.

scientists looked, they found very little leeway in how the universe was put together. Protons, neutrons, and electrons need to be very close to their observed masses and charges for atoms to form. The atoms of life (hydrogen, carbon, oxygen, and so forth) would be unstable if the strengths of the strong nuclear force, weak nuclear force, and gravity were not very near their current values. Changing strength of the electromagnetic force and the sizes of the proton and electron would prevent the molecules needed for life from forming. The size of the Big Bang and the current strength of gravity are needed for there to be enough time for life to appear. Also, all the billions and billions of stars and galaxies are needed to provide enough matter and space for a stable universe to exist long enough for life to exist. No wonder the atheist Hoyle had to struggle with the design "reflected by the superintellect that monkeyed with the universe."

Extradimensional Universe
Scientists are still trying to understand the earliest part of the Big Bang. Today the universe is cold, with an average temperature about 3K or -270° C or -454° F and vast, at least 15 billion light years across. (A light year is the distance light travels in one year or about 63 trillion miles.)

In the early, hot, dense universe, the four fundamental forces (strong nuclear, weak nuclear, electromagnetic, and gravity) would have been combined into one super force, and the elementary particles would have behaved differently from the way they behave today. Elementary particles are the smallest units of matter from which all other matter is composed. Several hundred elementary particles have been experimentally detected. Figure 4.4 classifies these elementary particles into three families. The three families are hadrons (nuclear particles), leptons (extranuclear particles), and elementary bosons, which carry the four fundamental forces between the particles (see fig. 4.5). The hadrons are composed of even smaller particles called quarks that exist in six forms (up, down, strange, charm, bottom, and top).

Today scientists have the paradoxical situation that one theory explains the early universe (quantum mechanics), but another theory is needed to explain the current universe (General Theory of Relativity). Since we are talking about one universe, scientists expect that we should be able to explain the whole history of the universe with just one theory. Today, scientists are trying to produce such a theory that would explain the behavior of the universe when it was small as well

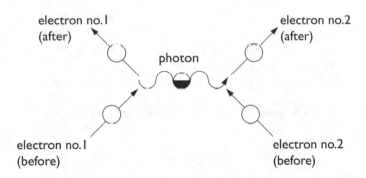

Fig. 4.5. How Particles Interact. Two electrons are moving up the page toward each other. A particle of light (photon) whizzes between them across the page. The photon carries the electromagnetic force between the two electrons. The two electrons are deflected or, like charged particles, repel each other. This picture is called a Feynman diagram, after Richard Feynman. A Feynman diagram can be drawn for the other bosons.

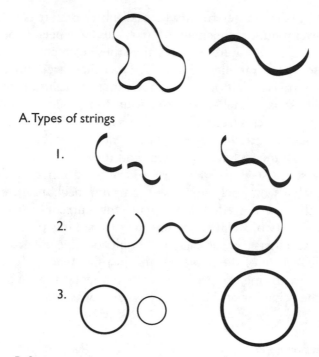

A. Types of strings

1.

2.

3.

B. String reactions
1. Two open strings join and form longer open strings.
2. Two open strings join and form closed strings.
3. Two closed strings join and form longer closed strings.

Fig. 4.6. Types of Strings and String Reactions.

as when it is large. One promising attempt is called String Theory.

Elementary particles formerly were thought to be zero-dimensional points. Scientists have found that a better model for understanding elementary particles in the early universe is to treat the elementary particles as one-dimensional loops of energy called "strings." These strings are not like small cords but rather like rotating, vibrating rubber bands. Strings can be closed or open and are capable of twisting, looping, combining, and separating as shown in figure 4.6. String Theory "is the only theory that self-consistently explains all the known properties of the known fundamental particles . . . , all the properties and principles of quantum mechanics, all the properties and principles of both special and general relativity, the operation of all four forces of physics, and all the known details of the creation event."[5]

For String Theory to work, the universe has to have ten dimensions. All of our lives, we have lived in the four dimensions of length, width, height, and time. Our ability to visualize is limited to three dimensions because our five senses can only directly detect the three spatial dimensions. Let us construct a multidimensional space by first visualizing a point (no dimension) as shown in figure 4.7. Now extend the point in a particular direction to form a line (one dimension). A one-dimensional space is called a one-brane, which is a play on the word *membrane*. Now move the line at right angles to itself to generate a square (two dimensions or two-brane). Move the square perpendicular to its plane to produce a cube (three dimensions or three-brane). Finally, move the cube at right angles to the three previous directions to produce a hypercube (four dimensions or four-brane). Although humans have no problem visualizing the point, line, square, and cube, humans cannot visualize the four-dimensional hypercube. One would be able to picture the four-brane hypercube if one could go beyond four-dimensional space into a five-dimensional space. Since we cannot go beyond the four dimensions, we are stuck picturing only three dimensions.

What happened to the other six dimensions of the universe that String Theory predicts? String Theory proposes that there was a dimensional split at 10^{-43} seconds after the Big Bang: "At that instant, the ten-dimensional expanding universe split into two: a six dimensional piece that permanently ceased expanding and never produced matter, and a four dimensional piece that became our dimensions of length, width, height, and time. That four dimensional system continued to expand and eventually produced matter and stars."[6] Figure 4.8 pictures this dimensional split as six dimensions

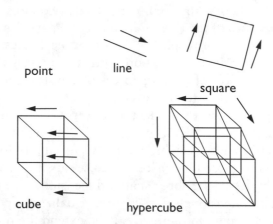

Fig. 4.7. Different Dimensions. Extend the point to form a line (1-D). Move the line at right angles to itself to produce a square (2-D). Move the square perpendicular to itself to form a cube (3-D). Move a cube at right angles to all three previous directions to yield a hypercube (4-D).

curled upon themselves in a compact manifold so small that scientists are unable to detect its existence with current instruments. The other four dimensions continue to expand toward "infinity."

Observations: If you have survived the last paragraph with your "brane" intact, you are probably thinking that it is nice that the universe has ten dimensions. But so what! How important is it that we have the three dimensions of space? Only in three-brane space could planets have stable orbits under the influence of gravity. Gravity obeys an inverse square law in three-brane space. This means that as the distance between objects is doubled, the force of gravity declines by one quarter. The force of gravity would drop off much faster in higher-dimension space; doubling the distances would cause a decrease in the force of gravity by one-eighth in four spacial dimensions and by one-sixteenth in five dimensions. Stable, approximately circular planetary orbits would be impossible in the four-brane or five-brane spaces. Atoms

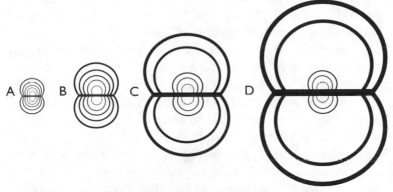

A. Ten-diminsional universe at beginning.
B. The ten dimensions continue and expand
until 10^{-43} seconds.
C. After dimensional split, only four dimensions
continue and expand.
D. Further expansion of only four dimensions;
the other six dimensions really curled up.

Fig. 4.8. The Ten-Dimensional Universe.

also would be unstable in any space other than three-dimensional space. In other dimensions the strength of the electromagnetic force would either cause electrons to spiral away from or spiral into the nucleus. Without atoms, chemistry and life itself would not exist. Finally, it is thought that distortion-free propagation of wave-based signals (such as radio, television, and microwave) require exactly three spacial dimensions.

Uncommon Earth
Each year we ask our upper-level students to give an in-class presentation on selected topics, such as whether there is life on the other planets of the solar system or whether there is intelligent life elsewhere in the universe. The students usually go beyond the science and really want there to be life elsewhere. They are like the characters in the movie *Contact* who

think all the space in the universe is wasted if we are the only life. Well, are we lucky to have the earth, or is it just one of thousands of planets teeming with life?

What is the place of the earth in the universe? To the ancients, the earth was the center of the universe. The earth was unique; it was imperfect and temporal while the heavens were perfect and eternal. The Polish astronomer Nicolaus Copernicus and his followers made the earth just one planet among others orbiting a minor star in the backwater of the Milky Way Galaxy. Astronomers Frank Drake and Carl Sagan, who estimated the number of planets with life and advanced civilizations in the Milky Way Galaxy, express this thinking in the Drake Equation.[7] The form of the equation is

$$N* \times f_p \times n_e \times f_l \times f_i \times f_c \times f_L$$

where (with Drake-Sagan estimate of value):

$N*$ = the number of stars in the Milky Way Galaxy (400 billion)

f_p = fraction of stars having planetary systems (1/3)

n_e = number of planets with environments suitable for life (2)

f_l = fraction of suitable planets where life occurred (1/3)

f_i = fraction of inhabited planets where intelligence arose

f_c = fraction of intelligent civilizations that developed communicative technology (fi X fc = 1/100)

f_L = fraction of planet's life with technical civilization (1/100,000,000)

Putting these estimates together, Drake and Sagan calculated

- the number of stars with planets could be 130 billion.
- the number of planets with environments suitable for life could be about 300 billion.
- the number of suitable planets where life occurred could be 100 billion.
- the number of planets with a technical civilization could be 1 billion.

- the number of technical civilizations in the Milky Way at one time could be 10.

The Drake-Sagan numbers imply that the earth is not uncommon. According to Drake and Sagan, the earth is one of 100 billion planets where life occurred and one of 1 billion planets where technical civilization developed. "Don't worry, be happy." If an advanced civilization had not developed on earth, there are one billion other places for it to develop. Such thinking is the basis of the SETI (Search for Extraterrestrial Intelligence) project. Begun in 1990, NASA funded a modest SETI project for a few years. The search is now privately funded.[8]

Recently scientists have been rethinking the assumptions behind the Drake Equation. The Drake Equation assumes that the earth is a common planet reproduced billions of times in the galaxy. Some scientists are beginning to think that the earth is an uncommon planet in an uncommon area of the galaxy. To decide whether Earth is an uncommon planet, one needs to consider the type of galaxy Earth is in, Earth's star location in the galaxy, the type of star the sun is, Earth's location in relation to the sun, the location of other planets in the solar system, the size of Earth's satellite, and the composition of Earth.

Galaxy type. Astronomers estimate that there are 100 billion galaxies, each containing billions of stars. The three types of galactic shapes are spiral, elliptical, and irregular. Most galaxies are elliptical. Elliptical galaxies contain older stars that have a low concentration of the heavy metals needed for life. Irregular galaxies are usually located near larger galaxies. Their irregular shape is thought to result from tidal interactions with the larger galaxy. Such interactions would create instabilities that would not favor the development of life. The sun is located in the Milky Way Galaxy, which is a spiral galaxy. Spiral galaxies are flattened disks that contain large populations of gas, dust, molecular clouds, and young stars that provide the environment for life to occur.

Location in galaxy. Even spiral galaxies can have dangerous environments. Within the Milky Way Galaxy there are compact, spherical groups of stars called globular clusters. Not only do globular clusters contain the oldest stars in the galaxy, but these stars are tightly packed together. In some cases the stars in a cluster are only a few billion kilometers away from one another. The age of the globular cluster stars and the star density both disfavor the occurrence of life. The star-packed center of a galaxy is also a dangerous place with black holes, supernovas, and stellar close encounters. The sun is located far from the galactic center (about 32,600 light-years) currently between spiral arms (fig. 4.9). As the sun rotates around the galactic center, it is thought that the sun spends 80 million years outside the spiral arms, 40 million years in, and so forth.

Type of star. A suitable star is one that will burn long enough for life to occur, one that does not rapidly change in energy output, and one without too much ultraviolet radiation emission. The sun is not a typical star; 95 percent of all stars are less massive than the sun. Less massive stars are less luminous, and thus a planet would have to be very close to the star to stay warm. But being close to the star is dangerous because of tidal effects. Also, at close distances the rotation of the planet becomes locked so that one side always faces the star, as is the case of the planet Mercury. This rotational lock causes one side of the planet to freeze, the other side to burn. Stars much larger than the sun have life spans too short for life to occur. It is estimated that 70 percent of all stars are binary or multiple stars. Binary or multiple stars contain two or more stars orbiting each other. Stable planetary orbits are hard to imagine in such systems. The sun is a single star. It is not the largest or smallest, the hottest or coolest type of star. It contains a lot of metals (building blocks for planets) and has had a stable output for billions of years.

Location of the earth in relation to the sun. Once one has a solar type star in the outer reaches of a spiral galaxy, one then has to determine if there is an ideal distance for a planetary

Fig. 4.9. Location of the Sun
in the Milky Way Galaxy.

orbit. The ideal distance is considered to be the distance from the star where the water in the ocean neither permanently freezes nor boils away. This turns out to be a range of distances called the habitable zone (fig. 4.10). A planet such as Venus, located closer to the sun than the habitable zone, would become too hot for life. A planet such as Mars, located farther from the sun than the habitable zone, would become too cold for life. With the earth at a distance from the sun of 1.0 AU (1.0 AU equals 93 million miles), the width of the sun's habitable zone is from 0.95 to 1.15 AU. Thus, the habitable zone for the sun is very narrow.

Location of other planets in the solar system. Just being in the habitable zone does not appear to be enough to ensure the

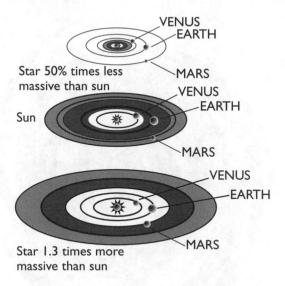

Fig 4.10. Estimates of Habitable Zones Around Stars.
Adapted from Peter D. Ward and Donald Brownlee,
Rare Earth (New York: Copernicus, 2000).

stability of life. Figure 4.11 shows the relationship of Jupiter
to the earth. Mars is smaller than the earth. Jupiter being near
Mars is thought to have attracted building material to itself
resulting in a smaller Mars. Thus, if the orbit of Jupiter had
been a little closer to the orbit of earth, then the earth could
have ended up as small as Mars. A smaller planet would not
support life since it could not retain its atmosphere.

Although Jupiter could have been a threat to the earth,
Jupiter in the right place can be a guardian for the earth.
Throughout the history of the solar system, planets have been
bombarded by asteroids and comets. Too many impacts can
melt the surface of a planet and sterilize the planet. What controls the impact rate? Computer modeling indicates that the
giant planet Jupiter acts as an asteroid and comet catcher.
Jupiter's gravity captures many asteroids and comets, preventing them from reaching the earth. Is there any evidence of
Jupiter-like planets around other stars? Yes, since 1995, at

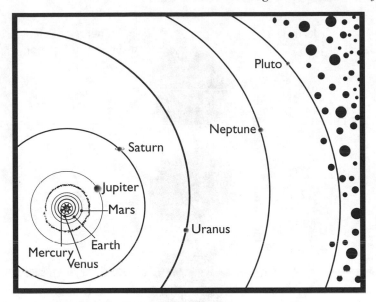

Fig 4.11. The Solar System. Note the relationship
between Earth and Jupiter.

least fifty planets orbiting stars other than the sun have been
discovered.[9] Only large planets like Jupiter can be detected.
All of these "Jupiters" are in bad orbits. Some are in elliptical
orbits far from the star. Elliptical orbits would create unstable
gravitational effects that would not "protect" any inner
terrestrial-like planets. Others of these "Jupiters" are in circular orbits close to the star. It is speculated that these
"Jupiters" formed far from the star and that their orbits
decayed. As the "Jupiter" spiraled inward, it would sweep
any terrestrial-like planets into the star. All other "Jupiters"
detected so far seem to prevent the occurrence of life.

Size of Earth's satellite. Earth has a satellite similar in size
to itself. (In the rest of the solar system, only Pluto has a satellite similar in size to itself.) The large moon stabilizes the tilt
axis of Earth and thus stabilizes the climate of Earth. The tilt
of Earth's spin axis has not varied by more than a degree or
two from its present value of 23 degrees. It is calculated that

Tilt Angle		Energy at Pole
		Energy at Equator
0°		0
22.5°		0.4
45°		0.9
60°		1.1
90°		1.6

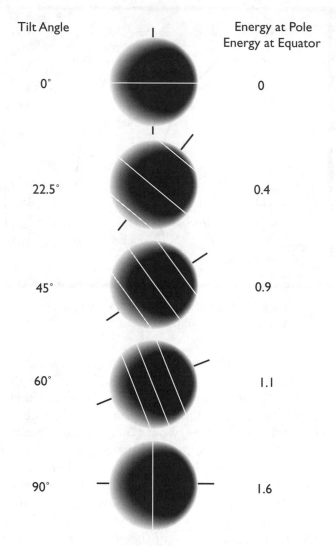

Fig 4.12. The Relationship Between the Tilt Angle and the Ratio of Solar Energy Falling on a Planet's Pole and Equator. Earth's tilt angle is 22.5. Adapted from Peter D. Ward and Donald Brownlee, *Rare Earth* (New York: Copernicus, 2000).

without the moon, Earth's tilt axis could vary by as much as 90 degrees. Figure 4.12 shows the relationship between the tilt axis of a planet and the amount of solar radiation falling on the planet's poles and equator. At a tilt of 0 degrees, no sunlight would ever reach the poles. At a tilt of 90 degrees, one pole would be exposed to sunlight for half a year while the other pole would be in darkness. Such fluctuations in the tilt axis would make it very difficult for life to exist.

The composition of Earth. Even with the right planet around the right star in the right location in a galaxy, the existence of life still could be difficult. The planet must possess a certain composition for life to flourish. The planet needs to contain *carbon* and other elements necessary for life (see fig. 4.1). The earth contains 0.05 percent carbon by weight while the rocky asteroids contain 4 percent carbon. It is thought that if the earth contained as much carbon as the asteroids, so much carbon dioxide would be produced as to cause runaway greenhouse overheating.

The planet needs *water* on and near its surface. The earth contains 0.1 percent water by weight while the asteroids contain 20 percent water. A planet needs enough water to buffer the global temperature but not too much to prevent shallow seas from occurring. Twice as much water as currently on earth is estimated to result in a water world. Such a water world would result in very few nutrients being available in the ocean because these nutrients come from land erosion. On the earth with its shallow seas, carbon dioxide is turned into limestone in these shallow seas and thus is removed from the atmosphere. A water world would have a runaway greenhouse effect because its deep waters would not be able to remove carbon dioxide in this way. Instead of a runaway greenhouse effect, the earth's temperature has remained stable. It is estimated that for the last 2 billion years the average temperature of the oceans has not exceeded 50 degrees Fahrenheit.

The planet needs an *atmosphere* containing oxygen and an ozone layer. Earth's atmosphere contains 20.9 percent oxygen

Fig. 4.13. Thirteen Major Plates of Earth's Crust. Arrows indicate the general direction of plate movement.

by volume. A greater concentration than this could result in hydrocarbons and plants being burned too easily. The atmosphere's oxygen concentration is maintained through oxidation of minerals and respiration of plants. The ozone layer is a region of the earth's atmosphere about 19 to 48 km (12 to 30 miles) above Earth's surface. In this layer, ozone concentrations of up to ten parts per million occur. The ozone layer protects life on Earth by absorbing some of the ultraviolet radiation from the sun.

The planet needs *heavy metals* such as iron and nickel in its core. This type of core generates a magnetic field that protects the planet from high-energy particles from outer space by repelling these particles. The planet also needs *radioactive elements* such as uranium. The heat from the radioactive decay in the inner regions of the planet helps maintain a constant planetary temperature.

Finally, a planet needs a thin outer *crust* of low-density material to allow for *plate tectonics* to occur. Earth's continents and oceans rest on a layer of rock called the lithosphere. The lithosphere consists of thirteen rock masses or plates (fig. 4.13). Plate tectonics is the theory that describes the motion of these plates. On the boundaries of these plates, earthquakes and volcanic eruptions tend to occur. The movements of the plates gradually rearrange the surface of the earth (fig. 4.14). The lithosphere needs to contain water to be able to bend and break, allowing the plates to move. Why is plate tectonics important? The movement of the plates helps regulate the carbon dioxide concentration in the atmosphere and thus the temperature of Earth. As discussed before, carbon dioxide is removed through weathering by the formation of limestone. Limestone at plate boundaries is subducted (pulled down) deep into the mantle, where it decomposes to release carbon dioxide. Thus, weathering and subduction work together to keep the carbon dioxide concentration in balance. The movement of the plates creates continents and shallow seas. Without plate tectonics rebuilding the continents, the continental land masses would ultimately be worn down by erosion. Plate tectonics helps make possible the earth's magnetic field. Earth contains a liquid iron-nickel core. Plate tectonics removes heat from this core, setting up convection currents. These convection currents in the spinning core create the magnetic field. In the absence of the magnetic field, high-energy particles from outer space could boil away the earth's atmosphere. Finally, plate tectonics, through rearranging the earth's surface, promote global biodiversity.

Observations: After listing all factors that make Earth uncommon, it is now obvious that Drake and Sagan overestimated the number of stars and planets that could have life. Rather than being one planet among billions, Earth now appears to be the uncommon Earth, the rare Earth. Again, Hoyle's superintellect has monkeyed with the universe by placing the sun far from the center of a spiral galaxy; locating Earth in the habitable zone of a typical star; locating Earth at a safe distance from Jupiter; providing Earth with the moon to stabilize its tilt angle and the climate of the Earth; providing Earth with the "right" amount of carbon, oxygen, heavier elements, and water; and providing plate tectonics to rebuild and replenish the earth. The data implies that Earth may be the only planet "in the right place at the right time."

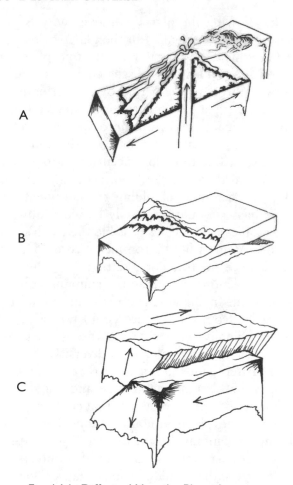

Fig. 4.14. Differing Ways the Plates Interact.
(A) Diverge along a volcanic ridge where new
crust is constantly being formed. (B) Converge
so that one plate must be subducted beneath
the other. (C) Scrape against another plate to
form a fault zone, which may produce violent
earthquakes. In each case, the plate motions
result from movement of the convecting
mantle below.

RESPONSES TO ANTHROPIC COINCIDENCES

The responses to evidence pointing to a created universe, a fine-tuned universe, and an uncommon earth depend upon one's worldview. In general the responses fall into two categories. Some observers regard the universe as the result of purely materialistic processes. Others believe the universe is the result of intelligent design.

Materialistic Processes Responses

Scientists who propose materialistic processes to explain the structure of the universe in many cases do not deny that the universe *appears* to be designed. Nonetheless, they not only deny that God was the designer; they deny that there is any designer. As astrophysicist George Greenstein states:

> As we survey all the evidence, the thought insistently arises that some supernatural agency—or, rather, Agency—must be involved. Is it possible that suddenly, without intending to, we have stumbled upon scientific proof of the existence of a Supreme Being? Was it God who stepped in and so providentially crafted the cosmos for our benefit? . . . A heady prospect. Unfortunately I believe it to be illusory. . . . I believe that the discoveries of science are not capable of proving God's existence—not now, not ever. And more than that: I believe that reference to God will never suffice to explain a single one of these discoveries. God is not an explanation.[10]

The following responses cover the range of materialistic explanations for the structure of the universe and the existence of intelligent life. We will divide the materialist responses into two classes: Anthropic Principles and non-Anthropic responses. Since the word *anthropic* means "of or related to human beings," the Anthropic Principles attempt to give a materialistic reason for the existence of humans. There are at least four Anthropic Principles: Weak, Strong, Participatory, and Final. Non-Anthropic responses attempt to provide materialistic explanations for the structure of the universe without the special emphasis on humans.

Accident of observation. This argument states that because we exist the universe must be so constructed to support life. Many unlikely (low probability) events had to have occurred or we would not be here. Maybe it was just incredible luck that the universe happened to have the right conditions for life. This argument states that just like someone wins the lottery even though the odds are very small, a universe that supports life occurred even though its odds of occurring were very small. This argument is called the Weak Anthropic Principle (WAP).

The Weak Anthropic Principle is a tautology; it states the obvious. If the universe was not fit for life, then we would not be here. Which is a larger act of faith, believing that the God of the Bible designed the universe or that the universe is the surprise result of a series of chance events?

Many-Possible-Worlds. Some scientists go beyond the tautology of the Weak Anthropic Principle to state that the universe *must* have those properties that allow life to occur. This latter statement is called the Strong Anthropic Principle (SAP). What material process can make these properties to be present? One explanation is to evoke the existence of multiple worlds (universes). One way to deal with the previously discussed very small probabilities is to propose billions of universes with our universe being the one with life. One version of the Many-Possible-Worlds proposal is to assume that the multiple universes followed one another in time. Billions of Big Bangs would be followed by expansion, then contraction to a Big Crunch, to be followed by another Big Bang and so forth. Each Big Bang-Big Crunch sequence represents one universe with its unique set of parameters. We exist in the universe that supports life. As we saw in chapter 3, David Hume proposed a similar theory in the eighteenth century.

Another version of the Many-Possible-Worlds proposal is to assume that billions of "universes" exist simultaneously. Because the word *universe* means the totality of things, these multiple "universes" are sometimes called multiple "worlds" and other times are labeled "miniuniverses" in a "super-universe." There are at least three flavors to the simultaneous Many-Possible-Worlds proposal. Two of the flavors arise from the inflationary Big Bang model with the third arising from quantum mechanics. During the time period discussed in the "Multiple Dimensions of Space" section, energy-matter fluctuations could have formed "bubbles" that individually inflated into miniuniverses. One flavor proposes that these miniuniverses are stacked one on top of the other in the multi-dimensions of space. Currently there would be no way to communicate between these miniuniverses. Recent interpretations of String Theory support this view. Another flavor proposes that these bubbles inflated into domains within one universe. Each domain would have its own set of properties. Our domain would be what we consider the universe. These domains are so far apart that again there is no communication between them. One interpretation of quantum mechanics is that every time a quantum event occurs the universe is split. Since there are billions of atoms and because all atomic and subatomic events are quantum events, this flavor would result in zillions and zillions of universes. To someone with a materialistic worldview, all three of these flavors do furnish enough universes to provide enough chances for our universe and life to occur.

The burden of proof resides on those making the Many-Possible-Worlds proposals. How scientific is a proposal that cannot be tested? If there is no way to detect the other worlds, how scientific is this proposal? As Martin Gardner states, "The many-worlds interpretation has been called a beautiful theory that nobody can believe."[11]

Man the creator. This proposal states that observers are needed to bring the universe into existence and is called the Participatory Anthropic Principle (PAP). The PAP also grows from an interpretation of quantum mechanics that states that the act of observing creates the reality; by choosing to observe the wave properties of the electron, the observer causes the electron to be a wave rather than a particle. A proponent of this interpretation of quantum mechanics as well as of the Participatory Anthropic Principle is the physicist John A. Wheeler. Wheeler states, "The Universe starts small at the big bang, grows in size, gives rise to life and observers and observing equipment. The observing equipment, in turn, through the elementary quantum processes that terminate on it, takes part in giving tangible 'reality' to events that occurred long before there was any life anywhere."[12] (Note that Wheeler capitalizes the word *universe* in his text.)

There are several concerns with PAP. Quantum events are at the heart of Wheeler's PAP. Yet quantum mechanics deals with micro not macro systems. The uncertainty of a quantum event approaches zero as the number of particles increases. The uncertainty involved in observing an electron would not be the same as that for the universe. Intelligence is not an exclusive factor in observing quantum events. Cloud chambers, Geiger counters, and photographic plates can record quantum events. Also, there are minds other than the human mind. Could a moth observe the moon and give it reality?

Creation of God. The Participatory Anthropic Principle is extended by the astronomer John Barrow and physicist Frank Tipler to what they call the Final Anthropic Principle (FAP): Intelligence must come into existence, and once it does it can never die out. They believe that life will spread beyond the earth to colonize all of space and to keep the universe from destroying itself and life. Using the terminology of the Roman Catholic paleontologist Teilhard de Chardin, Barrow and Tipler state, "At the instant the Omega Point is reached, life will have gained control of *all* matter and forces not only in a single universe but in all universes whose existence is logically possible; life will have spread into *all* spatial regions in all universes which could logically exist, and will have stored an infinite amount of information, including *all* bits of knowledge which it is logically possible to know. And this is the end."[13]

In a note to this text, Barrow and Tipler state, "A modern-day theologian might wish to say that the totality of life at the Omega Point is omnipotent, omnipresent, and omniscient!"[14] Thus, Barrow and Tipler are saying God does not exist now but that all of life is evolving into God.

The popular science writer Martin Gardner offers this evaluation of Barrow and Tipler's work: "What should we make of this quartet of WAP, SAP, PAP, and FAP? In my not so humble opinion I think the last principle is best called CRAP, the Completely Ridiculous Anthropic Principle."[15] By rejecting the notion of an eternal, transcendent Creator God, materialists have to propose more and more irrational options. As the Bible says, "See to it no one takes you captive through hollow and deceptive philosophy" (Col. 2:8a).

Inflexible fundamental constants. Not all who express a materialistic response agree with the Anthropic Principles. They would criticize the anthropic folks for putting a special emphasis on humans. One response is to use the Many-Possible-Worlds proposal to suggest that this is the only universe where life probably occurred. They further criticize the Anthropic Principles by saying that the fundamental constants have no choice in their values. They agree with Einstein when he said, "There are no arbitrary constants. . . . Nature is so constructed that it is possible logically to lay down such strongly determined laws that within these laws only . . . completely determined constants occur."[16] Scientists who hold this view are encouraged by the work of those trying to understand the earliest part of the Big Bang Theory: "The Grand Unified Theories" (GUT) have attempted to model the time in the early universe when the electromagnetic, strong nuclear, and weak nuclear forces were combined. The GUT results imply that the values of the electromagnetic force and the strong nuclear force are linked. If true, the values of these forces could not be individually fine-tuned. As we have previously discussed, String Theory is another attempt to understand the early universe. As the anthropic critic, physicist Gordon Kane says, "If the theory is right there will be no more to vary any of the constants the anthropic people like to vary."[17] So far, however, String Theory has not predicted the value of any of the constants: "If string theory pins down every physical constant, then the fine-tuning for life will turn out to be hard-wired into the mathematics."[18] Thus, design is not removed; design just moves from the constants to the underlying laws. The designer is still in the equations.

Observations. The Anthropic Principles seem to be proposing a "mystic" design without a designer. Is it scientific to believe that the future designs the past? It is amazing how the Many-Possible-Worlds model is becoming the materialistic response of choice. One sees it in popular magazines, such as *National Geographic.* The very vocal critics of design invoke the Many-Possible-Worlds model to say here is a "scientific" alternative to design. This model may feel good to the materialists, but it is not "scientific" if there is no way to falsify this model.

Intelligent Design Responses
Dirty Harry asks how lucky we feel. How lucky should we feel when we consider that the universe is similar to Goldilocks's porridge with every key parameter being just right? How many coincidences does it take for one to say that luck has nothing to do with it, that someone has designed it this way? Is one coincidence enough, two, three, or the approximately seventy coincidences for the fine-tuning of the universe and earth?[19] All these coincidences seem to point to either incredible luck or intelligent design. As we saw in the last section, many scientists can never, philosophically, go beyond a naturalistic explanation for the coincidences. Another example is geologist Peter D. Ward and astronomer Donald Brownlee whose book *Rare Earth*[20] concerns the earth's uniqueness; they never once address design issues nor acknowledge others who have made similar arguments within the context of design. As Ward has said, "We are just incredibly lucky. Somebody had to win the big lottery, and we were it."[21]

Surely there is some way to distinguish luck from design. The mathematician William Dembski has written extensively on how people determine whether an event is by chance or design. As Dembski writes, "The fact remains . . . that intelligent causes have played, are playing and will continue to play an important role in science. Entire industries, economic and scientific, depend crucially on such notions as intelligence, intentionality and information. Included here are forensic science, intellectual property law, insurance claims investigation, cryptography, random number generation, archaeology, and the search for extraterrestrial intelligence (SETI)."[22]

Thus, one sees that design inference is a legitimate concern of many areas of science. However, many scientists have been unable to transfer the design inference techniques to questions concerning the origin of the universe, structure of the universe, or origin of life. How does one determine if an event is designed?

How does forensic science work? When confronted with an event, the scientist must determine whether the event is the result of law, chance, or design. Dembski calls this decision process the *Explanatory Filter;* a flowchart representation of this filter is given in figure 4.15. Dembski proposes that contingency, complexity, and specification must be present in the event for design to be present. If there is no *contingency,* then the event is the result of an automatic process that had no choice in its output. Here the appeal would be to a natural law where things always occur this way. Next one needs to establish the presence of complexity. With *complexity,* the event is not so simple that it can be explained by chance. Finally, it is necessary to establish *specification,* a detailed, precise pattern associated with intelligent causes. Thus, Dembski proposes that *specified complexity* is how intelligent design is detected. A single letter of the alphabet, such as *C* is specified but not complex. A random drawing from a hat containing the twenty-six letters of the alphabet could result in the letter *C.* A string of letters *SDIERMNTYHJVM* is

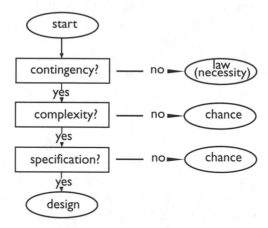

Fig. 4.15. The Explanatory Filter. Adapted from
William A. Dembski, *Intelligence Design* (Downers
Grove, Ill.: InterVarsity Press, 1999).

complex but not specified. A poem of Robert Frost is complex
and specified and the result of design.

Let us consider two events: radio signals received from CP
1919 by astronomers in England in 1967 and radio signals
received by the SETI investigators in the movie *Contact*
(fig. 4.16).

In these patterns, 1s represent beats or pulses and 0s represent pauses.

In 1967, graduate student Jocelyn Bell at the University of
Cambridge, England, discovered a pattern in the radio signals
from the celestial object CP 1919. The pattern was a pulse followed by a pause, pulse followed by a pause, and so forth
with a regular period of 1.33730199 seconds between pulses.
Bell and her research director Anthony Hewish determined
that the signals were not local but were coming from among
the stars. Because of the pattern in this radio signal, they considered the possibility that the signal was from a galactic civilization and nicknamed the source LGM for Little Green
Men.

In the movie *Contact,* the SETI investigator played by Jodie Foster also detected a radio signal from space that was a pattern of pulses and pauses. But this signal had a different pattern from that of the CP 1919 source. The *Contact* source had several pulses, then a pause followed by even more pulses followed by a pause, and so forth.

Let us use the Explanatory Filter to see if we can determine if either the CP 1919 or *Contact* source was possibly the result of intelligent design. Radio signals from space were first detected in 1932. The sun, Jupiter, the Milky Way Galaxy, other galaxies, supernova remnants, radio stars, and gas clouds all were discovered to emit radio signals. The intensity of these radio sources was steady or varied slowly with time;

Fig. 4.16.

Radio Signals.

Space Source CP 1919	Movie *Contact*
101010101010101010101010101010101010	1101110111110111111011111111111011111
101010101010101010101010101010101010	1111111011111111111111011111111111111
101010101010101010101010101010101010	1111111011111111111111111111111011111
101010101010101010101010101010101010	1111111111111111111111111011111111111
101010101010101010101010101010101010	1111111111111111111011111111111111111
101010101010101010101010101010101010	1111111111111111111011111111111111111
101010101010101010101010101010101010	1111111111111111111110111111111111111
101010101010101010101010101010101010	1111111111111111111111111111011111111
101010101010101010101010101010101010	0111111111111111111111111111111111111
101010101010101010101010101010101010	1111111111111111011111111111111111111
101010101010101010101010101010101010	1111111111111111111111111111111111111
101010101010101010101010101010101010	0111111111111111111111111111111111111
101010101010101010101010101010101010	1111111111111111111011111111111111111
101010101010101010101010101010101010	1111111111111111111111111111111111111
101010101010101010101010101010101010	1111111111111111011111111111111111111
101010101010101010101010101010101010	1111111111111111111111111111111111111
101010101010101010101010101010101010	1111111111011111111111111111111111111
101010101010101010101010101010101010	1111111111111111111111111111111111111
101010101010101010101010101010101010	1111111110111111111111111111111111111
101010101010101010101010101010101010	1111111111111111111111111111111111111
101010101010101010101010101010101010	1111111111111011111111111111111111111
101010101010101010101010101010101010	1111111111111111111111111111111111111
101010101010101010101010101010101010	1111111111111111111011111111111111111
101010101010101010101010101010101010	1111111111111111111111111111111111111
101010101010101010101010101010101010	1111111111111111111111111111111111101
101010101010101010101010101010101010	1111111111111111111111111111111111111
101010101010101010101010101010101010	1111111111111111011111111111111111111
101010101010101010101010101010101010	1111111111111111111111111111111111111
1010101010101010101010101010101010101010	1111111111111111111111111111111111111
10101010	11111111

In these patterns, 1s represent beats or pulses and 0s represent pauses.

no pulses were detected. Natural processes were proposed as the origin of these radio sources: the movement of charged particles, such as electrons and positrons, through magnetic fields. With the discovery of the pulsing signal in 1967, scientists had to determine whether this pattern was the designed signal from an alien civilization or the result of natural processes. How contingent is the CP 1919 signal? Within weeks three other sources with pulsing signals were discovered, each with a different period. Also, the signal from all these sources was not complex, just a repeating pattern of ons and offs. Scientists concluded that they had discovered recently predicted celestial objects called *pulsars*. Pulsar stands for pulsing radio source. Pulsars are believed to be neutron stars, the dense, rapidly spinning remains of burned-out supergiant stars. As the neutron star spins, a beam of radio waves sweeps through space. If the earth is in the path of this beam, a series of pulses followed by pauses results. Over five hundred pulsars have been identified in the Milky Way Galaxy.

How about the *Contact* signal? The *Contact* signal contained the following series of pulses separated by a pause: 2, 3, 5, 7, 11, 13, 17, 19, 23, 29, 31, 37, 41, 43, 53, 59, 61, 67, 71, 73, 79, 83, 89, 97, and 101. These numbers are the first twenty-five prime numbers. A prime number is a number, other than 0 or 1, that is only divisible by one and itself. In the case of the *Contact* signal, contingency is present as no known natural process can produce a sequence of prime numbers. No pulsar could theoretically produce such a pattern of signals. The *Contact* signal contains 1,126 bits representing the first twenty-five prime numbers. Suppose the signal contained only twelve bits (110111011111) representing the first three prime numbers: 2, 3, and 5? This sequence is too short to justify answering "yes" to the complexity question. A random process could by chance produce such a sequence. The *Contact* signal is much longer and is, thus, complex. But contingency and complexity are not enough to infer design. Specification also must be present. Flipping a coin 1,126 times will result in a complex sequence but without the pattern shown by the sequence of prime numbers. The *Contact* signal is not only complex but also contains the pattern of specified complexity. As the *Contact* character said, "This isn't noise; this has structure."

Observations: Many scholars from science and philosophy are saying that they see specified complexity in the universe's coincidences of having the right atoms, the right molecules, enough time, and enough space for life to occur. They also see design in the earth's coincidences of the right galaxy type, the location in the galaxy, the type of star, the earth's distance from the sun, the location of Jupiter, the size of the moon, and the composition of the earth. Or as biochemist Michael Behe says, "In other words, we apprehend design in highly improbable (complex) events that also fit some independently identifiable pattern (specification)."[23] Those who detect design include theists, deists, and atheists. Those in the theist camp include both young-earth as well as old-earth creationists. They all believe that design should be reinstated into science, that design is a valid, empirical tool for scientists to use.

THE NATURE OF THE DESIGNER

What does the evidence for intelligent design suggest about the Designer? As we previously stated, the Intelligent Design conclusions are consonant with the tenets of Christianity. One has to be cautious when the relationship between scientific theory and theological claims moves from consonance to apologetics. Scientific theories are never complete and do undergo refinements; a faith based on scientific theories appears to crumble when the scientific theory changes. A classic example of this dilemma occurred in the work of Thomas Aquinas who blended Christian theology with Aristotlean science, which included an earth-centered universe. Refinement of cosmology from an earth-centered model to a sun-centered model put a tremendous stress on the Thomist theology. A more recent example occurred when Pope Pius XII, in 1951, stated that the beginning of the Big Bang provided grounds for belief in God.

Although the design movement does not prove the existence of the "God of Abraham, Isaac, and Jacob," its findings do provide insight into theological issues.

A Creator

Far from being a challenge to biblical teaching, the current understanding of the Big Bang Theory supports the biblical teaching that the universe had a beginning and that space, time, and matter are finite.

Care for Living Things

The evidence of design suggests a Designer who has great care for living things, especially humans. This care is reflected in the vast amount of energy and matter committed to making the universe a pleasant place for life. For life to exist, the universe needs to be vast (13 to 15 billion light-years across) with an unbelievable amount of matter and energy (hundred-billion-trillion stars). The uniqueness of the earth suggests the great care the Designer took in preparing a home for humans. As Hugh Ross stated, "God invested heavily in living creatures. He constructed all these stars and carefully crafted them throughout the age of the universe so that at this brief moment in the history of the cosmos humans could exist and have a pleasant place to live."[24] This arrangement suggests a very caring Creator.

Multiple Dimensions of Space

The multiple dimensionality of the universe also suggests the caring nature of the Designer. The uncurled four dimensions of space and time provide a pleasant place for human bodies. These four dimensions provide for stable atoms in our bodies and stable orbits for our planets, among other things. Hugh Ross proposes that the extra dimensions beyond the four that we experience are a key to understanding many of the occurrences and doctrines of the Bible. Because of the insight he offers, we will briefly examine a few of the items discussed by Ross.[25]

God and time. The Bible makes it clear that God experiences time differently from humans.

For a thousand years in your sight are like a day that has gone by, or like a watch in the night [4 hours] (Ps. 90:4).

But do not forget this one thing, dear friends: With the Lord a day is like a thousand years, and a thousand years are like a day (2 Pet. 3:8).

Hugh Ross writes, "This biblical claim makes sense if God operates along one or more time dimensions independent of ours."[26] As shown in figure 4.17, if God has extra dimensional time lines available to him, then two events (A and B) that are the same "time" to him would appear to be different in length (A′ and B′) to us. The line T represents time as experienced by humans. Lines A and B are possible time lines available to God in the extradimensions. From God's perspective, the events occurring along lines A and B represent the same amount of time. However, when lines A and B overlap line T at distances A′ and B′, humans experience the former as involving a shorter time than the latter. Thus, to God a thousand years could be like a day to humans.

Jesus and locked rooms. An amazing postresurrection account is the appearance of Jesus to the disciples in the locked room: "With the doors locked for fear of the Jews, Jesus came and stood among them"(John 20:19). The disciples thought Jesus was a ghost. Jesus responded by saying, "Touch me and see; a ghost does not have flesh and bones, as you see I have" (Luke 24:39). To further confirm his physical presence, Jesus asked for food to eat: "They gave him a piece of broiled fish, and he took it and ate it in their presence" (Luke 24:42–43).

By moving into one of the extra dimensions, Jesus could bypass the barriers of the locked door. Once past the locked door, he could then move back into the four dimensions of his disciples. We cannot go beyond our dimensions; we cannot visualize how Jesus' movements would "look." However, we

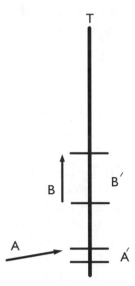

Fig. 4.17. God's Time and Our Time. The line
T represents time as experienced by humans.
Lines A and B are extradimensional time lines
along which God could operate. Although from
God's perspective, events A and B represent the
same amount of "time" humans would view A
as being shorter duration than B.

can model this event by considering a two-dimensional world
with two-dimensional beings (fig. 4.18). The two-dimensional
universe is like a rug. The two-dimensional beings are locked
behind the line A. Although to three-dimensional persons
(us), the rug beings look like circles, rug people appear to
each other as straight lines.[27] They cannot see beyond the line,
nor can they cross it. If a person using three dimensions steps
onto the rug at point B, the rug people will not know the person is there; line A blocks their view as a wall would block
our view. When the person steps to point C, the rug people
would be startled by the materializing of a new line (the foot)
into their world. To the three-dimensional person nothing
unusual has happened. The person has just been walking in
his/her three dimensions. Likewise, Jesus could just as easily

move around three-dimensional barriers by "walking" in the extra dimensions. As Hugh Ross wrote, "This six-dimensional . . . scenario may explain how Jesus entered the upper room to meet with His disciples after rising from the dead, or He may have chosen a different approach entirely. The point is not to assert one explanation above others but rather to suggest that His multidimensional capabilities offer Him countless ways to accomplish the feat—and the feat itself more than hints at His extra-dimensionality."[28] The universe modeled by String Theory is consistent with the universe described by the Bible.

A word of caution should be expressed at this point. While multidimensionality provides an intriguing explanation for postresurrection experiences, the explanation is a materialistic, naturalistic explanation. Though the other dimensions of physics have quite different characteristics from the four

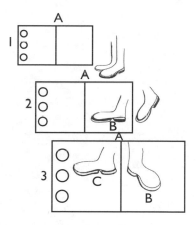

Fig. 4.18. Bypassing a Barrier by Using an Extra Dimension. 1. A three-dimensional person standing outside a two-dimensional space containing three two-dimensional beings (circles behind the line A). 2. The two-dimensional beings could not see the foot at point B. 3. The two-dimensional beings would see the outline of the foot at C.

dimensions we inhabit, they still represent aspects of the physical universe. Ross suggests that the resurrected Lord remains a physical being even though capable of moving from one physical dimension to another. We doubt that he means to imply a physical nature for the exalted state of the eternal Son, but the problem remains when attempting to provide a physical explanation for the resurrection. The Intelligent Design Movement must deal with the same problem to a certain degree as it seeks to establish physical evidence for a nonphysical being.

The Designer and God
While the characteristics of the universe give us insight into the nature of the Designer, these characteristics will always be an incomplete view of God. Finally, Robert Kaita cautions us: "While the universe reflects the Creator, it does not demonstrate his existence."[29]

CHAPTER FIVE

MARSHAL NEWTON TAMES
THE WILD, WILD UNIVERSE

*One may say the eternal mystery of the world is
its comprehensibility.*
—Albert Einstein

IT IS NOT TOO SURPRISING that Einstein was mystified by the
comprehensibility of the world (universe). The universe contains objects that range from the very
small and invisible to the very large and
visible (fig. 5.1).

Fig. 5.1
Relative Sizes and Distances in the Universe.

Object	Exponent	Meaning
Distance from Earth to nearest galaxy	10^{22}	ten sextillion meters
Diameter of Andromeda Galaxy	10^{21}	one sextillion meters
Distance from Earth to nearest star	10^{16}	ten quadrillion meters
Diameter of solar system	10^{13}	ten trillion meters
Diameter of sun	10^{9}	one billion meters
Diameter of earth	10^{6}	one million meters
Diameter of Mount Everest	10^{4}	ten thousand meters
Height of World Trade Center	10^{3}	one thousand meters
Human child height	1	one meter
Length of insect	10^{-2}	one hundredeth of meter
Width of paper thickness	10^{-5}	ten millionth of meter
Length of bacterium	10^{-6}	one millionth of meter
Diameter of large molecule	10^{-8}	one millionth of meter
Diameter of atom	10^{-11}	ten trillionth of meter
Diameter of nucleus	10^{-14}	ten quadrillionth of meter

For reference to the English system:
one meter = 0.0062 miles or 39.37 inches

125

There are all kinds of phenomena to consider: comets, meteorites, moon, rain, ocean waves, diamonds, salt, DNA, plants, and animals. How can we possibly hope to be able to explain all these phenomena? Yet we are able to comprehend the world using the methods of modern science. In this chapter, we will examine ideas from mathematics, physics, chemistry, and biochemistry that help make the universe comprehensible.

UNIVERSAL, MATHEMATICAL LAWS

[The universe] is written in the language of mathematics, and its characters are triangles, circles, and other geometrical figures, without which it is humanly impossible to understand a single word of it.
—Galileo Galilei, *The Controversy on the Comets of 1618*

Is Galileo correct in saying that the way to comprehend nature is to use mathematics? Most scientists would answer yes. A key figure in showing that mathematics is the language of nature was Isaac Newton, the marshal of this chapter's title. Newton's triumph was to unify terrestrial and celestial phenomena. Beginning with Aristotle (384–322 B.C.), people believed that the terrestrial domain was different from the celestial domain. Using qualitative, common-sense arguments, Aristotle observed that the earth underwent change and decay while the heavens seemed to be unchanging and eternal. Motion seemed very different in the two domains. On earth, rest seemed the natural state: a rock rolled quickly down a hill and stopped an arrow that flew from a bow and quickly stopped and so forth. In the heavens, everything seemed to be in constant motion: the moon, sun, planets, and stars constantly circled the earth. During the late Middle Ages and during the Renaissance, scientists began trying to quantify their observations, with the division between terrestrial and celestial domains continuing. The German astronomer

Johannes Kepler (1571–1630) used mathematics to show that the planets move around the sun in elliptical orbits. Meanwhile, the Italian scientist Galileo Galilei (1564–1642) used mathematics to explain the motion of projectiles and free-falling bodies.

It remained for the English mathematician and physicist Isaac Newton (1642–1727) to show that terrestrial and celestial motion could be explained by the same set of laws of motion (Law of Universal Gravitation and the three Laws of Motion). While a student at Trinity College, Cambridge, Newton learned of the work of Kepler and Galileo. After taking his Bachelor of Arts degree in January 1665, Newton fled Cambridge because of the Great Plague. Returning to his country home, he spent the next eighteen months laying the foundation for transforming science. During this eighteen-month period, he invented differential calculus, began developing the laws of motion and gravitation, invented the reflecting telescope, and showed that white light contains all the colors of the spectrum. Some eighteen months! After the Great Plague, Newton returned to Cambridge, where he was appointed Lucasian Professor of Mathematics in 1669.

Always fearful of criticism, Newton did not immediately publish any of his findings. In 1675, the German mathematician Gottfried Wilhelm Leibniz (1646–1716) independently discovered differential calculus and immediately published his findings. Newton spent the rest of his life fighting Leibniz over who invented differential calculus. In 1684, challenged by the British astronomer Edmond Halley (1656–1742), Newton began refining his ideas on motion. After eighteen months of intense work, Newton published in 1687 the *Philosophiae naturalis principia mathematica* (*The Mathematical Principles of Natural Philosophy*), or *Principia*, as it is commonly known. Newton's view of mathematics is reflected in the title of the *Principia*. He considered mathematics to be the undergirding principles of Natural Philosophy, as science was then called.

The *Principia* is considered the greatest scientific book ever written. Using the laws of motion and the universal law of gravitation, Newton explained phenomena that had been thought of as dissimilar; these included the causes of tides, the orbits of comets, the precession of the earth on its axis, and the effect of the sun's gravity on the orbit of the moon. This enabled him to address most of the problems of physics and astronomy. Newton united the work of Kepler and Galileo into one consistent theory. At last, the earth and heavens were united into one universe.

As can be seen in figure 5.2, precise mathematical expressions are used to describe motion. The success of these mathematical expressions led other scientists to look for quantitative expressions in their fields. For example, the French chemist and royal tax collector Antoine Lavoisier (1743–1794) carefully measured the amounts of the chemicals used in chemical reactions. Based on his studies, Lavoisier discovered the Law of Conservation of Mass (the mass of the

Fig. 5.2. Mathematical Expressions for Motion.

Second Law of Motion

The acceleration of a body is directly proportional to the net force acting on the body and inversely proportional to the mass of the body, or

$$a = \frac{F}{m}$$

where a represents the acceleration,
F represents the force, and
m represents the mass.

Law of Universal Gravitation

Every body in the universe attracts every other body with a force that is directly proportional to the product of their masses and inversely proportional to the square of the distance between them, or

$$F = \frac{GM_1 M_2}{r^2}$$

Where F represents the force of attraction between two bodies,
G represents the gravitational constant,
M1 represents the mass of one body,
M2 represents the mass of a second body, and
r represents the distance between the two bodies.

products equals the mass of the reactants). For this work, Lavoisier is considered one of the founders of modern chemistry; for his tax collecting, Lavoisier was guillotined by the French revolutionaries.

Two long-term trends resulted from the success of Newton's work. First, people came to believe that *mathematics is the language of nature*. Somehow the phenomena of nature followed a mathematical pattern. An interesting example of this belief involved NASAs *Pioneer 10* and *Pioneer 11* spacecraft. *Pioneer 10* was launched on March 2, 1972, and explored Jupiter while *Pioneer 11* was launched on April 5, 1973, and explored Jupiter and Saturn. These were the first spacecraft that would leave the solar system and journey into interstellar space.

Because there was a remote chance of contact with beings from other stars, Carl Sagan convinced NASA to include a message from earth to the stars. The message was etched on a six-inch-by-nine-inch gold-plated aluminum plaque. On the plaque a man and women, in classical models of Greek sculpture, stand in front of a drawing of the spacecraft. Also on the plaque are drawings showing which planet in the solar system launched the spacecraft, the relationship of the sun to fourteen pulsars, and the hyperfine transition of the neutral hydrogen atom.[1] In what language should this plaque have been written? Sagan argued: "The extraterrestrials cannot possibly understand English or Russian or Chinese or Esperanto, but they must share with us common mathematics and physics and astronomy. I believe that they will understand, with no great effect, this message written in the galactic language: 'Scientific.'"[2] At the heart of Sagan's assumptions is "common mathematics" of the binary number system, which uses only two digits, 1 and 0, and is used by computers for storage of numbers.[3]

The downside of the belief that mathematics was the language of nature was the bias that if one cannot describe a phenomenon mathematically, then one does not truly understand the phenomenon. This bias led to a reductionist view of nature: everything in nature should be describable in terms of physics. Simplistically, one would say biology is explained by the action of the atoms of chemistry, and chemistry is explained by the action of matter and forces of physics. This reductionism ignores that the whole can be greater than the sum of its parts.

The second result of the success of the Newtonian laws to explain motion in the terrestrial and celestial domains was the view that *the same laws apply throughout the universe.* The assumption is that the same laws of physics and chemistry apply to a rock on earth as well as to a star light-years away. Is the concept of universal laws valid? We test this concept every day. During a twenty-four-hour period, the rotation of the Milky Way Galaxy carries the earth about 12 million miles. Over a century's time, the earth travels about 400 billion miles. The Law of Universal Gravitation appears to apply to this 400 billion miles of space, or we would be floating by now. Likewise, the observed behavior of stars and galaxies thousands of light years away also can be described by the Law of Universal Gravitation.

Newton was a theist who believed that God created and constantly sustains the universe.[4] However, others interpreted Newton's ideas as a clockworklike description of the universe that led to a deistic view of nature; the universe was a machine that had been created by God. Once God had "wound up" the universe, he retired and let his laws keep the universe going. This deistic view gradually gave way to a totally materialistic view: everything can be explained by the interaction of matter and the laws of nature.

Observations: The success of physics has been built on the application of mathematical principles to physical problems. Because we are educated to solve physical problems using mathematical principles, we can easily miss the amazing fact that a mental construct (mathematics) has anything to do with the physical world. Why should anything as simple as the mentally constructed counting systems of arithmetic have anything to do with piles of stones or clusters of stars? This amazing utility of mathematics is a strong argument for design in which the mind corresponds to the universe.

ORDER AMONG THE ELEMENTS

Chemistry studies the material substance of the universe, the stuff we can hold, kick, feel, weigh, smell, see, touch, and taste.
—Carl H. Snyder, *The Extraordinary Chemistry of Ordinary Things*

One of the fundamental questions for chemistry is, *What is (are) the building block(s) of matter?* Are the building blocks composed of the four elements of the ancient Greeks (earth, fire, water, air)? Or is the number infinite with each substance made of its own unique building block? Gradually, chemists realized the number of building blocks was more than four but less than infinity. Each building block, called an element, is composed entirely of a single type of atom.[5] Since the beginning of recorded history, the number of known elements has grown from an original group of ten—antimony, carbon, copper, gold, iron, lead, mercury, silver, sulfur, and tin. The ten most abundant elements by mass in the earth's crust are oxygen (16 percent), silicon (28 percent), aluminum (8 percent), iron (6 percent), calcium (4 percent), sodium (2 percent), magnesium (2 percent), potassium (2 percent), titanium (0.6 percent), and hydrogen (0.1 percent). As of August 2000, 115 elements have been discovered, with the elements above Neptunium being synthetic elements produced by nuclear reactions.

A second fundamental question concerning the elements is, *Are the same building blocks common throughout the universe?* The spectrum of light from a star carries information regarding the elemental composition of the star. Atoms give off light when they are heated. The color of the emitted light can be used to identify atoms. Two dramatic events on earth caused by atoms emitting light are the colors of fireworks and the colors of the aurora borealis or northern lights. The colors of fireworks are due to the emissions of light by excited metal atoms (yellow—sodium, blue—copper, green—barium, and red—strontium). Likewise the colors of the aurora borealis are caused by a similar process involving excited atoms and ions (greenish-yellow and deep red—oxygen atoms, red—dioxygen ion, and violet and blue—dinitrogen ion).

When scientists used the same techniques to analyze the spectra of stars, they found that no matter how far away, or how hot, or how massive, all stars contained the same elements as found on earth. Thus, the same elements (building blocks) have been discovered throughout the universe.

A third fundamental question concerning the elements is, *Can the elements be organized?* At first it would seem that all the elements are different. Consider three solids: potassium, iron, and gold. Potassium reacts explosively with water. Iron slowly rusts in the presence of water. Gold hardly reacts with anything. Consider two gases: hydrogen and neon. Hydrogen reacts explosively with oxygen. (Remember the Hindenburg.) Neon hardly reacts with anything. Now we have two inert substances, but one is a colorful solid while the other is a colorless gas! Where is the pattern? There must be a pattern, or chemistry could not be studied as a science.

One possible way to organize the elements would be to collect all those elements of similar properties. One group of elements was observed to have a characteristic shine, to be good conductors of electricity and heat, and to be malleable and ductile. These elements are classified as metals and contain the familiar iron, gold, and silver. Others are labeled as nonmetals, which means they have properties opposite of metals and contain the familiar oxygen and nitrogen. Finally, there is a third group labeled metalloid, or semimetal, having both metallic and nonmetallic properties and containing the familiar silicon of semiconductors.

Since seventeen elements are nonmetals and seven are metalloids, most of the elements are metals. Except for mercury, all the metals are solids. Eleven nonmetals are gases, one is liquid, and five are solids. Vastly different chemistries can be observed for metals (remember potassium, iron, and gold) and nonmetals (remember hydrogen and neon). Thus, the metal/nonmetal/metalloid classification is too broad because of the large variance in physical properties and chemistries of the elements.

As more and more elements were studied, it was discovered that certain groups of elements reacted similarly. Lithium, sodium, potassium, and cesium all react with water, producing hydrogen gas. Lithium reacts the most slowly, while cesium reacts so violently that the force of the reaction destroys the reaction vessel. Helium, neon, argon, and krypton are all inert, colorless gases. Using information about the similar properties of groups of elements, in 1869, the Russian chemist Dimitri Mendeleev organized the sixty-three elements known in his day.

When the elements are arranged in order of their atomic number (number of protons in their nuclei), a tabular series of rows and columns results with the elements in each vertical column having similar properties. This tabular arrangement is called the periodic table (fig. 5.3). The elements in a column have similar properties because they have the same number of electrons in their outermost shell (energy level). The elements lithium (Li), sodium (Na), potassium (K), and cesium (Cs), in the left-most column, each has one electron in the outermost shell. This family of elements is called the alkali metals. The alkali metals are all soft silvery metals. In contrast to the metal iron, they can be cut with a dull knife. The alkali metals are the most reactive of all metals, reacting with air and water. They are never found as free metals in nature.

The elements helium (He), neon (Ne), argon (Ar), and krypton (Kr) are in the right-most column, each having eight electrons in its outermost shell.[6] These elements are called the noble gases and are colorless, odorless, unreactive gases. The reactivity of an element depends upon the number of electrons in its outermost shell.

Fig. 5.3. Periodic Table of the Elements.

1A	2A	3B	4B	5B	6B	7B	8B			1B	2B	3A	4A	5A	6A	7A	8A
1 H 1.00794																	2 He 4.002602
3 Li 6.941	4 Be 9.012182											5 B 10.811	6 C 12.0107	7 N 14.00674	8 O 15.9994	9 F 18.998403	10 Ne 20.1797
11 Na 22.989770	12 Mg 24.3050											13 Al 26.981538	14 Si 28.0855	15 P 30.973762	16 S 32.066	17 Cl 35.4527	18 Ar 39.948
19 K 39.0983	20 Ca 40.078	21 Sc 44.95591	22 Ti 47.867	23 V 50.9415	24 Cr 51.9961	25 Mn 54.938049	26 Fe 55.845	27 Co 58.933200	28 Ni 58.6934	29 Cu 63.546	30 Zn 65.39	31 Ga 69.723	32 Ge 72.61	33 As 74.92160	34 Se 78.96	35 Br 79.904	36 Kr 83.80
37 Rb 85.4678	38 Sr 87.62	39 Y 88.90585	40 Zr 91.224	41 Nb 92.90638	42 Mo 95.94	43 Tc (98)	44 Ru 101.07	45 Rh 102.90550	46 Pd 106.42	47 Ag 107.8682	48 Cd 112.411	49 In 114.818	50 Sn 118.710	51 Sb 121.760	52 Te 127.60	53 I 126.90447	54 Xe 131.29
55 Cs 132.90545	56 Ba 137.327	57 *La 138.9055	72 Hf 178.49	73 Ta 180.9479	74 W 183.84	75 Re 186.207	76 Os 190.23	77 Ir 192.217	78 Pt 195.078	79 Au 196.96655	80 Hg 200.59	81 Tl 204.3833	82 Pb 207.2	83 Bi 208.98038	84 Po (210)	85 At (210)	86 Rn (222)
87 Fr (223)	88 Ra (226)	89 +Ac 227.028	104 Rf (261)	105 Db (262)	106 Sg (266)	107 Bh (264)	108 Hs (265)	109 Mt (268)	110 (269)	111 (272)	112 (277)		114 (285)		116 (289)		118 (293)

*Lanthanide series:

58 Ce 140.116	59 Pr 140.90765	60 Nd 144.24	61 Pm (145)	62 Sm 150.36	63 Eu 151.964	64 Gd 157.25	65 Tb 158.92534	66 Dy 162.50	67 Ho 164.93032	68 Er 167.26	69 Tm 168.93421	70 Yb 173.04	71 Lu 174.967

+Actinide series:

90 Th 232.0381	91 Pa 231.03588	92 U 238.0289	93 Np (237)	94 Pu (244)	95 Am (243)	96 Cm (247)	97 Bk (247)	98 Cf (251)	99 Es (252)	100 Fm (257)	101 Md (258)	102 No (259)	103 Lr (262)

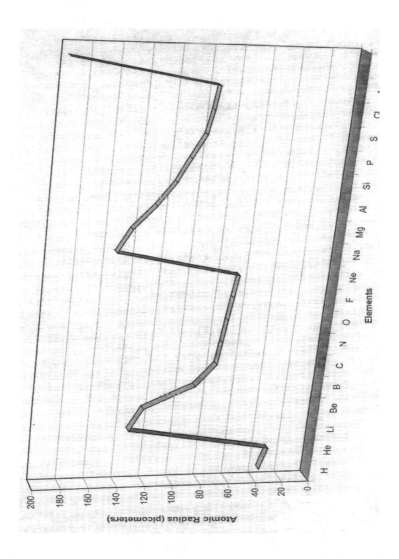

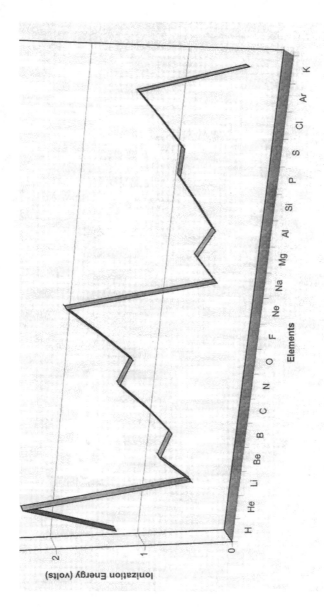

Fig. 5.5. Periodic Trend of Ionization Energies.

The electron configurations of the elements display a periodic variation with increasing nuclear charge (atomic number). Because the physical and chemical behaviors of the elements depend on the electron configurations, the elements show periodic variations in physical and chemical properties. In this section, we will examine two properties of an atom: atomic radius and first ionization energy.

The *atomic radius* is a measure of how large an atom is. One way to determine the atomic radius is from measurements of the distances between atoms in molecules. In figure 5.4, the atomic radius is plotted versus the atomic number for the first nineteen elements. Note that the curve tends to repeat, or is periodic. In general the atomic radius decreases as one moves from left to right across a horizontal row (period); compare Li to Ne and Na to Ar. The atomic radius generally increases as one moves from top to bottom within a vertical column (group); compare Li, Na, and K or He, Ne, and Ar.

The *first ionization energy* is the energy needed to remove an outermost electron from the neutral atom. The value of the first ionization energy is a measure of how reactive an element is. Atoms with a small ionization energy

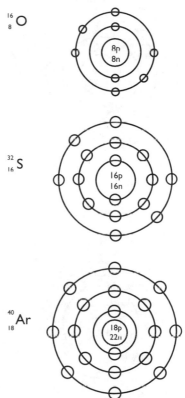

Fig. 5.6. Model of Atoms. The central area is the nucleus containing protons (p) and neutron (n). The electrons are in shells (energy levels) around the nucleus.

value are more reactive than atoms with a higher ionization energy value. In figure 5.5, the first ionization energy is plotted against the atomic number for the first nineteen elements. This results in a periodic trend. The ionization energy tends to increase as one crosses a period from left to right; compare Li to Ne and Na to Ar. The ionization energy tends to decrease

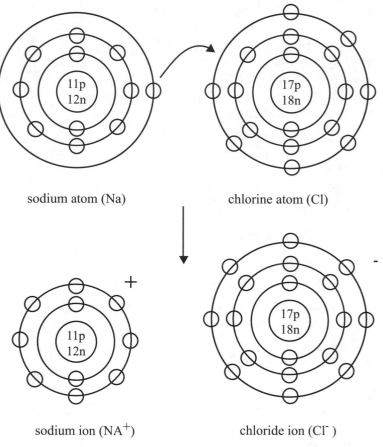

sodium atom (Na)   chlorine atom (Cl)

sodium ion (NA^+)   chloride ion (Cl^-)

Fig 5.7. Ionic Reaction. The metal sodium transfers an electron to the nonmetal chlorine forming table salt containing sodium and chloride ions.

as one moves down a group; compare Li, Na, and K or He, Ne, and Ar.

Chemists have transformed the way people live by building on the quantitative approach to the study of matter, on the fact that the number of building blocks (elements) is limited, and on the periodic relationships between the elements. Think what our life would be like if we removed plastics, such as, plastic wrap (polyethylene), Styrofoam, PVC pipe, and Teflon coated cookware from our homes. Or if we no longer had synthetic fibers: nylons, dacrons, rayons, or mylars. How would we deal with everyday pains without aspirin and Tylenol? Could we endure allergy season without antihistamines? Would our homes be as clean without Lysol? Think of all the diseases contained with the antibiotics: sulfa drugs, penicillins, and tetracyclines. Our clothes and bodies would be much dirtier without synthetic detergents and soaps. We would be unable to fax or photocopy. And finally, I would not be composing this chapter on a computer.

Atoms to Compounds

Chemists are interested in discovering how atoms react (combine) with one another to form collections of atoms called compounds. By knowing not only which atoms are present but also which atoms are bonded to one another, chemists gain an understanding of why Teflon produces a stick-free surface while polyethylene does not. In this section, we will examine the different ways atoms combine to form compounds.

Chemistry studies the interaction of the electrons of one atom with the electrons of another atom. The nucleus goes along for the ride. Models of several atoms are shown in figure 5.6. The nucleus contains the protons and the neutrons. The electrons are arranged in shells or energy levels.[7] The first (innermost) shell has the lowest energy and can hold a maximum of two electrons (oxygen, sulfur, and neon in the figure). The second shell can hold a maximum of eight electrons (sulfur and neon in the figure), while the third shell can hold a maximum of sixteen electrons. It has been observed that, in an uncombined atom, the outermost shell will never contain more than eight electrons (oxygen, sulfur, and neon in the figure).

An atom is most stable when it contains eight electrons in its outermost shell; hence, the unreactivity of the noble gases. Chemical reactions involve atoms shuffling electrons until each acquires eight electrons in their outermost shells (a noble gas electronic configuration). One way of shuffling the electrons is for one atom to loose electrons to another atom. Metals react with nonmetals in this manner. Metals lose electrons and

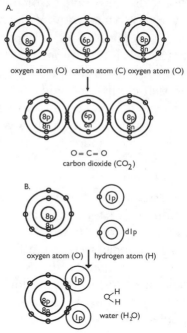

A.

oxygen atom (O) carbon atom (C) oxygen atom (O)

O = C = O
carbon dioxide (CO_2)

B.

oxygen atom (O) | hydrogen atom (H)

water (H_2O)

Fig 5.8. Covalent Reactions. A. The oxygen and carbon atoms share electrons thereby obtaining eight electrons in their outermost shell. B. The oxygen and hydrogen atoms share electrons. Oxygen obtains eight electrons in its outermost shell while hydrogen obtains only two electrons. Two electrons in hydrogen outermost shell is a stable arrangement because this arrangement is like the electronic arrangement of the Nobel Gas Helium.

become positive ions while nonmetals gain electrons and become negative ions. This reaction results in an ionic compound held together by an ionic bond. Figure 5.7 illustrates the reaction of the metal sodium with the nonmetal chlorine to form the ionic compound sodium chloride or table salt. Note that each ion now has eight electrons in its outermost shell.

Nonmetals react with nonmetals by sharing electrons. The reaction results in a covalent compound held together by a covalent bond. Figure 5.8, Part A, illustrates the reaction of carbon with oxygen to form carbon dioxide. In the covalent product, each atom has eight electrons in its outermost shell. The shorthand notation (O=C=O), called a structural formula, reveals two covalent bonds (double bond) between the carbon and each oxygen. Figure 5.8, Part B, illustrates the reaction of oxygen with hydrogen to form water. Note that in this covalent, compound oxygen has eight electrons in its outermost shell but hydrogen has only two. Hydrogen becomes like the noble gas helium, which has only two electrons, unlike the other noble gases, which have eight in their outermost shells. The shorthand notation for water reveals that there is one covalent bond (single bond) between oxygen and each hydrogen.

Covalent molecules come in two varieties: nonpolar and polar. Nonpolar molecules result when their atoms have an approximate equal sharing of electrons. Polar molecules result when two atoms share electrons unequally.[8] Chemists model this event by saying that the electrons spend more time orbiting one nucleus than orbiting the other. Oxygen has a greater attraction for electrons than does hydrogen. Thus, the electrons, in water, spend more time near the oxygen nucleus than the hydrogen nuclei. This results in the formation of a partial negative charge on the oxygen and a partial positive charge on the hydrogens. This separation of partial charges causes water to be a polar molecule. Whether a covalent molecule is polar or nonpolar affects many of its properties. Polar molecules are attracted to other polar molecules and ionic compounds. Nonpolar molecules are attracted only to other nonpolar molecules. These polarity relations determine solubilities. Sodium chloride (ionic) and sugar (polar) dissolve in water (polar). Oil (nonpolar) and dirt (nonpolar) do not dissolve in water (polar). As we shall observe, these polarity relationships determine many of the properties of the molecules of life.

Observations: Because we have been taught since elementary school that there are about one hundred chemical building blocks, we easily miss the astonishing fact that there are so few building blocks. We easily overlook the wonder that the same building blocks are present in the tiniest molecule as well as the largest galaxy. It is a tremendous help to chemists that once they know the properties of these one hundred or so elements, they can deal with the structure of granite or oil or a star or bones. This order throughout nature implies design.

Carbon: The Element of Life

Most of the molecules of life are covalent compounds resulting from the reaction of the nonmetal carbon with the nonmetals hydrogen, nitrogen, oxygen, and sulfur. Although carbon composes only 0.19 percent of the lithosphere and only 0.01 percent of the hydrosphere, carbon makes up 20 percent of the living organisms. The chemistry of carbon compounds is called organic chemistry. When these organic compounds are found in living organisms, the chemistry is called biochemistry. The following are some of the properties of carbon that make it an ideal candidate to be the key element in the compounds found in living organisms:

- forms stable, covalent carbon-carbon bonds
- forms characteristic three-dimensional structures
- reacts at functional groups
- forms energy-rich compounds

Carbon-carbon bonds. Carbon has the ability to form stable covalent bonds with other carbon atoms resulting in molecules containing thousands of carbon-carbon bonds (fig. 5.9). Carbon can form both single (saturated) and

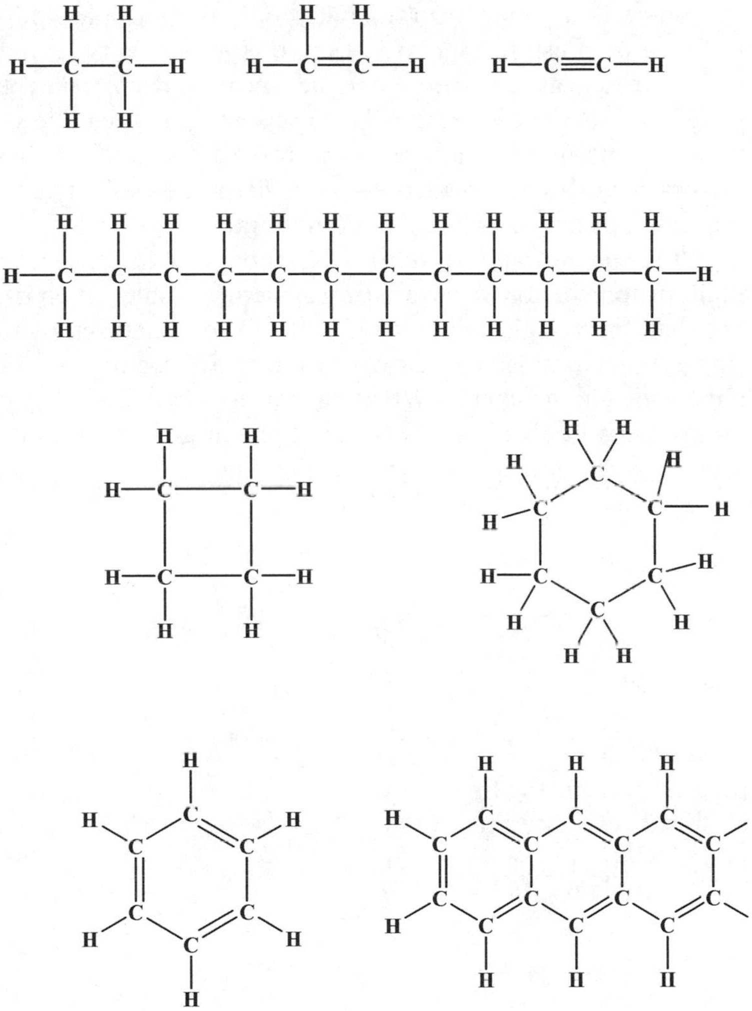

Fig. 5.9. Some compounds with carbon-carbon bonds.

multiple (unsaturated) bonds with other carbon atoms. These carbon-carbon arrays form the backbones of molecules found in living organisms. A great variety of forms results because these carbon-carbon arrays can be linear (chains) or cyclic (rings). Further variety results because some arrays can be saturated while others may be unsaturated. When all of these factors have been considered, over 90 percent of all compounds turn out to be organic compounds.

Three-dimensional structures. Carbon can form a maximum of four bonds. A tetrahedral structure results when carbon has four single bonds (fig. 5.10). The structures of the single-bonded molecules shown in figure 5.9 are not flat but have a zig-zag geometry. When carbon is bonded to another atom with a double bond, a trigonal planar geometry results. Two different arrangements are possible in some double-bonded carbon compounds. The cis arrangement (Latin *cis,*

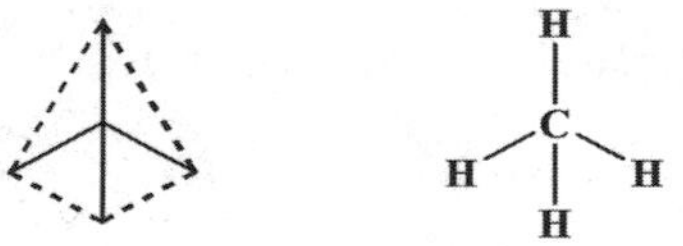

A. The tetrahedral arrangement around the carbon atom.

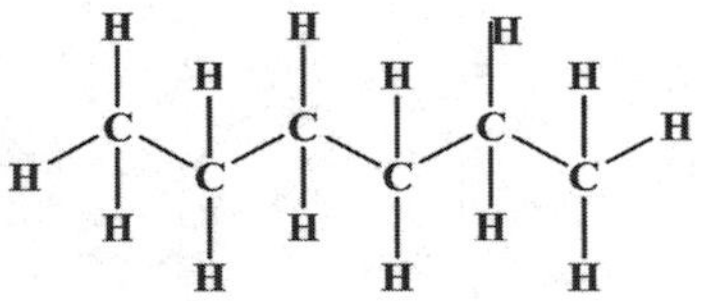

B. Zig-zag geometry

C. Cis and trans geometry

Fig. 5.10 Three-Dimensional Geometries of Carbon Compounds.

"on this side") occurs when two groups lie on the same side of the double bond. The trans arrangement (Latin *trans*, "across") occurs when two groups lie across the double bond. Many reactions in living organisms involve the shapes of molecules. The chemistry of vision involves light converting the cis isomer of retinal (the vision molecule) to its trans isomer. The detection of odors is thought to result from molecules of certain shapes fitting closely on the receptor sites of olfactory nerve endings. Enzyme action depends upon molecules of certain shapes fitting into pockets of the enzyme molecule. No other chemical elements form as many shapes as carbon.

Functional groups. Additional variety results because the energy involved in forming carbon-carbon bonds is not much different from forming carbon-hydrogen or carbon-oxygen bonds. By attaching hydrogen, nitrogen, or oxygen groups to the carbon-carbon backbones, many different biological molecules can easily be formed. These groups attached to the carbon-carbon backbone are called functional groups (fig. 5.11). The chemistry of an organic molecule, regardless of its size, is largely determined by its functional group. For example, all molecules have the properties of an alcohol when the OH fragment is bonded to carbon. Thus, whether the OH is bonded to one carbon or to a ten-carbon chain or to a five-carbon ring, they are all alcohols. The alcohol group is an important functional group in carbohydrates. The ester group is important in lipids (fats and oils), while the amide, amine, and carboxylic acid groups are important in proteins.

Energy-rich compounds. Most organic compounds are rich in hydrogen. Or a chemist would say they are reduced. They have a lot of potential energy available for reacting with oxygen. In contrast most inorganic carbon compounds such as carbon dioxide and carbonates are oxygen rich or oxidized. They do not have the potential for further reaction with oxygen.

Although organic molecules have the potential to react with oxygen, they do not spontaneously react with the atmosphere. If they did spontaneously react, then life could not have been based on carbon because the needed compounds already would have reacted with oxygen. A spark is needed to cause natural gas or gasoline to react with oxygen. Living organisms moderate this reaction by the use of enzymes.

Carbon Dioxide

Carbon dioxide is a simple gas molecule composed of two oxygen atoms double bonded to a carbon atom: O=C=O. The ultimate source of carbon in living organisms is carbon

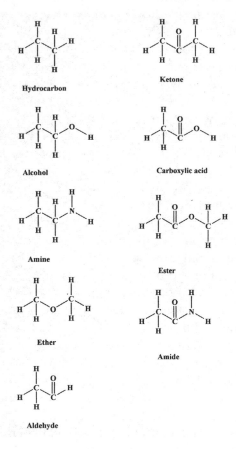

Fig. 5.11. Functional Groups.

dioxide. Through photosynthesis, plants remove carbon dioxide from the air and convert carbon dioxide into the chemicals of life. By eating plants, animals transfer the carbon to their bodies.

Carbon dioxide has several properties that make it an important molecule for life. At the temperatures associated with living organisms, carbon dioxide is found in nearly the same concentration in air as in water. Among the gases, this is a unique property for carbon dioxide. Being in nearly the same concentration allows carbon dioxide easily to exchange between air and water or between living organisms and their surroundings.

When animals process food during metabolism, carbon dioxide and water are the two waste products. One could say that animals get energy by converting carbon compounds to carbon dioxide. An average person produces about a kilogram (2.2 pounds) of carbon dioxide each day. This amount of waste would be very difficult to remove if carbon dioxide were not a gas. Gases cross the cell membrane by diffusion that does not require energy because the gas spontaneously flows from high pressure to low pressure. In contrast, liquids and solids have to be pumped across the membrane.

Once the carbon dioxide gas diffuses through the cell membrane into the blood stream, the carbon dioxide is hydrated to form carbonic acid, H_2CO_3. Carbonic acid is a weak acid and partially disassociates into the bicarbonate (HCO_3) ion. A mixture between a weak acid and the salt of a weak acid (the bicarbonate) forms a buffer. A buffer maintains the acidity or basicity of a solution by neutralizing any acid or base added to the solution. Or the buffer maintains a constant pH for the solution. The normal pH of blood is 7.4. Blood pH below 7.4 is called acidosis, with the blood pH above 7.4 being called alkalosis. If the pH of the blood should rise above 7.8 or fall below 7.0, the result can be fatal. The body regulates the amount of carbon dioxide in the blood and hence the pH by regulating the rate of breathing.

Carbon dioxide also has an important role in regulating the earth's temperature. When sunlight strikes the surface of the earth, some of the light energy is absorbed while the rest of the energy is reflected back into the atmosphere. Carbon dioxide absorbs some of this energy thereby moderating the earth's temperature. Without this greenhouse effect of carbon dioxide, the average temperature of the earth would be similar to that of the moon: an average of -22° C or -6° F rather than the earth's 14° C or 57° F. This is the natural greenhouse effect. Currently, scientists are trying to determine if our industrialized societies are causing an enhanced greenhouse effect (the bad one). A carbon dioxide level above that produced by living organisms could raise the average earth's temperature high enough to disrupt the earth's ecosystems.

Why Not Silicon?
I remember, as a child, watching a B movie about scientists creating life based on silicon. At first, life based on silicon seems reasonable since carbon and silicon are in the same family in the periodic table. Thus, why not silicon?

Silicon does lie below carbon in the periodic table, but the properties of silicon differ greatly from carbon. Carbon is a nonmetal while silicon is a metalloid that lies on the boundary between nonmetals and metals. Thus, the chemistry of silicon is different from that of carbon. Although carbon-carbon, carbon-hydrogen, and carbon-oxygen bonds have about the same energy, silicon-silicon bonds are easier to form than silicon-hydrogen or silicon-oxygen. Thus, the great variety of compounds seen for carbon is not seen for silicon.

As we just discussed, carbon dioxide, being a simple gaseous molecule, is critical for life processes. Silicon dioxide is a polymeric solid called quartz. Silicon does not form double bonds like carbon does in carbon dioxide. The structure for silicon dioxide is an extended structure with single bonds between the silicon and oxygen atoms. Thus, it would be much harder for a living organism to excrete a kilogram of solid quartz than a kilogram of gaseous carbon dioxide. For this reason, many chemists and biologists do not think that silicon could be the element around which a living organism could be formed.

Observations: Because its compounds are everywhere, it is easy to overlook the fact that carbon is a unique element. The carbon atom's ability to bond easily to itself and other elements results in structures found in oil, trees, dogs and cats, plastics, and people. By removing carbon from nature, we not only would lose most of the variety in the chemical compounds in the universe, but we would lose life itself. The unique chemistry of carbon suggests design.

WATER

Ocean, n: A body of water occupying about two-thirds of a world made for man—who has no gills.
—A. Bierce

Before we leave chemistry, let us examine one very common but unusual molecule, water. We have "water, water, everywhere," as Coleridge wrote[9]—in rain, snow, rivers, oceans, lakes, underground streams, swimming pools, plants, animals, and people. Water is the most abundant compound on the earth. Yet this common compound is very strange. The following properties of water, which we experience every day, make water a unique substance:

- Water is a liquid at room temperature.
- Solid water (ice) floats.
- Water has a high heat capacity.
- Water has the highest heat of vaporization of all known substances.
- Water has a large surface tension.
- Water is an excellent solvent.

Boiling Point
If one considers the hydrogen compounds of the first member of the carbon, nitrogen, oxygen, and halogen families, all of

these hydrogen compounds (CH_4, NH_3, and HF) are toxic and/or corrosive gases except for water (H_2O), which is a nontoxic, noncorrosive liquid. The properties of water are anomalies since its properties do not fit the expected periodic trends. For most families of compounds, the observed periodic trend is that as the molecular weight of a compound increases its boiling point also increases. The hydrogen compounds made from the members of the carbon family (carbon, silicon, germanium, and tin) are an example of this periodic trend (fig. 5.12). Part B of the figure presents the

Part A. Molecular Weights & Boiling Points		
Molecule	Molecular Weight	Boiling Point
CH_4	16.04	-161.5
SiH_4	32.09	-111.8
GeH_4	76.63	-90.0
SnH_4	122.73	-52.0

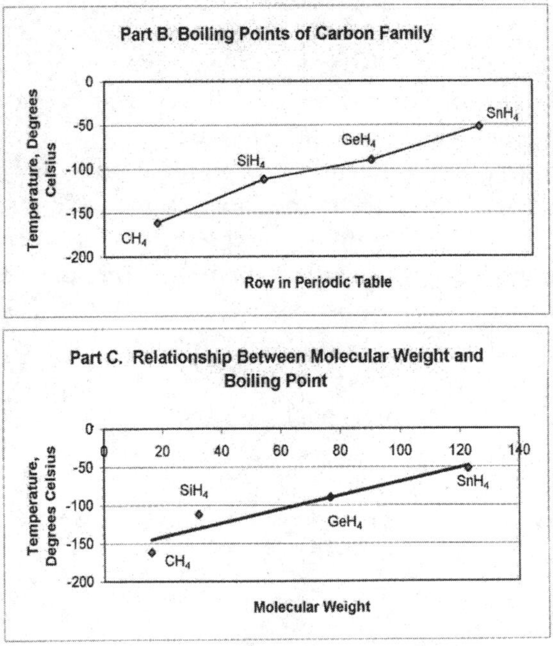

Part B. Boiling Points of Carbon Family

Part C. Relationship Between Molecular Weight and Boiling Point

Fig. 5.12. Hydrogen Compounds
of the Carbon Family.

periodic distribution of boiling points; all are gases at room temperature. Figure 5.12 Part C presents the relationship between the molecular weight of a compound and its boiling point. The periodic trend observed is that as the molecular weight increases the boiling point increases.

Figure 5.13 extends the data on the hydrogen compounds to the nitrogen family (nitrogen, phosphorus, arsenic, and antimony), oxygen family (oxygen, sulfur, selenium, and tellurium), and the halogens (fluorine, chlorine, bromine, and iodine). Ignoring the first members of each family, the clear periodic trend is that the boiling points all increase with increasing molecular weights. Three of the first members (ammonia, hydrogen fluoride, and water) show anomalous behavior, water having the greatest anomaly. If the oxygen family behaved like the carbon family, the expected boiling point of water would be near -100° C, not the observed +100° C!

The unique properties of water result from its molecular structure. The shape of the water molecule is similar to an isosceles triangle (fig. 5.14) with the distance between the oxygen and hydrogen nuclei being 9.65 nanometers with the H-O-H angle being 104.5 degrees. The water molecule is held

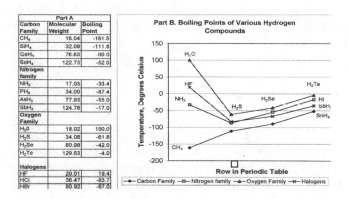

Fig. 5.13. Boiling Points of Various Hydrogen Compounds.

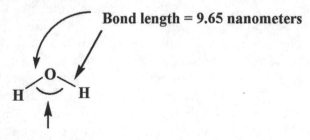

Bond length = 9.65 nanometers

Bond angle = 104.5 degrees

Fig. 5.14. Isosceles Triangular Shape of Water.

together by sharing electrons between the oxygen and the hydrogen atoms. As we discussed previously, the oxygen atom has a greater attraction for the shared electrons than does the hydrogen atoms. Thus, the electron density shifts from the hydrogen atoms and builds up around the oxygen atom, making water a polar molecule. The hydrogen atoms of one water molecule are now electrostatically attracted to the oxygen atom of another molecule. This attraction forms a strong bond between the molecules called the hydrogen bond. In water, the hydrogen bonding extends from molecule to molecule until a three-dimensional polymer with a tetrahedral structure is formed (fig. 5.15). The energy required to break all these hydrogen bonds is great; thus, water boils at the very high, anomalous temperature of 100° C.

Ice Floats

The hydrogen bond-formed, three-dimensional structure is very rigid in ice. As shown in figure 5.16, this is a very open structure. This is not a very compact arrangement as each molecule in this structure has only four neighbors. Many solids are packed more compactly with arrangements where each molecule has up to twelve neighbors.[10] Upon the melting of ice, about 15 percent of the hydrogen bonds are broken; the percent broken is low because of the strong tendency of the water molecule to hydrogen bond. Breaking these hydrogen bonds disrupts the pure tetrahedral structure. In the liquid state some water molecules would have more than four neighbors, making liquid water more compact and less open than solid water. Since liquid water is more compact (takes up less volume) than solid water, ice is less dense and floats.

Ice floats, and aquatic life survives the winters. As water freezes, ice forms only on the surface of the river or lake, leaving liquid water below it for marine life to exist. The surface ice insulates the water and aquatic life below. If ice were denser than liquid water, the ice would sink upon freezing and accumulate on the bottom. During the summer, the ice on the bottom would not melt. Year by year, more and more ice would accumulate until all aquatic life would be eliminated.

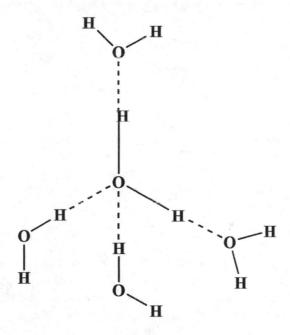

Fig. 5.15. Three-Dimensional Structure of Water. Hydrogen bonding between □ water molecules results in a tetrahedral structure. Solid lines denote□ covalent bonds. Dashed lines denote hydrogen bonds.

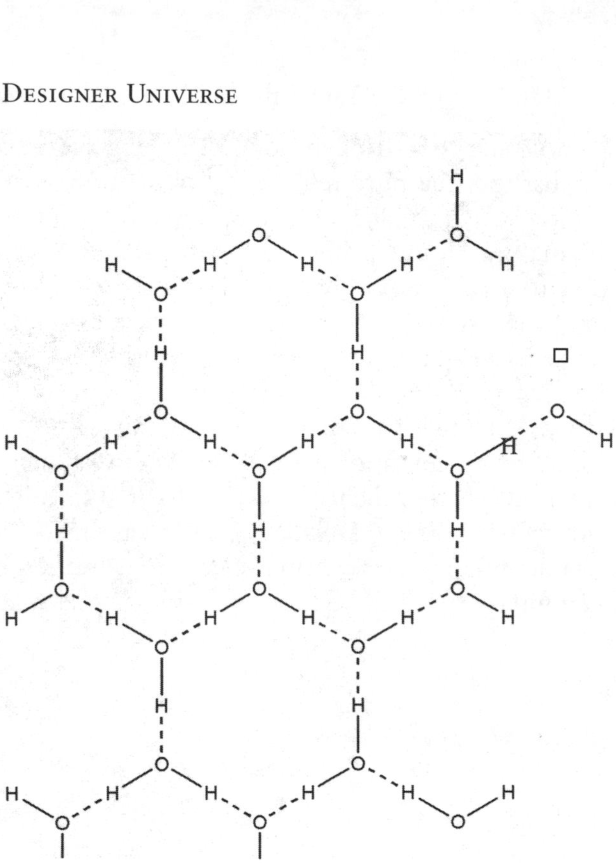

Fig. 5.16. Structure of Ice. A fragment of one layer of the ice structure □ is shown. Dashed lines represent hydrogen bonding.

Thus, floating ice is much more important than just as an addition to one's tea.

High Heat Capacity
The heat capacity (specific heat) is the amount of heat required to raise the temperature of one gram of a substance by one degree Celsius. The greater the heat capacity the longer it takes for the substance to warm up. Water has a large heat capacity and thus heats up very slowly—"a watched pot never boils." The heat capacity of water is about ten times larger than that of copper or iron (fig. 5.17) and about twice as large as simple organic liquids. The absorption

Fig. 5.17. Heat Capacity of Some Substances.

Substance	Heat Capacity
Water	4.18
Ethyl alcohol	2.43
Aluminum	0.901
Iron	0.449
Copper	0.384

The heat capabilities are measured at 25 degrees and are in units of joules per gram-degree Celsius.

of heat by water causes the vibration and breakage of its hydrogen bonds. Thus, the extensive hydrogen bonding in the three-dimension structure of water results in a large heat capacity.

The oceans cover about 72 percent of the earth's surface with 97.2 percent of the world's water. About 2.1 percent of the water is in the ice caps and glaciers. Fresh water in lakes, rivers, and ground water amounts to only 0.6 percent with the remaining 0.1 percent in the form of brine wells and brackish waters. All of this water moderates the climate of the earth. During the daylight hours, these large bodies of water absorb and store heat from the sun. At night, the waters slowly release the heat. These processes prevent extreme temperature variations.

High Heat of Vaporization
The heat of vaporization is the quantity of heat necessary to change one gram of liquid water to vapor without a temperature change. It is a measure of how easily a liquid will evaporate. Water has the highest heat of vaporization of any known substance (fig. 5.18). This high heat of vaporization makes water a great coolant through the process of evaporation. As can be seen in figure 5.18, the heat of vaporization of water is almost five times higher than the two common rubbing alcohols, ethyl and isopropyl. Living creatures use the evaporation of water as a cooling mechanism.

Fig. 5.18. Heats of Vaporization of Various Liquids.

Liquid	Heat of Vaporiation (calories per gram)
Water	540
Ethyl alcohol	204
Isopropyl alcohol	159
Acetone	125
Ethyl acetate	102
Ethyl ether	89.3
Chloroform	59

Water's high heat of vaporization also affects the earth's weather. The hydrologic cycle involves the movement of water from the oceans to freshwater sources and from the freshwater sources back to the ocean. The cycle begins with the evaporation of surface waters, which absorbs about 30 percent of the solar energy reaching the earth. The energy is released as this water condenses, resulting in precipitation, sometimes in the form of thunderstorms. This precipitation replenishes the freshwater sources.

Large Surface Tension
Surface tension is the resistance of a liquid to spreading out and increasing its surface area. Surface tension allows a water strider to move across water and causes water to bead on a waxy surface. Because of water's strong intermolecular hydrogen bonds, it has a very large surface tension, even larger than glycerin and ethyl alcohol. The large surface tension of water allows plants and trees to use capillary action to carry water and nutrients to their leaves.

An Excellent Solvent
All our lives we've heard that water is the "universal solvent." It has unusual solvent properties because it is both a polar molecule and a hydrogen-bonding molecule. It is able to dissolve both ionic substances, such as salts, as well as polar

compounds, such as sugars. Because of its solvent properties, water is the premier biological solvent allowing the transportation of carbohydrates, fats, proteins, and nucleic acids throughout an organism. Also, since water contains both the H^+ of an acid and the OH^- of a base, water is an excellent solvent for both acids and bases.

But all our lives we've also heard that oil and water do not mix. That means that not even water is really a "universal solvent." Water does not dissolve nonpolar compounds. Oil and water do not mix because oil is nonpolar and water is polar. Many biological molecules, such as enzymes, contain parts of their structure that are polar and other parts that are nonpolar. When an enzyme is placed in water, the enzyme molecule twists and turns so that its polar parts (hydrophilic parts) are on the outside of the molecule and its nonpolar parts (hydrophobic parts) are on the inside, away from the polar water molecules. The resulting shape of the enzyme enables the molecule to catalyze biochemical reactions in the cell. Cell walls and cell membranes are also formed by similar hydrophilic and hydrophobic interactions. A lipid is another type of biological molecule that contains hydrophilic and hydrophobic components. One end of the lipid is polar and is called the head, while the rest of the molecule is nonpolar and is called the tail (fig. 5.19). The main structure of membranes is a lipid bilayer of two rows of lipid arranged tail to tail with the heads on the outside interacting with the water within and without the cell.

Observations: Water is so common that we easily miss its uniqueness. Using the trends of chemistry, we would expect water to be a gas at room temperature or for ice to sink in our iced tea. Either one of these properties would be enough to make the earth very hostile to life. The high heat capacity and heat of vaporization of water further moderate the climate of the earth. Water is a unique molecule; some people consider that a mark of design.

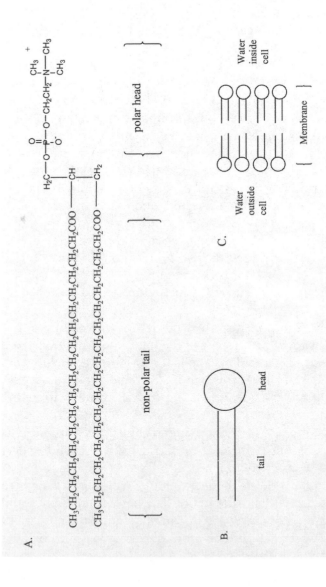

Fig. 5.19. A Lipid. A. Chemical structure of a typical lipid. B. Symbolic representation of lipid. C. Lipid bilayer found in cell membranes.

WHERE'S THE BEEF?

Design is not so much a set of facts as it is a way of reasoning.

—Nancy Pearcey

Mathematics and Physics

Key question: does mathematics really describe nature? Several responses to the question have been proposed.

The conventionalist view. The conventionalists[11] would state that the mathematical equations are provisional models of reality. They give us a partial truth. The model (type of mathematics) changes as one's knowledge of nature increases. The model is just curve-fitting, the modification of the mathematics until it fits reality.

Ptolemy (c. 100–c. 165 A.D.) started with a geometric model of the circle to model the orbit of Mars. When that did not work, he kept adding circles upon circles until he reproduced the orbit of Mars. The conventionalist would say that Newton did the same thing. Newton started by solving the differential equation involving Mars and the Sun. The elliptical orbit predicted does not exactly fit the orbit of Mars. Adding other masses, such as Jupiter, will more closely reproduce the orbit of Mars. The conventionalist would say, "We are still curve-fitting, but we're doing it on the basis of a more versatile vocabulary of the solutions of differential equations rather than on a vocabulary of 'ready made' simple curves such as circles."[12]

The Platonic view. This second view believes that mathematical objects exist independently of our knowledge of them. When one discovers mathematical concepts, one is discovering the "blueprint" of nature. The mathematical concepts are more than just mental constructs. The Platonist would say that the conventionalists have not really explained why mathematics is so unreasonably effective.[13]

How can something as abstract as a number be broadly applied to physical objects? The mathematician Richard W. Hamming asks, "Is it not remarkable that 6 sheep plus 7 sheep make 13 sheep; that 6 stones plus 7 stones make 13 stones? Is it not a miracle that the universe is so constructed that such a simple abstraction as a number is possible? To me this is one of the strongest examples of the unreasonable effectiveness of mathematics."[14]

The unreasonable effectiveness of mathematics is also reflected in the fact that "what we predict from the manipulation of mathematical symbols is realized in the real world."[15] In 1873, James Clerk Maxwell (1831–1879) published the fully developed form of his equations describing the behavior of visible light. Maxwell's equations predicted that visible light had "brothers and sisters" in the electromagnetic spectrum. This prediction was confirmed by Heinrich Rudolph Hertz (1857–1894) in 1887 when he discovered radio waves. Soon microwaves, infrared, ultraviolet, X rays, and gamma rays were discovered to be part of the electromagnetic spectrum. Manipulations of mathematical equations led to a greater understanding of nature.

An even more amazing example of the unreasonable effectiveness of mathematics concerns cases where types of mathematics were developed abstractly without any reference to nature. Yet, many of these mathematical types were later shown to describe nature better than previous mathematical concepts. One example is non-Euclidean geometry, which was developed independently early in the nineteenth century by Carl Friedrich Gauss (1777–1855), Nikolay Ivanovich Lobachevsky (1793–1856), and Janos Bolyai (1802–1860). Euclidean geometry is the geometry usually taught in high school. Euclidean geometry fits common sense: one line is drawn parallel to a given line through a given point not on the line. Non-Euclidean geometry allows more than one line to be drawn parallel to a given line through a given point not on the line. At first non-Euclidean geometry was considered useless, even monstrous. Einstein later showed that it describes astronomical space more precisely than Euclidean geometry.

Another example of "bizarre" mathematics is fractal geometry developed by Benoit B. Mandelbrot (1924–). A fractal is an irregular geometric figure with the property that when any given part of the figure is enlarged or reduced a similar shape is maintained. Zooming in for a closer view of a nonfractal object tends to smooth out its irregularities. As in the case of non-Euclidean geometry, fractals at first were considered bizarre and useless. Mandelbrot later suggested that coastlines, clouds, mountains, and trees are fractal in shape. A cloud keeps its detailed shape whether viewed from the ground or an airplane. A rock looks like the mountain from which it came. On an atlas, the eastern coastline of the United States looks like a fairly smooth line with a length of two thousand to three thousand miles. On a more detailed map of just the United States, this coastline now has bays and inlets; the coastline now is a more complex line with a length of four thousand to five thousand miles. At the greater magnification of a person walking along the coastline, the path becomes very ragged with a length of over fifteen thousand miles. The bizarre fractal geometry seems to describe some parts of nature better than the smooth curves of Euclidean geometry.

Whether one sees design in the "unreasonable effectiveness of mathematics" depends upon one's philosophy, one's worldview, or one's frame of reference. As the quote from Nancy Pearcey states, whether one sees design does not depend upon the "facts" but upon how one reasons about those facts. Both the conventionalist and the Platonist see how mathematics is applied to physics problems. Their worldviews determine whether they see a model or design.

Chemistry
Key concepts: Consider a handful of organizable building blocks, the unique chemistry of carbon, and the extraordinary properties of water. Materialists would explain these

phenomena in terms of the interaction of matter and forces. They would say that it is not surprising that there are so few elements. Since the atomic nucleus is a very small space, electromagnetic repulsion between increasing numbers of protons will eventually overpower the attractive effects of the strong nuclear force and tear the nucleus apart. They would also attempt to use electromagnetic interactions to explain the chemistry of carbon and the properties of water.

It is true that many aspects of chemistry can be explained as the forces of physics. Yet, there is much about chemistry that has not been calculated by the use of the forces of physics. Happily, chemists still need to go into the laboratory to discover what happens when two substances are mixed. Even if the dark day were to come where all chemistry could be reduced to a series of calculations, the possibility of design would not be removed. The argument for design would only be moved back to the laws of nature as discussed in chapter 4.

As Nancy Pearcey stated, whether one sees design depends upon one's reasoning or worldview. Chemistry does reveal an astonishing set of facts that do have the appearance of design. Rather than getting lost arguing this or that point, however, one should look at the big picture. The big picture reveals a universal science in which one hundred or so elements form the basis of matter throughout the universe. The chemistry that makes carbon unique gives it the properties required for life. The remarkable properties of water allow it to provide a wonderful external environment for life as well as a wonderful internal medium for life. Likewise, carbon dioxide has the right properties for removing carbon-based waste from living organisms.

CHAPTER SIX

DESIGNER GENES

Biology is the study of complicated things that
give the appearance of having been designed with
a purpose.
—Richard Dawkins

THE COMPLEXITY AND INTERDEPENDENCE of living organisms was used as evidence for design. As the quote of Dawkins shows, to many people, Darwinian evolution implies that what others thought was design was really the result of the adaptation of organisms to their environment by natural processes. In this chapter, we will consider the difficult question of whether living organisms show evidences of design.

WEB OF LIFE

The marks of design are too strong to be gotten over.
—William Paley

This section will review certain areas of biology that appear to be designed. We will look at the relationships between organisms, review the anatomy that undergirds the organism, and examine the biochemistry that powers the organism.

Interdependence of Living Organisms

When natural philosophers or naturalists (later called scientists and biologists) began studying living organisms, they noticed that many organisms depend on one another to exist. They seem to be made for one another. They have the correct shape or color for the mutual benefit of one another. From the thousands of cases that we could consider, we will examine pollination, nutrient-exchanging species, camouflage, mimicry, and birds' beaks.

Pollination. Flowering plants depend upon external agents to transfer pollen from the male part of one flower to the female part of another flower. Bees, moths, wasps, flies, and hummingbirds are common pollinating agents. Scientists discovered that the color, shape, and odor of the flowers coordinated well with the physiology of the pollinating agent. Bees can see ultraviolet, blue, and yellow parts of the spectrum. Bees are attracted by sweet, aromatic, or minty odors. They alight on a petal before exploring the flower; they do not hover like hummingbirds. Bees are active during the day. Scientists discovered that flowers that bees pollinate have "colors" in the ultraviolet, blue, and yellow range; they have petals that the bees can alight on before moving on to the nectar and pollen; they have a sweet, aromatic, or minty odor; and they are open during the day.

Hummingbirds, unlike bees, see red well but blue poorly; they have a poor sense of smell; and they like to hover. Another set of flowers exists that are red, have almost no odor, and do not have landing platforms. These flowers are pollinated by hummingbirds. Figure 6.1 illustrates how the shape of the popular garden plant, the columbine, varies from pollinator to pollinator. In contrast to hummingbirds and bees, moths are active at night. The flowers that moths pollinate open at dusk, are mostly white, and have strong odors to guide the moths.

Another interesting relationship between the flowers pollinated and the pollinators concerns the shape of the nectar tubes of the flowers and the shape of the tongues or bills of the pollinators. There is a good correlation between the curvature and length of the nectar tube of the flower and the curvature and length of the tongue of the bees and moths or

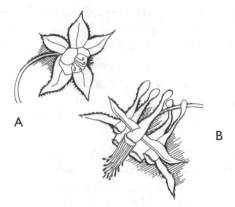

Fig. 6.1. Structures of Columbine Flowers Correlated with Anatomy of Pollinators. (A) *Aguilegia ecalcarata,* pollinated by bees. (B) *Formosa,* pollinated by hummingbirds. The length and curvature of the bees' tongue and the hummingbirds' bills are correlated with the length and curvature of the nectar tubes of the flower. Adapted from V. Grant, "The Fertilization of Flowers," *Scientific American,* June 1951.

curvature and length of the bill of the hummingbird (fig. 6.1). The fit is remarkable.

Other flowers are pollinated by short-tongued flies. These flies feed on carrion, dung, and blood. They are attracted by vile rather than sweet odors. They depend upon detecting vile odors more than depending upon vision to detect food. Thus, the flowers that these flies pollinate are dull-colored and vile-smelling. These flowers also are shaped so that the fly is temporarily trapped. This entrapment ensures that the fly becomes covered by pollen.

In the above cases, the relationships are between a general class of pollinator and a general class of flower. In some cases the relationship is very specific and extreme. One specific relationship is between the flower, Scotch broom (*Cytisus scoparius*), and certain bumblebees. The stamens spring up and dust the underside of the bee with pollen only when the right type of bumblebee enters the Scotch broom flower. An extreme example is the mirror orchid, *Ophrys speculum*. The shape and color of the flower of this orchid resembles the shape and color of the female of one wasp species. When the male wasp attempts to copulate with the orchid, he is covered with pollen which the male wasp spreads from flower to flower.

Exchange of nutrients. Termites eat wood, but termites could not digest the wood if it were not for the protozoa that live in their intestinal tract. Yet the protozoa do not digest the wood; bacteria living in the protozoa digest the wood. Residing in the termites provides a safe home and steady food supply to the protozoa and bacteria. The latter provides the termites carbohydrates from the digestion of the wood. Cows eat grass. Yet cows cannot digest the cellulose in the grass. The cellulose is digested by microorganisms that live in the cow's digestive tract. Being in the cow's digestive tract provides the bacteria with a steady source of food, while the bacteria provide the cows with carbohydrates from the cellulose. Humans have a similar relationship with bacteria in their intestines that synthesize vitamin B_{12}. The bacteria are provided with a steady source of food, and they provide the humans with a vitamin that humans cannot synthesize.

In the far northern part of North America, Europe, and Asia lies the tundra. In this extreme climate are found lichens. Lichens have a symbiotic relationship between a fungus and a green alga (cyanobacterium). The body of a lichen is composed of three layers. A lower layer of fungus and a top layer of fungus shield the photosynthetic cells of the alga in the middle. Their association enables them to live in the extreme conditions of the tundra where neither could survive alone. The fungus apparently benefits from the photosynthetic activity of the alga. The alga apparently benefits from the water-retaining properties of the fungal layers.

Camouflage. Many animals, because of their color and/or shape, blend into their surroundings so well that they are nearly undetectable. Animals that fly or swim are dark on their topside (dorsal) and lighter in color on the underside (ventral). Thus, from below these animals blend into the sky or surface waters, and from above these animals blend into the darker earth or stream bottom. Other animals such as lizards (chameleons), frogs, and fish can change colors to match their backgrounds. Flounder are uniform in color against a uniform colored sea floor but become spotted in color against a spotted background. Some animals change color with the seasons. The ptarmigan, arctic fox, and snowshoe hare are brown in the summer but white in the winter. The pupa of certain butterflies have two color forms. If the pupae are developing in green vegetation, the pupae will be green and resemble a leaf. If the pupae are developing against a brown background, the pupae will be brown and resemble rotting wood. Certain insects (*Phyllium pulchrifolium*, beautiful moving leaf) resemble the leaves upon which they rest. This resemblance is so thorough that the insect has the vein pattern of a true leaf and includes coloration that resembles insect-infected holes in real leaves.

Mimicry. Some harmless animals (the mimic) resemble more dangerous or poisonous animals (the model). This resemblance results in protection from predators or some other benefit to the mimic. In the southeastern United States, the nonpoisonous scarlet king snake, *Lampropeltis triangulum*, resembles the very poisonous coral snake, *Micrurus fulvius*. Bees and wasps are brightly colored and are known for their painful stingers. Flower flies, which do not have stingers, have black and yellow markings similar to bees or wasps and are even found on flowers eating nectar. The pipevine swallowtail is a poisonous butterfly avoided by birds. Its color pattern is mimicked by the females of the black swallowtail, the tiger swallowtail, and the biana fritillary, but the males of these species do not mimic the color pattern of the pipevine swallowtail. Both sexes of the red-spotted purple butterfly, which are in the same range as the pipevine swallowtail, mimic the pipevine swallowtail's color pattern. Another type of mimicry is shown by snapping turtles and angler fish. The snapping turtle's tongue resembles a worm.

The angler fish have lures that resemble worms. In both cases it is thought that this mimicry of worms lures fish within reach.

Bird beaks. When naturalists studied birds, they noticed that there were many different types of bird beaks. They also observed that each type of beak was of the right shape for the food-gathering habits of the bird. Figure 6.2 displays some typical bird beaks. Some birds have beaks suitable for cracking seeds and nuts. The crossbill feeds on the seeds of conifer cones. Each species and subspecies of crossbill have beaks shaped for a particular size and shape of conifer cone. The hawfinch feeds on tough, large seeds of the wild cherry and damson. Its massive bill can exert a pressure of about two hundred pounds per square inch (fourteen kilograms per square centimeter). Other birds have beaks suitable for

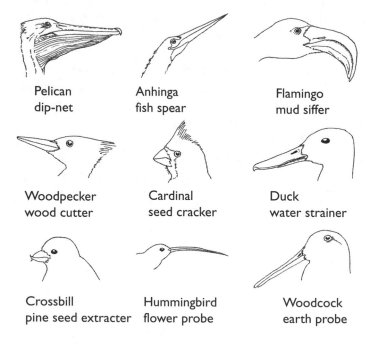

Pelican dip-net	Anhinga fish spear	Flamingo mud siffer
Woodpecker wood cutter	Cardinal seed cracker	Duck water strainer
Crossbill pine seed extracter	Hummingbird flower probe	Woodcock earth probe

Fig. 6.2. Bird Beaks Associated
with Different Kinds of Feeding.

fishing or feeding in water. The pelican has a long bill with a pouch suspended from the bill and throat. This arrangement acts like a net to scoop up fish. Ducks and flamingos have bills lined with bony notches for straining plant and animal matter from the water. Some birds have beaks suitable for hunting insects. The cactus wren has a long, curved beak for catching insects. Woodpeckers have sharp, straight, chisel-shaped beaks with long, extensile tongues. They use their sharp beaks to chisel into the wood and work the insects out with their long tongues. Other birds have beaks suitable for probing flowers. We already have discussed the humming-bird. The shape and curvature of the hummingbird's slender bill corresponds to the shape and curvature of the flower favored by each species of hummingbird. Some birds have beaks suitable for probing mud or sand. The spoonbill has a long broad beak to shovel through mud in search of food. The sandpiper is a common shore bird which catches small fish and invertebrates as it probes the sandy or muddy shore with its long bill. The heron has a long, sharp, pointed bill. The heron hunts by waiting in shallow water or on land to spear prey with its long bill.

human   cat   horse   whale   bird

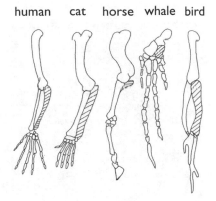

Fig. 6.3. Homologous Stuctures. The bones of the
vertebrate forelimbs display a similar pattern.
Adapted from Sylvia Mader, *Inquiry into Life,*
8th ed. (Dubuque, Ia.: Wm.C. Brown Publishers, 1997).

Observations: The interdependence of living organisms gives a strong appearance of design. The correlation between the eyesight of pollinators and the color of flowers is truly amazing. Also astonishing is the fit between the shapes of flowers and the tongues and bills of the pollinators. How much design went into termites depending upon protozoa that depend upon bacteria? The camouflage and mimicry of animals again give the appearance of design. By looking at the relationships of organisms today, one does not know how much they have changed over time and how any changes may have affected the relationships.

Comparative Anatomy
When scientists examine the insides of the plants and animals, they find structures and patterns that seem made for the particular plant or animal. We will examine two cases: homologous structures and the bodies of birds.

Homologous structures. Comparing the anatomies of a variety of vertebrates reveals a common architecture. The forelimbs of vertebrates are used for running (horse), swimming (whale), climbing (cat and human), and flying (bird). In spite of all these different functions, all these forelimbs contain the same set of bones. Figure 6.3 shows that all these

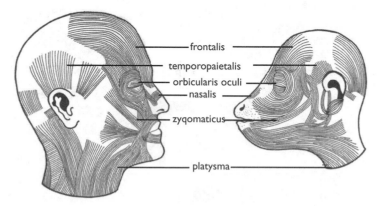

frontalis
temporopaietalis
orbicularis oculi
nasalis
zyqomaticus
platysma

Fig. 6.4. Similarities Between Facial Muscles of Humans and Monkeys.

forelimb bones are organized in a similar manner. Since these forelimbs contain the same relative pattern, they are called homologous structures. Another example of homologous structures is the similarity between the facial muscles of humans and monkeys (fig. 6.4). Because the human has more facial muscles, a human can make more facial expressions than a monkey can.

Bodies of birds. Birds have bodies that appear to be made for flight. The efficiency of flight depends upon how light the body is. One way birds have a lighter framework is through the construction of their bones. Many bones are hollow instead of being filled with marrow, and these bones are connected to a system of air sacs. The bones of the skull and pelvic girdle are fused for lightness and strength. The wing needs to provide strong support for the large flight feather; this support is provided by the fusing of the digital and wrist bones of the forelimb (see fig. 6.3). Birds need powerful muscles to power the flight stroke. Powerful muscles need a firm anchor. This anchor is provided by the large, overdeveloped breastbone. In flightless birds the breastbone is reduced in size. Large amounts of energy are consumed in flight. Thus, the hearts of birds are large and well developed. The complexities of flight require keen eyesight. Thus, it is not surprising that the eyesight of birds is several times better than man's. The complexities of flight also require complex muscle coordination; the cerebellum, the part of the brain that controls muscle coordination, is large in birds.

Observations: When one examines the anatomy of organisms, design again seems to be present. Living organisms seem to be built along similar patterns, whether one is talking about forelimbs or muscles. The bodies of birds are amazing machines that appear to be made for flight.

Biochemistry

When scientists began exploring below the anatomical level, they discovered that all living organisms contain similar chemical compounds and reactions. Biochemistry is the branch of chemistry that deals with these chemical compounds and reactions.

Cellular hierarchy. Figure 6.5 shows the hierarchical arrangement of the chemicals found in living organisms. Simple inorganic molecules (carbon dioxide, water, and nitrogen) are taken in by living organisms and converted through the intermediate compounds to the building-block molecules. The building-block molecules are covalently linked to form the macromolecules. Simple sugars combine to form carbohydrates (sucrose, starch, glycogen, and cellulose). Amino acids link to make proteins (muscles, enzymes, and connective tissue). Fatty acids combine with glycerol to form lipids (fats

Fig. 6.5. Hierarchy of Molecular Organization of Life.

The Cell

Organelles — Nucleus, Mitochondria, Chloroplasis, Endoplasmic reticulum

Supramolecular assemblies *Particle mass* $10^6 - 10^9$ — Lipoproteins, Ribosomes

Macromolecules Mol Mass 10^3-10^9 — Carbohydrates (polysaccharides), Lipids, Proteins, Nucleic Acids

Building Blocks Mol mass 100–350 — Simple sugars, Fatty acids / Glycerol, Amino acids, Nucleotides

Intermediates Mol mass 50–250 — Photpho-pyruvate / Malate, Acetate / Malonate, ∞-Keto acids, Ribose / Carbamyl phosphate

Preceptors from the environment Mol mass 18–44 — CO_2, H_2O, N_2

Adapted from Albert L. Lehninger, *Biochemistry* (New York: Worth Publishers, 1970).

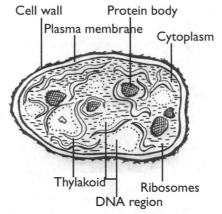

Fig. 6.6. Prokaryote Cell. These cells
lack a nucleus. The DNA is in direct
contact with the cytoplasm.

and oils). Nucleotides combine to form nucleic acids (DNA and RNA). These macromolecules form the four large classes of compounds found in living organisms: carbohydrates, lipids, proteins, and nucleic acids.

Different macromolecules associate together to form supramolecular complexes, the next level of organization. For example, lipids and proteins associate together to form lipoproteins. Two lipoproteins are high-density lipoproteins (HDL) and low-density lipoproteins (LDL). Coronary heart disease is associated with elevated levels of LDL while HDL seems to reduce a person's risk of developing coronary heart disease. Another supramolecular complex involves the ribosomes, which are associations of proteins and nucleic acids. The ribosome is the site for protein synthesis in the cell.

The next level of organization is the assembly of the supramolecules into organelles. The organelles are membrane-enclosed structures within a cell. Examples of organelles include the nucleus (contains chromosomes that control the function of the cell), mitochondria (produce energy for the cell through cellular respiration), chloroplasts (contain chlorophyll and is the site of photosynthesis in

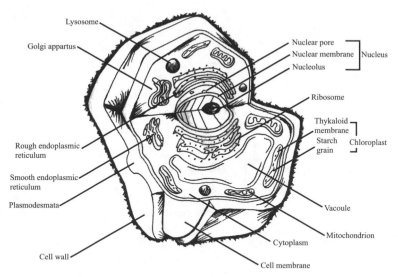

Fig. 6.7. Plant Cell. This type of cell is surrounded by a rigid cell wall. The cell contains a nucleus as well as other membrane surrounded organelles.

plants), and endoplasmic reticulum (system of interconnected tubules and sacs that functions in the transport of materials in the cell).

Finally all these hierarchical components are organized into a cell. The cell is the smallest unit capable of carrying out the functions of life. Some cells are complete organisms, such as a protozoa. Other cells, such as a muscle cell, are specialized parts of multicellular organisms. The smallest cell (mycoplasmas) is about 0.1 micrometer in diameter. The largest cell (ostrich egg yolk) is about 8 cm. (3 in.) in diameter. All cells are surrounded by a membrane. The inside of the cell is a water-rich environment (cytoplasm) containing genetic material (DNA), which contains the instructions for the functioning of the cell.

Cells come in two types: prokaryotes and eukaryotes. Examples of prokaryotes are unicellular bacteria and cyanobacteria. The prokaryote cell lacks a nucleus. The DNA is in direct contact with the cytoplasm (fig. 6.6). Eukaryotic cells are found in plants (fig. 6.7) and animals (fig. 6.8). In eukaryotic cells the DNA is separated from the cytoplasm by a membrane. The eukaryotic cells also contain the membranous organelles. Generally, plant cells differ from animal cells in that plant cells have a cell wall, chloroplasts, and a large vacuole.

Macromolecules. As discussed previously, the major cellular components are made of the four major classes of macromolecules (carbohydrates, lipids, proteins, and nucleic acids). The distribution of the macromolecules in the *Escherichia coli* cell are shown in figure 6.9. If we exclude the exoskeleton and storage materials, the four classes of macromolecules are found in these proportions in all types of cells. As can be seen again in figure 6.9, proteins are the most abundant macromolecule.

Not only do the macromolecules occur in the same proportions, but they have the same functions in all cells.

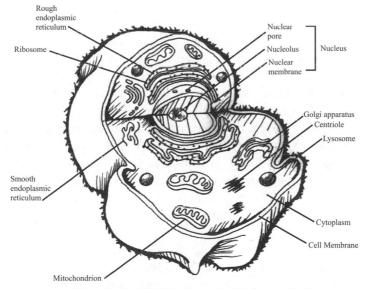

Fig. 6.8. Animal Cell. This type of cell is surrounded by a flexible cell membrane. The cell contains a nucleus as well as other membrane-surrounded organelles.

Fig. 6.9. Macromolecules in E. coli Cells.

Substance	Percent total weight
Water	70
Protein	15
Nucleic acids	
DNA	1
RNA	7
Carbohydrates	3
Lipids	2
Building-block molecules and intermediates	2
Inorganic ions	1

Adapted from Albert L. Lehninger, *Biochemistry* (New York: Worth Publishers, 1970), 20.

Carbohydrates occur as monosaccharides such as glucose and fructose, disaccharides such as sucrose and lactose, and polysaccharides such as starch and glycogen (energy storage molecules) or cellulose (structural elements). Lipids are the major components of membranes and for energy storage (fat). Proteins serve as catalysts (enzymes), communication (hormones), and structural elements (muscles, collagen, and keratin). Nucleic acids store and transmit genetic information.

One difference between the macromolecules is that the nucleic acids and proteins are informational due to their structure while polysaccharides and lipids are not (fig. 6. 10). Each nucleotide contains one of four different bases symbolized by the letters *A, T, G,* and *C*. The sequence of these bases in the nucleic acid encodes the hereditary information contained in DNA. Likewise, each protein contains information in its sequence of amino acids. In contrast, polysaccharides do not contain information in their sequences. The polysaccharide starch is just a repeating sequence of the building block

Fig. 6. 10. Informational and Noninformational Macromolecules.

Informational

Nucleic Acid (DNA)
-A-C-G-T-G-A-A-C-G-T-T-A-

Protein
-Phe-Arg-Arg-Ala-Lys-Trp-Lys-Met-

Noninformational

Polysaccharide
Glu-Glu-Glu-Glu-Glu-Glu-Glu-Glu-Glu

Lipid
$-CH_2-CH_2-CH_2-CH_2-CH_2-CH_2-CH_2-CH_2$
The letters A, C, G, and T symbolize the four bases in DNA.
Three-letter abbreviations such as Ala, Arg, Lys, Met, and Trp,
are used to symbolize the amino acids that make up a protein. In the polysaccharide, glucose is symolized by Glu.
The CH_2 are the repeating units in the fatty acid part of
the lipid.

glucose. Lipids are also noninformational since they involve
the repeating of CH_2 units.

Observations: It is amazing that the same chemistry is
found in all living organisms. Does this fact reflect the construction of all living organisms on a common chemical
design? What an astonishing fact that organisms contain the
same genetic code. Even more amazing, the cells of all organisms from the smallest one-cell bacterium to the largest multicellular whale contain information. Was this information
designed into the cells?

DESIGNER GENES:
FLOW OF INFORMATION IN THE CELL

For centuries one of the great mysteries of life was how characteristics of the parents were transmitted to their offspring.
Where in the organism was the hereditary information

stored? How was it encoded? Was it located in one part of the cell? Did this information also control the day-to-day activities of the organism?

The first step in answering these questions was taken by the Austrian/Czech Republican monk Gregor Mendel (1822–1884), who spent seven years studying garden peas. He discovered the rules of heredity and published his findings in 1866. His work was forgotten for thirty-four years until it was rediscovered in 1900. While Mendel's work was being overlooked, scientists in the 1870s developed microscopic staining techniques. By staining the nucleus of the cell, scientists discovered that it was full of tiny threads. These threads were labeled chromosomes or "colored bodies" from the Greek words *chromo* (color) and *soma* (body). The German biologist August Weismann (1834–1914) conjectured in the 1880s that chromatin, the component that chromosomes are made of, was probably responsible for heredity. In 1874, the Swiss biochemist Johann Friedrich Miescher (1844–1895) analyzed the nonprotein material in the nucleus and determined that its chemical identity was an acid that he named nucleic acid. Today this acid is called deoxyribonucleic acid or DNA. By 1909, the name *gene* had been coined to describe parts of the chromosome that carry traits. In 1941, the American geneticist George Beadle (1903–1989) and the American biochemist Edward L. Tatum (1909–1975) showed that one gene is responsible for synthesizing one enzyme that catalyzes a particular reaction. For this work, Beadle and Tatum received the Nobel Prize in 1958. Since the chromosome contains protein as well as nucleic acid, scientists were trying to determine if this protein stored hereditary information. In 1944, the Canadian bacteriologist Oswald Avery (1877–1955) showed that DNA alone was responsible for the hereditary traits. His work influenced the English biologist Francis Crick (1916–) and the American biologist James Watson (1928–) to investigate the structure of DNA. In 1953, Watson and Crick reported that DNA consisted of a double helix (spiral staircase). For their work they received the Nobel Prize in 1962. The genetic code was shown to be a triplet combination of the DNA bases. For this work, the American biochemist Marshall Warren Nirenberg (1927–), the American biochemist Robert Holley (1922–1993), and the Indian-American geneticist Har Gobind Khorana (1922–) shared the 1968 Nobel Prize. Scientists also realized that another nucleic acid, ribonucleic acid or RNA, was involved in carrying the genetic information from inside the nucleus to protein synthesis sites outside the nucleus.

Deoxyribonucleic Acid (DNA)

The DNA in a human cell is at least two meters (6.6 feet) long.[1] Yet this DNA is stored in a nucleus only about five micrometers in diameter. How is this possible? The human chromosome is about 25 percent DNA and 75 percent protein. This protein is involved in packing the DNA. The protein forms a scaffold around which the DNA coils. The protein-DNA package continues to coil until a chromosome forms. During cell division the extremely compact chromosomes are duplicated into two daughter chromosomes. By the end of mitosis (the process of cell division), the daughter chromosomes have separated, and a copy of each chromosome ends up in the two daughter cells. In this way, the hereditary information is duplicated and passed on to the new cells. Does the structure of DNA help us understand how the hereditary information is copied? Yes, it does. Watson and Crick in their original publication stated, "It has not escaped our notice that the specific pairing we have postulated immediately suggests a possible copying mechanism for the genetic material."[2] Let us review the structure of DNA and examine how this structure explains the reproduction of hereditary information.

DNA is a polymer made by stringing together nucleotide molecules. The nucleotides from which deoxyribonucleic acid is formed consist of three parts—phosphate group, a pentose sugar (deoxyribose), and a nitrogen base (fig. 6.11). There are four possible nitrogen bases. Two of the bases are pyrimidines

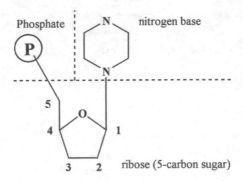

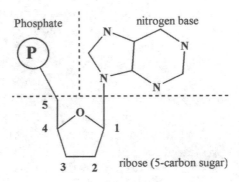

Fig. 6.11. Representative Nucleotides.

containing one ring, and two are purines containing two rings. The names of the bases are pyrimidines (thymine or T and cytosine or C) and purines (adenine or A and guanine or G). Nucleotides combine to form the DNA polymer. The backbone of the polymer consists of the sequence: phosphate-sugar-phosphate-sugar. The nitrogen bases extend from the side of the backbone (fig. 6.12). Using the numbering system in figure 6.11, scientists designate one end of a DNA strand as 5′ and the other end as 3′. The term *primary structure* is used to describe the sequence of bases along the backbone of a DNA strand. The sequence of the bases is read from the 5´ end to the 3´ end. Thus the sequence of bases AGCT is not equivalent to the sequence TCGA. Since the base sequence in a strand can be in any order, tremendous variability results. In a chromosome with about 140 million base pair, $4^{140,000,000}$ possible combinations are possible. No wonder each living organism is unique.

The term *secondary structure* is used to describe the three-dimensional pattern for the DNA molecule. The secondary structure of DNA consists of two strands that twist about each other to form a double helix (fig. 6.13). In the DNA

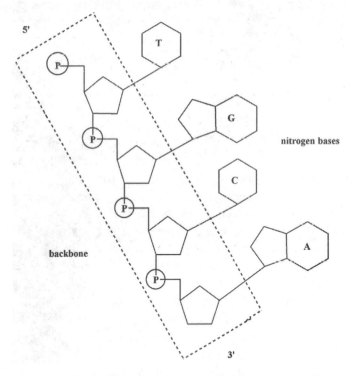

Fig. 6.12. DNA Backbone. Each strand has a backbone composed of □ phosphate-sugar sequences. The sequence of bases is read from the 5'□ end to the 3' end. In this example, the sequence is read as TGCA rather□ than ACGT.

5'   3'

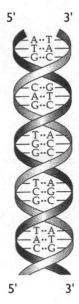

5'   3'

Fig. 6.13. The DNA Double Helix.
Base A always pairs with base T.
Base C always pairs with base G.

double helix, the two strands run in opposite directions. At each end of the double helix, there is one 5´ end and one 3´end. In the double helix the strand backbones are on the outside with the bases pointing toward the inside. The two strands are held together by hydrogen bonding between bases on the two strands. The base A on one strand always pairs with the base T on the other strand, whereas the base C always pairs with the base G. These base pair combinations are known as complementary bases.

Each organism has a unique number of chromosomes. Tomatoes have twelve pairs of chromosomes, dogs have thirty-eight pairs, and humans twenty-three pairs. Genes are the units of heredity. They are carried by the chromosomes and are arranged in a line along the chromosome. Each gene is a segment of DNA that codes for one protein molecule. Each gene is a section of the DNA molecule in the chromosome. The gene is the specific sequence of the four bases (A, C, G, and T) along this section of DNA and can contain from about one thousand to two thousand bases. Thus, transmission of genetic information involves copying of the DNA strands in the chromosomes. How is a DNA strand copied?

The DNA double helical arrangement provides a template for the copying process. The old strand acts as a mold (template) for the new (daughter) strand formed. The duplication of the DNA molecule is called replication. The first step in replication is the unwinding of the double helix. The unwinding

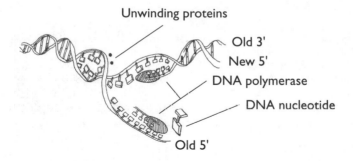

Fig 6.14. Duplication of DNA. The unwinding
proteins unzip the double helix.

can start at either end or in the middle. Special enzymes
(unwinding proteins) attach themselves to one of the DNA
strands, cause the hydrogen bonds between the bases to
break, and bring about the unzipping of the double helix
(fig. 6.14). The next step in replication is the pairing of the
complementary bases. The necessary nucleotides are in the
fluid surrounding the unzipping DNA. Once a free base T
comes in contact with a base A on the parental strand, they
stick together through hydrogen bonding. The final step in
replication is joining the complementary bases to form the
daughter strand. The enzyme DNA polymerase joins the complementary nucleotides into the backbone of the daughter
strand. Interestingly, the polymerases only work from 5′ to 3′.
The two complementary strands are connected in different
ways. The new 5′ to 3′ strand is continuously synthesized by
the polymerase. For the new 3′ to 5′ strand, the polymerase
can only synthesize short fragments of about one thousand
nucleotides. Another enzyme, DNA ligase, eventually joins
these fragments together to complete the 3′ to 5′ complementary strand. The complementary strand synthesized continuously is called the *leading strand*. The complementary strand
made from fragments is called the *lagging strand*.

Replication is a semiconservative process in that two of the
four strands are new. The information that was contained in

Fig. 6.15. Types of RNA.

Type	Percent	Approx. # of Bases
Message RNA (mRNA)	5	1200
Transfer RNA (tRNA)	15	70–90
Ribosomal RNA (rRNA)	80	1800

the original DNA is now contained in each of the duplicates. When the cell divides, this information will end up in each daughter cell.

Ribonucleic Acid (RNA)—A Second Type of Nucleic Acid

In eukaryotes, DNA is located in the nucleus. Yet protein synthesis takes place outside the nucleus. What transfers the information encoded in DNA out into the cell? Before we can discuss this, we need to discuss another type of nucleic acid found in cells. RNA or ribonucleic acid is found both in the nucleus and cytoplasm. Like DNA, RNA is a polymer made from nucleotides. Unlike DNA, RNA is a single strand, uses the pentose sugar ribose rather than deoxyribose, and contains the pyrimidine base uracil (U) rather than the base thymine (T). There are three types of RNA. *Messenger RNA* (mRNA) contains a strand of bases that are complementary of a section of DNA. This type of RNA carries the genetic information from the nucleus into the cycoplasm. Messenger RNA has a short life span; it is synthesized as needed and then degraded. *Transfer RNA* (tRNA) is a small nucleic acid that carries amino acids to the protein synthesis site. There is a different tRNA for each of the twenty amino acids. The third type of RNA is *ribosomal RNA* (rRNA). Protein synthesis occurs in the ribosome. The ribosome is a supramolecular assembly that is about 65 percent rRNA and 35 percent protein. A ribosome is composed of two parts. The larger part has an affinity for tRNA; the smaller part has an attraction for mRNA. In animal cells, ribosomes are bound to endoplasmic recticulum organelle. Figure 6.15 contains information about the three types of RNA.

Fig. 6.16. The Genetic Code.

UUU Phe	CUC Ser	UAU Tyr	UGU Cys
UUC Phe	UCC Ser	UAC Tyr	UGC Cys
UUA Leu	UCA Ser	UAA END	GUA END
UUG Leu	UCG Ser	UAG END	UGG Trp
CUU Leu	CCU Pro	CAU His	CGU Arg
CUC Leu	CCC Pro	CAC His	CGC Arg
CUA Leu	CCA Pro	CAA Gln	CGA Arg
CUG Leu	CCG Pro	CAG Glnl	CGG Arg
AUU Il3	ACU Thr	AAU Asn	AGU Ser
AUC Ile	ACC Thr	AAC Asn	AGC Ser
AUA Ile	ACA Thr	AAA Lys	AGA Arg
AUG Met & START	ACG Thr	AAG Lys	AGG Arg
GUU Val	GCU Ala	GAU Asp	GGU GLY
GUC Val	GCC Ala	GAC Asp	GGC Gly
GUA Val	GCA Ala	GAA Glu	GGA Gly
GUG Val	GCG Ala	GAG Glu	GGG Gly

In each group, the left-most triples (for example, UUU) refers to a set of bases on the mRNA molecule. The right-most triplet (for example, Phe) is a three-letter abbreviation for an amino acid. The word *START* signals the beginning of the gene sequence. The word *END* refers to the ending of the gene sequence. As can be seen, many amino acids are coded for by more than one base triplet.

To express an inheritable trait, the information contained in DNA must be expressed as the correct sequence of amino acids in a protein. Since the information (the DNA) is inside the nucleus and the protein synthesis occurs outside the nucleus, a way has to exist for transferring the information outside the nucleus. The way living organisms carry out this process is to transfer the information contained in a DNA molecule to RNA molecules. The information carried by the RNA molecules is then used by cell organelles to synthesize proteins. A summary of the process is

$$\text{DNA} \xrightarrow{\text{transcription}} \text{mRNA} \xrightarrow{\text{translation}} \text{protein}$$

Transcription describes the process of transferring information from DNA to messenger RNA. How is the information written in DNA and RNA? As we mentioned in the previous historic sketch, the information is written in a triplet combination of the DNA bases. For each gene, there is a triplet combination that signals the start of the gene, followed by the triplet codes for each amino acid in the protein, followed by a triplet combination that signals the end of the gene. The genetic code is listed in figure 6.16.

In each group, the left-most triplet (for example UUU) refers to a set of bases on the mRNA molecule. The right-most triplet (for example, Phe) is a three-letter abbreviation for an amino acid. The word *START* signals the beginning of the gene sequence. The word *END* refers to the ending of the gene sequence. As can be seen, many amino acids are coded for by more than one base triplet.

Transcription begins with a segment of the DNA molecules unwinding at the point where the gene is located (fig. 6.17). The *ribonucleotides* needed to synthesize the mRNA assemble along the unwound DNA strand. They assemble in a complementary fashion. Opposite each G on the DNA there will be a C on the mRNA; the other base pairs are C with G, A with U, and T with A. The enzyme *RNA polymerase* joins the

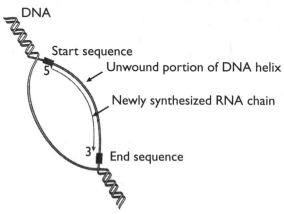

Fig. 6.17. Synthesis of mRNA from DNA.

complementary ribonucleotides into the backbone of the mRNA.[3] Interestingly, the code between the start sequence and end sequence contains segments that seemingly do not code for anything. The base triplets that code for an amino acid are called *exons* and the noncoding triplets are called *introns*. The mRNA transcribed from the DNA contains both exons and introns. Somehow, enzymes know how to cut out the introns and splice together the exons before the mRNA is used to synthesize a protein. If the introns were left in the mRNA, the synthesized protein would not function properly. The modified mRNA moves out of the cell into the cytoplasm.

Translation is the process by which the information contained in the mRNA is used to assemble the protein. This process is called translation since it involves translating the language of the nucleotide triplets into the language of individual amino acids. The translator is the transfer RNA molecule. A simplified cloverleaf structure of tRNA is shown in figure 6.18. The molecule is a single chain, but base pairing allows the molecule to fold back on itself.

Translation or protein synthesis involves four steps: activation, initiation, elongation, and termination. *Activation* involves attaching an amino acid to a tRNA molecule. Once an amino acid is activated with energy from *ATP* (the body's energy storage molecule), the enzyme *tRNA synthetase* binds the amino acid to the tRNA molecule (fig. 6.18). Since there is one tRNA for each amino acid, somehow the synthetase enzyme recognizes which amino acid should join to which tRNA molecule.

Initiation involves all three types of RNA (messenger, transfer, and ribosomal). Protein synthesis occurs in the supramolecular assemblies called ribosomes. The ribosome contains two subunits. The smaller ribosomal unit is made of one rRNA molecule and several proteins, and the larger ribosomal subunit is made of two rRNA molecules and several proteins. Among these proteins is the enzyme that will join the amino acids to form the protein. During initiation the mRNA, carrying information needed to synthesize one

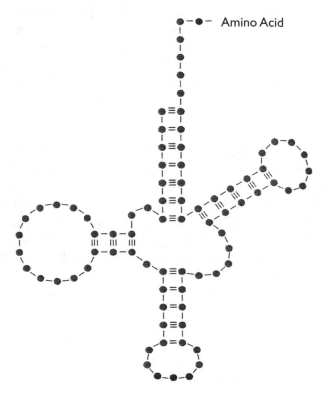

Anticodon base triplet

Fig. 6.18. Simplified Cloverleaf
Structure of tRNA.

protein, binds to the smaller ribosomal subunit (fig. 6.19). The first tRNA molecule binds to the first ribonucleotide triplet (*codon*) of the mRNA. The area of the tRNA molecule shown in figure 6.18 labeled *anticodon* binds in a complementary fashion to the codon of the mRNA.[4] Once the tRNA molecule has bound to the mRNA, the larger ribosomal subunit combines with the smaller ribosomal subunit. The larger subunit has two binding sites. The site on the left of figure 6.19 is called the *P site* because this is where the growing protein molecule will be attached. The other site is called the *A site* because this is where the tRNA will bring the next amino acid.

Elongation involves connecting the amino acids to form a protein. The next tRNA binds to the vacant P site (fig. 6.20). The enzyme *transferase* links the two amino acids together. The ribosome moves along the mRNA releasing the first tRNA. Another tRNA will bind to the resulting vacant A site. This amino acid will be joined to the other two. The ribosome moves along the mRNA continuing the process until the last amino acid is attached.

Termination occurs when the END condon is reached. *Releasing factors* cut the protein from the last tRNA. The mRNA is released. The two subunits of the ribosome come apart.

Using the information from one mRNA, five to eight ribosomes will usually be simultaneously synthesizing 5 to 8 copies of the same protein. In mammals, it takes about 3 minutes to join 300 amino acids. Insulin is a small protein

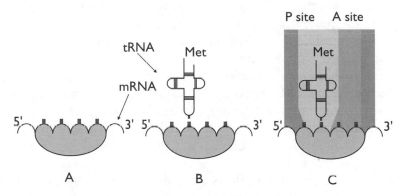

Fig. 6.19. Initiation of Protein Synthesis. A. The mRNA molecule binds to the smaller ribosomal subunit.
B. tRNA binds to mRNA. C. The larger ribosomal subunit binds to the complex. Adapted from Bettleheim and March, *General, Organic and Biochemistry* (Forth Worth: Saunders College, 1998).

containing 51 amino acids; on the other hand, a large protein like hemoglobin contains a total of 574 amino acids.

Proteins are used for structure (collagen in bone), contraction (muscles), catalysts (enzymes), hormones (insulin), antibodies (gamma globin), and transport (hemoglobin). Proteins have four different structures called primary, secondary, tertiary, and quaternary. The *primary structure* is the sequence of the amino acids that results from the translation process. A protein must be linked in the right sequence for a protein to function properly. For example, hemoglobin contains 574 amino acids. Sickle-cell hemoglobin differs from normal hemoglobin in only 2 out of these 574 amino acids. The *secondary structure* of a protein results from the chemical interactions between amino acids in the chain that creates a three-dimensional structure. One such structure is the alpha helix, a three-dimensional structure in the form of a right-handed screw. A *tertiary structure* results from further chemical interactions with the secondary structure components. This tertiary structure gives the protein a *lock-and-key* relationship to other molecules. By having a certain tertiary structure, the protein acts like a lock that only certain molecules can fit into like a key. Without the correct tertiary structure, the protein cannot catalyze specific chemical reactions. A *quaternary structure* results if the protein is composed on two or more chains of amino acids. Each chain has its own primary, secondary, and tertiary structure. In the quaternary structure, the chains are held together by chemical attractions. Both insulin (two chains) and hemoglobin (four chains) have quaternary structures. The change of two amino acids in sickle-cell hemoglobin affects all structural levels. To degrade or *denature* a protein is to change one or more of these structural levels.

The Human Genome Project

A *genome* is the complete DNA sequence of any organism. An average human has 46 chromosomes with approximately 40,000 genes. Each chromosome consists of a single DNA

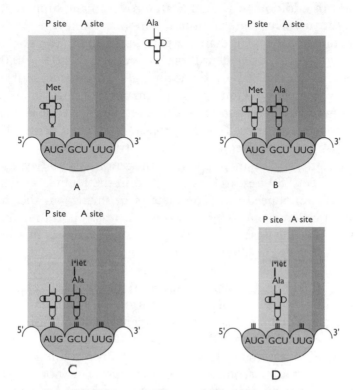

Fig. 6.20. Elongation Phases of Protein Synthesis.
A. Second tRNA approaches empty A site.
B. The tRNA binds to the A site. C. The two
amino acids are connected. D. The ribosome
moves along the mRNA releasing the first tRNA
and generating a vacant A site. Adapted from Bettleheim and March, *General, Organic and Biochemistry*
(Fort Worth: Saunders College, 1998).

molecule. The DNA of an average human contains approximately 3 billion base pairs. The *Human Genome Project,* a joint project of the U.S. Department of Energy and the National Institutes of Health, began in 1990 with a 13-year goal of determining the location of the genes in the 46 human chromosomes as well as the sequencing of all the DNA base pairs. In addition to United States government support, the project involves international support from the United Kingdom, France, Germany, Japan, and China. The goals of the project include identifying the approximately 40,000 genes in human DNA, determining the sequences of the approximately 3 billion bases in human DNA, providing this information to the public, and addressing the ethical, legal, and social issues raised by the project. In 1998, a private U.S. company, Celera Genomics Corporation, began a private-sector attempt to map the human genome in 3 years. In December 1999, researchers involved in the Human Genome Project announced the complete sequencing of the first human chromosome. Chromosome 22 was found to contain 33.5 million bases. A total of 545 genes, ranging in length from 1,000 to 583,000 bases of DNA, were detected. These efforts reveal that chromosome 22 is implicated in the workings of the immune system, schizophrenia, birth defects, congenital heart disease, mental retardation, and cancers such as leukemia. On June 26, 2000, President Clinton with British Prime Minister Tony Blair announced that the Human Genome Project and Celera Genomics Corporation had completed an initial sequencing of the human genome. They reported that 97 percent of the bases had been decoded; the other 3 percent were considered unsequenceable and irrelevant. Continuing to refine their data, the project will present a final draft of the human genome within 3 years.

Sequencing the human genome promises potential benefits for:

- molecular medicine: improved diagnosis of disease, earlier detection of genetic predispositions to disease, better drug design, gene therapy
- microbial genomics: biofuels, environmental monitoring of pollutants, safe toxic waste cleanup
- risk assessment: caused by radiation exposure, caused by mutagenic chemicals, caused by cancer-causing toxins

- DNA identification: identify suspects, exonerate persons wrongly accused, identify endangered species
- agriculture: produce disease- or insect- or drought-resistant crops, produce healthier crops and animals, produce more nutritious crops

Sequencing the human genome includes potential concerns for:

- privacy: preventing your genome information from being used in employment decisions
- genetic determinism: preventing society from assuming if one has a certain gene, one will automatically have a certain set of traits
- patenting: preventing patented genetic information from delaying the above-discussed benefits
- genetic modification: preventing a rush to improve on the genetic text to obtain the "perfect" offspring

Although the DNA of the human genome has been 97 percent sequenced, much work remains to be done. The DNA base sequences must be analyzed to determine how many genes humans have. Once researchers know the code for the gene, they must figure out what protein is produced. Once they identify the protein, they must determine what this protein does and how it interacts with all the other cellular proteins. This final stage is called *proteomics,* the cataloging and analysis of every protein in the human body. Proteins are much more complex than DNA, which has only three to four levels of structure. As we stated before, proteins are used for structure (collagen in bone), contraction (muscles), catalysts (enzymes), hormones (insulin), antibodies (gamma globin), and transport (hemoglobin). How a protein behaves depends upon its structure. During fall 2000, the National Institute of General Medical Sciences provided $20 million to fund a series of research centers to study a branch of proteomics called *structural genomics.* Over these next ten years, these centers will try to determine the maximum number of distinct shapes that proteins adapt. At this time, they estimate that there are about five thousand distinct shapes.

Observations: The flow of information from the DNA to the RNA to the protein is even more complicated than described in this section. Many supporting enzymes have been left out for narrative clarity. The major challenge for those denying design is the origin of the information contained in the DNA. Did all the parts of this complicated system have to be present for it to begin working, or could it be built up gradually from its parts? A challenging question is this: If enzymes (proteins) are required to make messenger RNA from DNA, where did the enzyme come from before the first mRNA was synthesized. All the parts seem designed to work together as a unit.

WHERE'S THE BEEF? ADAPTATION NOT DESIGN

Biologists must constantly keep in mind that what they see was not designed, but rather evolved.
—Francis Crick

In the description of the interactions of biological organisms in the first part of this chapter, it was very difficult not to include the word *adaptation*. When one opens a biology text of any level, one reads that everything is adapted to its environment. If design is mentioned, it is to state that what appears to be design is really adaptation. The modern biology text would say that hummingbirds and columbine flowers were not designed so that the bill and nectar tube fit but environmental changes selected those hummingbirds and columbines most adapted to survive resulting in the observed fit.

Why does modern biology deal with adaptation rather than design? The watershed event was the publication of *The Origin of Species* by Charles Darwin. Although a thorough discussion of Darwin's theory of evolution by natural selection is beyond the purpose of this text,[5] the modern formulation of

Darwin's theory contains the following points. The physical characteristics of each member of a species vary due to genetic variations. As the members of a species daily compete for limited resources, some will have characteristics that will make them more competitive. Those members better suited to the environment will more likely produce more offspring. Thus, they are selected by the environment to survive and reproduce. Through the generations, natural selection causes certain organisms to become adapted to the environment. Darwin replaced design with adaptation: "The sum total of the accidents of life acting upon the sum total of the accidents of variation thus provided a completely mechanical and material system by which to account for the changes in living forms."[6]

If we consider again the organisms discussed in the "Interdependence of Living Organisms" section of this chapter, modern biologists would say that natural selection over a long period of time resulted in the amazing fit between pollinators and flowers, the symbiotic relationships discussed, the amazing way organisms camouflage themselves, clever mimicry, and each bird's having a beak matched to its food source. Darwin also pointed out that in some cases there are surprising matches between the bird and its food source:

> How strange it is that a bird, under the form of a
> woodpecker, should prey on insects on the ground;
> that upland geese which rarely or never swim, should
> posses webbed feet; that a thrush-like bird should dive
> and feed on sub-aquatic insects; . . . and so in endless
> other cases. But on the view of each species constantly
> trying to increase in number, with natural selection
> always ready to adapt the slowly varying descendants
> of each to any unoccupied or ill-occupied place in
> nature, these facts cease to be strange, or might even
> have been anticipated.[7]

In regard to the comparative anatomy examples, Darwinists would say that these examples are explained "on the theory of descent with slow and slight successive modifications."[8] In

Fig. 6.21. Differences in DNA Base and Protein Amino Acid Sequences.

Pairs of Organisms	Percent Difference in DNA Base Sequences	Pairs of Organisms	Amino Acid Differences in Hemoglobin
human/chimpanzee	2.5	human/gorilla	1
human/gibbon	5.1	human/rhesus monkey	8
human/old world monkey	9.0	human/mouse	27
human/new world monkey	15.8	human/chicken	45
human/lemur	42.0	human/frog	67
mouse/rat	30.0	human/lamprey	125

regard to homologous structures, Darwin stated, "We may further venture to believe that the several bones in the limbs of the monkey, horse, and bat, were originally developed, on the principle of utility, probably through the reduction of more numerous bones in the fin of some ancient fish-like progenitor of the whole class."[9]

In regard to biochemistry, the modern biologist emphasizes that all living organisms share a common biochemistry, or as Darwin said, "Nevertheless, all living things have much in common, in their chemical composition, their cellular structure, their laws of growth, and their liability to injurious influences."[10] Modern biologists use the degree of difference between DNA base sequences or amino acid sequences to indicate the degree of relatedness between organisms (fig. 6.21). Currently, an exciting research area regarding the beginning of life is trying to determine which came first DNA, RNA, or proteins. At present, there is no consensus concerning these questions, which amount to a more sophisticated variation of "what came first, the chicken or the egg?" Because components of DNA and proteins cannot spontaneously join in water, one proposal involves the formation of RNA first. Ribonucleotides can join in water to form RNA. Also, certain RNA can act as enzymes. In this proposal, RNA would be the first self-replicating information-storage molecule. Because of its structure, this RNA molecule would be capable of evolving by natural selection. This RNA would catalyze the formation of proteins. Later, the more complex DNA molecule would be synthesized. Much work still needs to be done, however, to answer all the questions that arise.

WHERE'S THE BEEF? ADAPTATION AND DESIGN

The result of these cumulative efforts to investigate the cell—to investigate life at the molecular level—is a loud, clear, piercing cry of "design!"
—Michael J. Behe

Even before the publication of *The Origin of Species*, scientists were trying to determine whether one species could change into another species. One scientist who dealt with this question was the Swedish naturalist Carolus Linnaeus (1707–1778). Linnaeus developed the binomial system for classifying and organizing plants and animals. His system is called binomial nomenclature because it assigned a unique two-word Latin name to each organism. The first word refers to the genus to which the organism belongs while the second word refers to the species. For example, the dog has the scientific name, *Canis familiaris*, where *Canis* (dog) is its genus name and *familiaris* (of the family) is its species name. The complete classification system is kingdom, phylum, class, order, family, genus, and species. His inspiration for a classification system was his belief in design and in God's original creation of "fixed kinds" as stated in the first chapter of

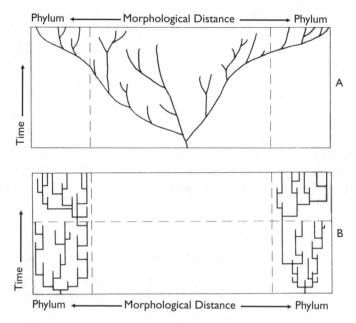

Fig. 6.22. Two Views of How New Organisms Arise.
A. Gradualism assumes all animals began with a
common ancestor. Gradual changes lead to new orders,
classes, and phyla. B. Since the Cambrian Period (about
570 million years ago), the fossil record shows changes
within phyla but no change between phyla. After a major
extinction (dashed line), rapid variation within the phyla
occur. Adapted from the American Scientific Affiliation,
Teaching Science in a Climate of Controversy, 1986.

Genesis. His faith in God the Creator convinced him that
there would be common characteristics within similar types
of organisms that would allow him to classify them. In addition, this belief spurred Linnaeus to search to see how the
concept of "fixed kinds" fit into his classification scheme. At
first, based on his observation of limited numbers of species
in Scandinavia, he thought that species referred to the Genesis
"kinds." As he was exposed to more organisms from other
areas, he became convinced that species can change and that
the genus level corresponded to the "fixed kinds." Finally, he

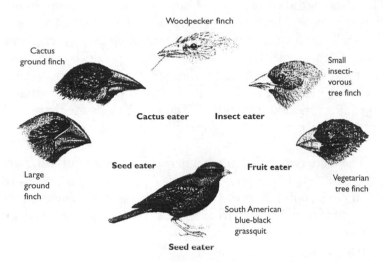

Fig. 6.23. Finches of the Galapagos Islands. These birds were important to Charles Darwin in developing the theory of evolution. The island finches closely resemble the South American grassquit.

revised his thinking to propose that the order level corresponded to the "fixed kinds." Currently, the American Scientific Affiliation (ASA), an organization of evangelical scientists, proposes that the fossil record supports species changing into other species. They propose that body types (Phyla) were finalized in the Cambrian period, and all changes occur in either the class, order, family, genus, or species categories.[11] In contrast to the ASA proposal, current evolutionary theory proposes gradual descent from a common ancestor with changes involving all the classification categories from kingdom to species. Figure 6.22 contrasts the two views.

Almost everyone recognizes that organisms undergo adaptation. A dramatic example was the recent change in the beaks of the Galapogos Islands finches, divided into thirteen species and placed in three genera. Darwin proposed that the Galapogos Islands finches descended from mainland finches that migrated to the islands (fig. 6.23). Peter and Rosemary

Grant have studied the finches since 1973. The Grants found that the finches' beak types varied with the climate. During a dry spell when large, hard-shelled seeds are the only available food, finches with large, strong beaks reproduce more successfully. During the wet season, small, easily-opened seeds become more available, and smaller beaked finches reproduces more successfully.[12] The finches indicate that some organisms can be rapidly adapted by changing environmental conditions.

There are two major areas where some scientists think purpose and design are reflected in biology. The two areas are *irreducible complexity* and *information systems*. These scientists propose that these areas cannot be totally explained by material and mechanical processes. They state that these areas indicate design.

Irreducible Complexity

The American biochemist Michael J. Behe argues, in his book *Darwin's Black Box,* that the cellular biochemistry is too complex to be explained by a series of mutations. As Behe states, "Life is in the details, and it is molecules that handle life's details. Darwin's idea might explain horse hoofs, but can it explain life's foundations?"[13] Behe is not a "young-earth creationist." He states, "I have no reason to doubt that the universe is the billions of years old that physicists say it is. Further, I find the idea of common descent (that all organisms share a common ancestor) fairly convincing, and have no particular reason to doubt it."[14] We need to quote Behe extensively to understand what he means by irreducible complexity.

> By *irreducibly complex* I mean a single system composed of several well-matched, interacting parts that contribute to the basic function, wherein the removal of one of the parts causes the system to effectively cease functioning. An irreducibly complex system cannot be produced directly (that is, by continuously improving the initial function, which continues to

work by the same mechanism) by slight, successive modifications of a precursor system, because any precursor to an irreducibly complex system that is missing a part is by definition nonfunctional. An irreducibly complex biological system, if there is such a thing, would be a powerful challenge to Darwinian evolution. Since natural selection can only choose systems that are already working, then if a biological system cannot be produced gradually it would have to arise as an integrated unit, in one full swoop, for natural selection to have anything to work on.[15]

When one considers the process of protein synthesis that we discussed in this chapter, one sees a very complex process that operates like a factory. In the central office (the nucleus) are the plans (DNA) for making all the factory's products (proteins). The plans for one product are copied (mRNA) and modified (introns removed) and carried out to the factory floor. The plans are fed into the computer (ribosome) that controls the machine (ribosome) that makes the protein. Meanwhile, forklifts (tRNA) are returning from the supply room with the parts (amino acids). The barcode (anticodon) on each part is read to ensure that the protein is assembled in the correct order. The shop floor is so designed that an assembly line can be set up with several machines (ribosomes) simultaneously reading the plans (mRNA). This way several copies of the protein can be made at one time. Once the protein is assembled, it is taken into the shape room, where it is allowed to take on its final three-dimensional shape (secondary, tertiary, and quarternary structures).

Behe describes other complex biochemical processes that he views as molecular machines: solar-powered machines (photosynthesis), electrical machines (nerve impulses), swimming machines (cilium), blood-clotting machines, and so forth. As Behe states, mutations and natural selection explain many of the behaviors and structures discussed in the first part of this chapter. The challenge for those expressing only a materialist explanation is to show how mutations and natural selection explain the complex and highly interdependent molecular systems. At present the concept of design seems to be a more viable explanation.

Yet many say that injecting design (faith) into the information gathering, knowledge formation process results in a dead end. They say once God is invoked, further exploration is ruled out. An example of this thought process is represented by Robert Pennock in the *Tower of Babel* when he discusses Behe's book. Pennock writes, "The most that Behe has done there is to point to a number of interesting research problems. One wonders why he, as a biochemist, does not begin the research himself. . . . Of course, Behe has no motivation to pursue the research himself, since he thinks he already knows the answer—biochemical complexity was produced by the intentional action of an intelligent designer. With intelligent-design theory, Behe has found a way to save himself a lot of work."[16]

Pennock is confusing how to carry out an experiment with how to interpret an experiment. The worldview of the experimenter will influence what questions are asked and how the experimental results are interpreted.[17] The example of Linnaeus reveals that his use of design made many positive contributions to the accumulation of knowledge. Design did not stifle the acquisition of knowledge but provided the insight needed to advance understanding at many key points.

Information Systems
Where did the information contained in the DNA molecule come from? On the one hand the DNA molecule confirms the materialist view of nature because all the cell's functions depend on the physics and chemistry of DNA. The components of DNA obey the same chemistry as all other molecules. There is no new chemistry involved in the phosphate groups reacting with the sugars to form the backbone of DNA. The usual chemistry is involved with the bases bonding to the backbone or from one strand to the other strand. As we discussed previously, the materialists spend their effort trying to

determine how DNA or RNA could arise from just the inter-action between matter and force. The materialist approach overlooks the question of how information became incorpo-rated into the DNA molecule.

Materialists hoped that the structure of DNA would solve the information question. As a review of figure 6.12 reveals, in a strand there are no chemical bonds between the bases. Thus, there are no chemical rules to determine the order in which the bases will be attached to the backbone. The base T can be followed by G or C or A or another T. Another approach is to look outside the DNA molecule. Maybe DNA or RNA formed on a mineral crystal. Crystals are self-ordering. Maybe the crystal's order formed the template for the synthesis of the nucleic acid. Crystals are highly ordered. In table salt (sodium chloride) each sodium ion is followed by a chloride ion that is followed by a sodium ion that is fol-lowed by a chloride ion, and so forth. Because the structure of a crystal is repetitive, a crystal has low information con-tent. If a nucleic acid were constructed like a crystal, then it could have a pattern like GAGAGAGA. This crystal-like pat-tern for a nucleic acid would not contain all the variety found in biological nucleic acids.

A different approach to the information content of DNA is provided by the chemist-philosopher Michael Polanyi.[18] Polanyi accepted the fact that materialists define life like a machine (forces and matter). Then he asked what makes some-thing a machine. Is it the material from which the machine is composed, or is it the function of the machine? Consider a pile of iron filings and a pair of scissors. There is no difference in the two at the atomic level. Where they differ is in their func-tion. (A similar argument by Paley is discussed in chapter 3.) Polanyi is saying that for any machine (non-biological or biological), we have to look beyond the physical-chemical components to the organizational function or purpose.

Using Polanyi's reasoning, what is the function of the DNA molecule? DNA provides the instructions for the growth and reproduction of a cell.[19] Instructions or information is independent of the medium. The information in this book is written in ink. Someone could copy the contents in pencil, crayon, or face paint. Likewise, the information in DNA can be written in nucleotide bases. Once a section of DNA is sequenced, its information is stored in a computer and can be transferred by a scientist to a colleague in a note written in ink. The colleague can then use the ink message to synthesize a copy of the DNA using nucleotide bases. The message (information) does not depend on the medium. One has to look outside the medium to discover the origin of the information.

We have stated that DNA contains information, but what makes a string of letters (bases) convey a message? In human languages there are arbitrary rules that make one string of letters a message and another string meaningless. In English, the string of letters *b-o-y* has meaning but the string *y-o-b* does not. In Spanish, the sequence to give the equivalent English meaning is *e-l c-h-i-c-o*. These are arbitrary letter combinations. There is nothing inherent in the letters that give meaning to these combinations. Sometimes, the same combination has drastically different meanings in different languages. The sequence *g-i-f-t* brings you a present in English but a poison in German!

What conferred meaning to the sequence of bases in the DNA molecule? What established the linguistic rules that "endow what otherwise would indeed be ordinary molecules with symbolic properties?"[20] From our everyday experience, intelligence is required to confer meaning to a sequence of letters. Intelligence implies design. As we saw in the case of Behe's irreducibly complex argument, many scientists dismiss appeal to design as being nonscientific. Some say that design is just the old god-of-the-gaps argument. Yet design in terms of information is not based on a gap in our knowledge but on the growth in our knowledge.

Is design good science or even science? Many believe that there is an obvious boundary separating science from pseudoscience. Although concepts such as observability, testability, repeatability, and falsifiability have been proposed, there is no universally accepted boundary. In fact, boundaries are philosophically tainted. The philosopher of biology David Hull states that these arguments "tend to be suspiciously self-serving designed to put one's opponents at a disadvantage while shoring up one's own position."[21]

What about the argument that science is guided by the principle of uniformity, or that existing processes can explain past processes? Scientists are comfortable invoking natural processes. Scientists observe that water erosion on earth results in long, narrow trenches. When similar trenches are observed on waterless Mars, scientists propose that water in the past caused erosion on Mars. Most current scientists would say that it would not be appropriate to invoke intelligent cause. Yet the skeptic David Hume, whom we discussed in chapter 3, wrote, "The same rule holds, whether the cause assigned be brute unconscious matter, or a rational intelligent being."[22] Thus, the principle of uniformity should be neutral in regard to the kind of cause. In our everyday experience, the only sources of information are intelligence. Around us, we see intelligent agents creating newspapers, books, musical scores, computer programs, plans for buildings, and so forth. The principle of uniformity suggests that intelligence was involved in the origin of DNA. Currently this seems like the strongest evidence for design.

CHAPTER SEVEN

AWE AND WONDER

HOW MUCH EVIDENCE does it take to prove a case? The question of evidence for a Designer of the universe is not like a normal scientific experiment in which observation leads to a description of how something happens. Ultimately, the question of design concerns why something has happened. In this case the something is the entire universe and everything in it. We have seen that the new Intelligent Design Movement is concerned with developing criteria for demonstrating why the universe appears to be designed.

Why do people see patterns? Why do we gaze into the sky at the clouds passing overhead and see a ship in full sail or a Yorkshire terrier? Why do old ladies collect driftwood from a stream or seashore and give the different pieces names; like Jonah's whale, the church mouse, or Dick Wittington's cat? They see a form or pattern that resembles something else. They know it is not the thing they have named it, yet they see a pattern. They do not believe a sailing ship with full rigging is making its way across the sky. They do not believe an old, warped stick is actually a whale. Yet they see correspondence and analogy. This is the stuff of poetry. Is this what people see when they say that the universe looks as though someone designed it?

On the surface, the situations seem the same, but they are quite different. It is one thing to say a stick looks like a snake and quite another to say that someone has fashioned a stick to look like a snake. Persons who see a ship in the clouds have a sense of satisfaction with themselves for being clever enough to "create" a ship where there is no a ship. This sort of exercise in imagination rarely results in awe and wonder. It has more a self-congratulatory feel to it. The awe and wonder comes when we gaze upon the clouds as clouds. Even when we know that they have resulted from a combination of relative humidity, temperature, barometric pressure, and wind it is possible to lose ourselves in gazing at the clouds. No longer are we entranced with our ability to imagine a ship. We are drawn into the cloud as a work of art.

Awe and wonder involves more than the perception of a design, which is the experience of seeing the ship in the clouds. Awe and wonder involves knowing something lies behind the clouds. Seeing a pattern is an act of human creativity. Awe and wonder, however, comes with recognizing the personal while observing the impersonal. It produces a surprise. The mind organizes what it sees to establish patterns.

Worldviews also affect how we see or accept the patterns of life. Different worldviews give people different patterns of life, yet minds all over the world perceive design behind nature. Is this common occurrence the example of mind perceiving mind? Does this perception of design relate to the remarkable way that mathematics, a mental construct, corresponds to the world (as we saw in chapter 4)? Rather than dismissing a phenomenon as "just" a mental construct, does the phenomenon not point to a relationship between the mind and what the mind perceives?

The remarkable matter is not that differing cultures, theologies, and philosophies disagree over the meaning of design but that they agree over the *fact* of design. Psychology does not "work" like the hard sciences that have a clear advantage in how they observe their object of study. The subject that psychology studies is no more observable than God is observable. Psychology deals with secondary matters (affects). It gropes after the created intentions of the human mind, but the mind cannot be observed, only inferred. It can be revealed by itself, yet it cannot be verified as having truly revealed itself. This is the same problem with knowing God empirically: God can be perceived secondarily in nature through the affects of creation, and God can be self-revealing.

In his study of why people believe in God, Michael Shermer discovered that the most common reason people give for their own belief in God (28.6 percent) is the "good design" of the universe.[1] Oddly, they give quite a different answer for why they think other people believe in God. They most commonly believe that other people believe in God because belief gives them comfort or purpose (26.3 percent). Most people believe that very few people (6 percent) believe in God because of the good design of the universe. We may recognize God, but we doubt that others will!

A CHANGING PATTERN

In the opening chapter we saw that the idea of design has been present in most cultures all over the world, but the idea has rarely involved proving the existence of the Designer. The idea has more frequently involved knowing the Designer. It involves the difference between knowing something and proving something. It involves the difference between knowing something and reflecting on what one knows. The first three chapters of this book explored the better-known varieties of ways that people have thought about design religiously, philosophically, and scientifically.

What attracted the attention of people to nature in the first place so that they thought it represented the handiwork of someone? The answer to that question lies buried in the past, but the history of the discussion reveals several dimensions at which the question of design operates. The religions of the world describe nature as revelatory of something or someone, or perhaps many someones. In antiquity, people began using the method of philosophy to reflect on the human experience of nature, as we saw with Plato and Aristotle. From the time of the Enlightenment, people began using the scientific method to reflect on the human experience of nature. To understand the underlying and fundamental consideration of design, however, we need to recall that the discussions began with people who already believed something about what or whom was responsible for nature. In the West, the tools of philosophy and science were employed to help believers gain a deeper grasp of faith rather than to prove the existence of the one in whom they had faith. At least this situation prevailed until the Enlightenment, or Age of Reason, when many scientists were adopting a mechanical model of the universe in keeping with the technological and scientific advances of the day.

The mechanical model coincided with a growing tradition in natural theology to view empiricism as the dominant and the only certain means to true knowledge. People of devout piety pushed this understanding, including Bishop Butler and the authors of the *Bridgewater Treatises*. An earlier taxonomy of knowledge would have given place to revelation, experience, tradition, rationalism, and empiricism. By the time of Tennant in the twentieth century, however, we find Christians who no longer recognize the validity of any of these ways of knowing except empiricism.

The last three centuries have witnessed a loss in the variety of the palette of ways of knowing. The palette has shrunk from many complementary ways of knowing that mutually informed one another to only one or two recognized ways of knowing. This transition corresponds to the general fragmentation of knowledge over the last three centuries. We have witnessed an explosion in some kinds of knowledge, but a poverty in other areas of knowledge.

In compiling the *Bridgewater Treatises,* the authors believed that by the sheer accumulation of data, the force of their argument would prove overwhelming. The complexity of the question, however, suggests that evidence must be drawn from a wider range of experience. For three hundred years, however, Christians have abandoned the interrelated fabric of human knowledge. Calvin planted the seeds of modern skepticism with his dichotomy of specific revelation and general revelation. He considered the general revelation of God found in nature unhelpful to people as a result of their fallen minds. Descartes succeeded in separating considerations of the spiritual from the physical with his dichotomy of mind and body. Pascal succeeded in separating spiritual experience from the domain of reason with his dichotomy of reason and feelings. Butler despised religious experience and looked to empiricism alone as the only legitimate basis of knowledge. On this basis, the natural theology tradition entered into dialogue with science. One might argue, however, that they had nothing left to bring to the conversation.

In John Wisdom's parable of the gardener that we introduced in chapter 3, we saw the gridlock that occurs when two people presented with the same evidence have different responses to the data. One person looked about and said that a gardener had been at work. Another person looked about and simply saw an old garden. Both people saw the pattern of a garden, but one of the people raised the issue of the presence of personality. In all of the discussion of design, it is possible to lose sight of the reason for the discussion. The design has evoked in people an awareness of the personal. Not everyone acknowledges this experience of the personal, but an overwhelming number of people do experience it. Sheer numbers do not prove the case, but it does help focus the question. Empiricism is a valid and helpful means of gathering data, yet the data require interpretation.

The design argument does not operate the way a scientific experiment works. First of all, it has been developed and used for centuries by people who already know what it is they hope to demonstrate. Thus, it does not have as its primary purpose the discovery of new truth. The argument was developed by people who already had firm convictions about the origin of the physical world. On the other hand, the argument has a compelling staying power that has survived many scientific revolutions. The argument transcends the scientific frameworks in which it has been stated as well as the philosophical frameworks in which it has been rationalized.

The argument from design is not really a proof for the existence of God. Design rarely operates as a proof in any culture.

It usually operates as a declaration of faith. The Bible and other religious traditions do not prove God's existence by design even though they affirm the evidence of design. Instead, design explains what kind of God exists and what kind of universe exists. Different religious traditions have differing views of what kind of God exists and what kind of universe exists. Their differing accounts of the nature of design reflect these variations.

Even Aristotle's "proofs" are not really proofs at all for the existence of God. Instead, they are aspects of his explanation of the workings of the physical world. He is not so much concerned with proving the existence of God as he is concerned with disproving Plato's understanding of universal ideas. Design is merely an aspect of one extended argument in Aristotle, and perhaps the least important.

Belief in an Intelligent Designer forms the foundational article of faith for Islam, Judaism, and Christianity. Within these faiths design does not function as a proof but as a "self-evident truth." The act of design and creation bestows a sacredness on the physical world (often forgotten in the modern period) such that it is wrong to deface (pollute) what God has made or to act in a way contrary to God's design. Even in nontheistic religions we find a strong awareness of the sacredness of the physical world, though often this awareness comes through the perception of the divine within the physical order rather than through the perception of the physical order as the result of the creativity of the divine.

Since the eighteenth century, the design argument has had strong opposition. Certainly Augustine and Calvin held that one could never come to true knowledge of God through philosophical arguments, but they did not oppose the argument as Hume did. They opposed the argument as people of faith who believed that God had designed the world and that the world gave compelling evidence of its design. They simply believed that people who did not already believe in God as Creator could not discover this truth from their own interpretation of the evidence. Thus, even those who opposed the argument affirmed its conclusion as well as its premises! People believed in and experienced design even if they did not believe it could prove the existence of God.

Now the entire playing field has changed. Aristotle and Aquinas pointed to the design of nature that everyone could see and accept. From the self-evident truth of design, they argued toward the Designer even though they had entirely different concepts of God and the nature of the universe. In the twentieth century, however, the argument has added an additional step. The culture no longer publicly accepts the notion of design and direction, goal and purpose for nature. Now the argument focuses on the demonstration of *intelligent* design. People still may perceive what has the appearance of design, but they question the validity of their own experience of nature. In the breakdown of knowledge spurred on by Descartes's dichotomy of mind and body, design became enmeshed with the empirical dimension of science. With the growth of Deism and the adoption of empiricism as a primary method of theology at the same time that specific revelation diminished in importance, the need to prove design itself became of greater concern than proving the Designer.

Plato, Augustine, Calvin, Descartes, and Pascal all understood the fundamental flaw of empiricism. Sensory experience does not lead to the absolute certainty we might wish as the quantum physicists have pointed out in the twentieth century. Science has a history of proving things that in the end were later disproved by alternative theories and evidence that will be replaced by new breakthroughs. Jesus discussed the inadequacy of empirical evidence to establish his identity because of the mental framework within which people evaluated the evidence. Though the Gospels contain many instances in which he performed miraculous deeds, Jesus refused to provide a sign as evidence of his identity. In response to Peter's famous statement of faith in him as Christ, Jesus remarked, "This was not revealed to you by man, but my Father in heaven" (Matt. 16:17).

Yet we find that God always gives a tangible, observable, concrete basis for faith. For Thomas, faith came through *touching* (John 20:24–28). For the two disciples on the road to Emmaus, faith came by *seeing* (Luke 24:28–31). In the Bible, God consistently provided a concrete basis for faith that related the spiritual experience to the bodily experience; as Paul said, "Faith comes from *hearing*" (Rom. 10:17). Aristotle, Aquinas, Butler, Buckland, and Tennant understood the flaw of ignoring sensory experience as the eastern religions tend to do. Do we need a new synthesis of the two great epistemological species of descent from Plato and Aristotle? Probably not, for that would suggest that Plato and Aristotle represent the original thesis and antithesis of knowledge when, from a biblical perspective, they would more accurately represent the beginnings of the Western tradition to fragment knowledge.

BEAUTY

Beauty itself doeth of itself persuade
The eyes of men without an orator.
—William Shakespeare, *The Rape of Lucrece*

Beauty is in the eye of the beholder.
—Margaret Wolfe Hungerford, *Molly Brown*

As discussed in chapter 5, Newton's success came from using one set of equations to describe motion both on the earth and in the heavens. Many educated people began to look at the universe as a deterministic clockwork universe. To many people, nature was no longer warm and fuzzy; nature was now a cold machine. The poets of the Romantic Movement revolted against this view of nature and against science. To the Romantics, scientists were heartless cads who had cut beauty out of nature. As William Wordsworth (1770–1850) wrote in "The Tables Turned":

> Sweet is the lore which nature brings;
> Our meddling intellect
> Misshapes the beauteous form of things
> We murder to dissect.

Or as Johann Wolfgang von Goethe (1749–1832) wrote in *Faust:*

> Unless you feel it, you will never achieve it.
> If it doesn't flow from your soul . . .
> Your listener will not believe it . . .
> Gray and ashen . . . is every science,
> And only the golden tree of life is green.

The life of Charles Darwin can be cited as an example of how science destroyed the enjoyment of nature. In his letters, Darwin laments the loss of his enjoyment of literature, poetry, music, and natural beauty.[2] Darwin states, "I am a withered leaf for every subject except Science. It sometime makes me hate Science."[3] Also, a quick examination of some recent introductory astronomy, biology, chemistry, and physics texts reveals no listings of the words *awe, beauty, splendor,* or *wonder* in their indexes.[4] Is there no beauty or wonder in modern astronomy, biology, chemistry, or physics? Surprisingly, these terms also were not found in many texts dealing with the interaction of science and faith.[5]

Natural Philosophical Beauty
As the historian of science John Brooke has pointed out, earlier forms of the design argument did include the appreciation of beauty.[6] The German astronomer Johannes Kepler (1571–1630) searched for harmony in the relationships of the planets. When he discovered that the planets followed an elliptical orbit, he felt that he was hearing the music of God. The beauty of gemstones captivated the English chemist Robert Boyle (1627–1691). Boyle, believing that nature was constructed along a plan of simplicity and economy, envisioned that the external shape of crystals resulted from a regular arrangement of particles. The English scientist Robert

Hooke (1635–1703) used the microscope to explore nature. Hooke was impressed by his observation that at the microscopic level nature was not only functional but also beautiful. The ornamental beauty of fish scales or fly eyes impressed him. He was amazed that under the microscope human artifacts (edge of a razor) looked imperfect compared to the artifacts of nature. For Hooke, this beauty and perfection pointed toward a Designer. The English physicist Isaac Newton (1642–1727) looked for beauty in a mathematical undergirding of nature. He felt that the beauty of colors or the solar system was based on simplicity of mathematical ratios. The Swedish naturalist Carolus Linnaeus (1707–1778) used the principles of economy and beauty to develop a classification scheme for living organisms. The British geologists William Buckland (1784–1856) and Hugh Miller (1802–1856) were attracted to the beauty of fossils. One fossil that attracted them was that of the ammonite, an extinct marine mollusk with a coiled shell containing a series of chambers. The shapes of these fossils reminded the geologists of human architecture. As Buckland wrote: "The general principle of dividing and subdividing the ribs, in order to multiply supports as the vault [of the shell] enlarges, is conducted nearly on the same plan, and for the same purpose, as the divisions and subdivisions of the ribs beneath the groin work, in the flat vaulted roofs of the florid Gothic Architecture."[7]

Buckland and Miller believed that since the artifacts of nature and humans shared architecture principles, there was a designer of nature. Even Darwin (1809–1882), in the early part of his career, was attracted to beauty. Desmond and Moore describe Darwin in the Brazilian rain forest: "Seated on a mossy log . . . his feelings flowed. 'Twiners entwining twiners,' his pencil twitched, 'trees like hair—beautiful lepidoptera—Silence—hosannah.'"[8]

Physical Beauty
Modern physics continues this emphasis on beauty. Particle physics studies the properties of the particles found inside

atoms. Particle physicists depend heavily on mathematical formulations to "describe" the subatomic world. In many cases, there are no instruments powerful enough to test some of the predictions of these mathematical formulations. A challenge for modern science is to determine the criteria for verifying particle physics theories. Ideas proposed and used have included "agreement with data," "coherence with other accepted theories," "simplicity," and "beauty." Beauty! To paraphrase Tina Turner, "What has beauty got to do with it?" The British physicist and Nobel laureate Paul Dirac (1902–1984) was a hard-nosed empiricist; it was reported that if you asked Dirac about the weather, he would go open the door and check before answering! Yet Dirac is famous for using beauty as a criterion for truth. Dirac stated that "it is more important to have beauty in one's equations than to have them fit experiment. . . . It seems that if one is working from the point of view of getting beauty in one's equations, and if one has a really sound instinct, one is on a sure line of progress. If there is not complete agreement between the results of one's work and experiment, one should not allow oneself to be too discouraged, because the discrepancy may be due to minor features that are not properly taken into account and that will get cleared up with further developments of the theory."[9]

The American physicist and Nobel Laureate Steven Weinberg (1933–) included the chapter "Beautiful Theories" in his recent book *Dreams of a Final Theory.*[10] Weinberg stated that it is "rather spooky . . . that something as personal and subjective as our sense of beauty helps us not only to invent physical theories but even to judge the validity of theories."[11] For Weinberg and others, a beautiful theory is one that displays simplicity and inevitability. We have all seen a painting or heard a musical score to which we would not want to add or remove anything. This feeling that it was inevitable that all the components would be there is what the physicists mean by beauty.

The chemist and philosopher Michael Polanyi believed that a great theory is one that has "an inarticulate component acclaiming its beauty, and this is essential to the belief that the theory is true."[12] For example, Weinberg remarked, "I believe that the general acceptance of general relativity was due in large part to the attractions of the theory itself—to its beauty."[13] Weinberg won the Nobel Prize for proposing the electroweak theory uniting the weak nuclear force with the electromagnetic force. When this theory was proposed, it clashed with experimental results. Its beauty encouraged scientists to continue to check to see if their experimental results were in error. The superstring theory was discussed in chapter 4. This theory is convincing to many not because someone has seen a string (which they have not) but because of the wonder of its beauty. Science appears to be converging with the Romantic poets. In his "Ode on a Grecian Urn," John Keats (1795–1821) said, "Beauty is truth, and truth beauty." This statement is reflected in the remarks of the American physicist and Nobel Laureate Charles H. Townes (1915–): "The beauty of nature elicits a response from both our scientific and our poetic modes of understanding. . . . We scientists, seeing a simple relationship that seems beautiful, intuitively think it likely to be true. Both scientists and theologians give themselves to the truth that transcends and invites us."[14]

False Beauty

Sometimes, one's taste leads to a preference for "tacky paintings" or false theories. As Weinberg stated, "Just as in our appreciation of music or painting or poetry, this sense of [beauty] is a matter of taste and experience."[15] The Dane Tycho Brahe (1546–1601) was the greatest astronomer of his day, yet he rejected the Copernican model of the solar system because this model had an "ugly" gap between the planets and the nearest stars. Before discovering that planets move in elliptical orbits, Kepler wasted years trying to find a model of the solar system based on the "beautiful" shapes of the five Platonic solids.[16] The British chemist Humphry Davy

(1778–1829) opposed John Dalton's atomic theory because Davy thought it was more beautiful to have one type of matter; ironically Davy continued to discover elements, thereby supporting Dalton's theory that matter was divided into several building blocks. More recently, Albert Einstein, Louis de Broglie, and Erwin Schrodinger (key players in the founding of quantum mechanics) opposed the probabilities associated with quantum mechanics. It did not fit their sense of the aesthetic, to paraphrase Einstein, for God to play with dice. As the examples in this section reveal, a sense of beauty does not always point toward how nature behaves. The other criteria discussed in the previous section also must be applied.

Not a Natural Beauty
If the aesthetic was a topic in natural philosophy and is a topic in particle physics, why do we not find the aesthetic in many introductory science books? One reason that many texts do not index words such as *awe, beauty, splendor,* or *wonder* could be because of the view that science should be objective, rational, and empirical. In this view, scientists are to remove their emotions, be objective, and be logical. Each type of literature has its own style of writing. Scientific writing in many cases uses an unemotional and precise style that the Romantic poets hated. Yet this cannot be the only reason for not mentioning the aesthetic, because there are emotions and hunches in science. Einstein stated, "When I examine myself and my methods of thought, I come close to the conclusion that the gift of fantasy has meant more to me than my talent for absorbing positive knowledge."[17] Charles Misner thought Einstein saw the majesty and splendor of the universe:

> I do see the design of the universe as essentially a religious question, that is one should have some kind of respect and awe for the whole business. Its very magnificence should not be taken for granted. In fact that is why I think Einstein had so little use for organized religion, although he strikes me basically as a very

religious man. Einstein must have looked at what the Christian preachers said about God and felt that they were blaspheming. He had seen much more majesty than they had ever imagined, and they were just not talking about the real thing.[18]

Another reason that the aesthetic is not found in many modern texts could result from the new view of the "beautiful" in light of Darwin's theory of evolution. Characteristics of organisms are now discussed in terms of the utility that resulted from natural selection, not in terms of their awe and wonder reflecting a Designer. The ammonite structures that impressed Buckland and Miller as beautiful architectural forms are now described as forms that were useful in the ammonite's struggle for survival: "The reduction of beauty to utility, orchestrated by the Darwinians, marked the passage of an era: 'Those colours which so fascinated the poet or artist, and which seem to be spread in such royal lavishment over copse and meadow and heath, have all their purpose to fulfil; they have to serve as an attraction to insects which effect the fertilisation of the flower.'"[19]

Another challenge to beauty is the presence of what some say are imperfect forms. Those wonderfully beautiful structures of the natural philosophers are considered imperfectly designed by evolutionists. An example of this common argument is given by the American biologist Kenneth Miller:

> Because intelligent design works from a clean sheet of paper, it should produce organisms that have been optimally designed for the tasks they perform.[20]

> To adopt the explanation of design, we are forced to attribute a host of flaws and imperfections to the designer. Our appendix, for example, seems to serve only to make us sick; our feet are poorly constructed to take the full force of walking and running; and even our eyes are prone to optical errors and lose their ability for close focus as we age.[21]

In chapter 6, we discussed the American biochemist Michael Behe's concept of irreducible complexity. Since Behe has written some of the best criticisms of the perfect design argument, we will quote him extensively:

> The most basic problem is that the argument demands perfection at all. Clearly, designers who have the ability to make better designs do not necessarily do so. For example, in manufacturing, "built-in obsolescence" is common—a product is intentionally made so it will not last as long as it might, for reasons that supersede the simple goal of engineering excellence. Another example is a personal one: I do not give my children the best, fanciest toys because I don't want to spoil them, and because I want them to learn the value of a dollar. The argument from imperfection overlooks the possibility that the designer might have motives, with engineering excellence oftentimes relegated to a secondary role. Most people throughout history have thought that life was designed despite sickness, death, and other obvious imperfections.[22]

The perfection critique also naively assumes that organisms do not change over time. Miller implies that what we see today is what we would have seen yesterday. In chapter 6, we discussed how some organisms could be adapted by changing environmental conditions. Thus, because an organism may show a history of adaptation does not rule out the possibility of design.

A FLAWED DESIGN?

A friend who serves as president of a denominationally related Christian college has occasion to attend meetings of pastors. At one of these meetings the preacher of the day waxed eloquent about the loveliness and serenity of nature as he referenced the manicured lawns and well-kept flowerbeds outside. On such a day, he asked, how could anyone doubt the existence of God? Upon leaving the meeting, the college president noticed a baby squirrel playing in the grass. At that moment, down from the heights came a hawk and scooped up the little squirrel for its lunch! The president observed that the preacher had not mentioned episodes like the demise of the squirrel in his sermon.

A common argument against awe, wonder, and beauty is the presence of cruelty and evil. Nature is viewed as "red in tooth and claw": herbivores always being stalked by carnivores, aging alpha males being thrown out of the tribe by youthful challengers, terrible parasites, or devastating plagues. This critique also has a personal tone. Weinberg writes, "I have seen a mother die painfully of cancer, a father's personality destroyed by Alzheimer's disease, and scores of second and third cousins murdered in the Holocaust. Signs of a benevolent designer are pretty well hidden."[23] Weinberg's arguments have an emotional tone, rather than the objective, rational, and empirical tone of science. It is interesting that this critique appeals to a sense of justice, of right and wrong. Yet the alternative proposed to design is a materialist account based on the interaction of forces and matter. What does cruelty, evil, or injustice mean in this materialist account? Why should one event be "better" if all organisms are adapting to the "neutral dictates" of natural selection?

Those who oppose the idea of design because of the presence of "evil" or bad things that happen have undergone a subtle shift in their own response from one of intellect to emotion. The fact that ugliness, thorns, death, pain, suffering, and chaos are present in the world does not disprove design. Infestation by termites does not prove a house did not have an architect. Vandalism does not prove a house did not have an architect. Arson does not prove a house did not have an architect. Sloppy homeowners who do not paint or carry out the garbage do not prove a house did not have an architect. These matters simply raise questions about the situation of the house since it was built. The presence of suffering in the world appears to be a recurring theme of people who oppose the idea that the world bears evidence of design. The presence of suffering may raise questions about the adequacy of the design or the character of the architect but not about the issue of design itself. As to what the presence of suffering tells us about the designer, we must look to other sources of evidence to explore the character of the designer, but only after establishing the existence of such a being. It does no good to jump the gun and argue against such a being on the basis of the being's character. Recognizing ugliness, pain, and evil, however, suggests an equally perplexing problem. How do we account for goodness, truth, and beauty? Some would say that these qualities are only mental constructs in the mind. If so, we are left to explain ugliness, pain, and evil in the same way. The Buddha accepted this conclusion and resolved that all of physical existence is an illusion. He accepted the reality of the perception of design, but he denied the reality of the design that we perceive!

Hume raised the issue of pain and suffering as evidence against design in the eighteenth century when the mechanical model of the universe was all the rage. The design Butler saw and that Paley would describe was that of a machine. Hume argued that the presence of bad things in the universe demonstrates a flaw in the design of the machine. He argued that a good, all-powerful God would not design a machine with such a serious flaw. Those who bring up the flaw usually do so as though it were a secret that religious people somehow seek to ignore or deny. Actually, the heart of religion involves the acknowledgment of the flaw. Plato spoke of the flaw as a shadow. Aristotle spoke of it as the problem of change and decay as opposed to the eternal perfection of the heavenly realm. The Buddha spoke of it as an illusion, and the entire focus of his approach to religion is to get over the illusion. For Muslims, Jews, and Christians, the problem is sin, and the purpose of religion is to solve the problem of sin. In contrast to the popular view of sin as merely "breaking the rules," these religions view sin as cosmic in scope, striking at the very heart of physical and spiritual reality.

The Christian religion is the story of nature, including people, from creation to completion. Page after page of the Bible deals with flawed people and their impact on one another and on nature. It is the story of intimate contact between the Creator and the creature toward an ultimate goal that has not yet appeared. It is a story in which the struggle has meaning and represents an aspect of the goal. The coming of Christ into the world to participate in physical, human life defined by the experience of both birth and death forms the focal point of the completion of people.

The Christian worldview, which Weinberg has attacked, does provide the basis for judging events. The life of Jesus provides the basis for judging human actions. While demanding that evil be opposed, this worldview explains why human actions alone cannot overcome evil. As the science writer Kitty Ferguson states, "Those who believe in the biblical God point out that the biblical description of the world situation is, sadly, on target, and that the biblical explanation for our human predicament and the problem of evil—though we may not like or accept the explanation—fits."[24]

If the universe is seen as a completed work at its inception, then the complaint of flawed design has merit. If the universe is a vast machine, then the static idea of creation makes sense. It was made and started. Now it runs on its own. The Deists held to this view, but they also popularized this view with a reading of the first chapter of Genesis in which God created the heavens and the earth. As a work of art in progress, however, the complaint of flawed design does not hold. The universe is not finished and neither are people. As we demonstrated in *Science and Faith: An Evangelical Dialogue,* the first chapter of Genesis as written in its original Hebrew stresses that God *began* to bring the creation about, which is a continuous action.[25] It also stresses the completed action of creation. English translations tend to deal with this seeming contradiction by placing all of creation in the past tense as completed action in the past. Hebrew has no tense—neither past, present, nor future. It has completed action and continuing action.

Genesis stresses that in the ages of creation, God continues to be involved in creation. It also stresses, however, that in the totality of creation, God completes the work.

Thus, the problem of pain and suffering is the problem of incompletion. The presence of pain and suffering does not preclude design. It is the design of the artist, however, rather than the design of the engineer. It is the artist painting on a great canvas. It is the sculptor chipping away at an enormous block of marble until all of the roughness is gone and only the design in the artist's mind remains. It is the play in progress. It is the song being sung. The Hindu might say that it is the dance of the dancer that only exists as the body of the dancer moves.

PERCEIVING THE PERSONAL

The power of nature to evoke awe and wonder in people constitutes the primary way that people experience the personal through nature. In gazing upon a brilliant sunset, a terrible electrical storm, or a serene mountain pool, people often speak of an experience of wonder. Some would identify it with the experience of worship. Yet others who have a purely materialistic orientation will claim to have had similar experiences listening to a Beethoven symphony or observing a painting by Botticelli. This similarity of experiences can be explained in at least two ways. Reference to the moving, rapturous experience in response to some form of creative, artistic expression by humans suggests that the "religious" experience people have in response to nature is merely an internal human response to certain sensory stimuli. It also suggests, however, that what people dub a "religious" experience should more properly be called a "personal" experience in which a human responds to a perception of the personal behind a collection of sensory stimuli. The music of Beethoven and the sunset suggest an artist. A random set of noises at different frequencies does not produce the same effect in a person that a carefully designed set of tones by Beethoven produces. Rather than evidence for the absence of an artist for nature, the experience of rapture over human artistic expression provides evidence that similar effects have similar causes.

A stream of nineteenth- and twentieth-century philosophers and theologians devoted themselves to exploring the experiential dimension of faith. They had no interest in exploring natural philosophy. People such as Søren Kierkegaard, Friedrich Schleiermacher, Rudolf Otto, and William Hocking continued a trajectory away from sensory experience that dates back to Descartes and Pascal. They were concerned with religious experience without cognitive content. The fact that they abandoned the idea of revelation as well as empiricism does not in any way diminish the significance of their insights into the narrow realm of experience that they separated from other ways of knowing. Otto in particular explored the universal phenomenon of religious experience. He referred to the encounter between people and the personality behind nature by the Latin terms *mysterium tremendum et fascinans*. By these terms he meant that people have a mysterious encounter in the context of sensory experience that takes them beyond the sensory. This experience has a tremendous dimension to it that elicits fear. Yet the perception of "the other" fascinates so much that we feel drawn to it. These terms may prove helpful in considering how the notion of intelligent design involves more than just the observable facts.

Mysterium—Modest Personality

The human response to nature as design involves more than the mere recognition of pattern, order, system, regularity, probability, and predictability. When people perceive the world as an artifact, is it the artifact that they perceive or the personality behind the artifact that they perceive? Does the world serve as a mediator of the personality responsible for the world? This is a different question than, Does the world give evidence of design? The second question may be an attempt to rationalize the first question and resolve it with an empirical methodology. As we have seen in chapters 1 and 2, peoples around the world assumed the first question until relatively recently.

Much of the discussion of design since the time of Newton has focused on the perception of the universe as a great machine. In this model the perception of design has increasingly depended upon the power to demonstrate how the universe is like a machine rather than to see how the universe is the result of creativity. The two are not quite the same thing. Is the universe more like a machine as the Deists suggested, or a body as Plato suggested, or a work of art as the Bible suggested? Is God an engineer or an artist?

Tremendum—The Problem of Evil

The imperfection in the universe is a major objection to the idea that some intelligence designed the universe. Hume objected to design on these grounds. Darwin was driven to find a naturalistic explanation for life that would let God off the hook. Following the Holocaust this issue has contributed to theological conversation about God's possible involvement in the world. Many have reasoned that it is better not to have a God at all than to have one who could allow evil. Why would a great intelligence create a world filled with evil and suffering? Notice that the question involves emotion and values more than it involves a simple empirical inquiry into whether the universe shows evidence of design.

At a recent international gathering of scientists and theologians in Oxford, we engaged a prominent physicist and a prominent molecular biologist in conversation about God's relationship to time. In independent conversations, both men who hold scientific and theological degrees opted against the notion that God stands outside time. The conversations took quite some time to work through all of the issues, but the final determining issue for both men, and they both used the same language, was that they felt "uncomfortable" with the idea that God knows what is going to happen. The emotional concern for human freedom governed the terms in which they considered the question.

Freedom and suffering have an intrinsic relationship to each other. In order for the possibility of freedom or non-determinacy, the possibility of pain and suffering must also be present. Without this basic openness of the universe that we can detect at the subatomic level in quantum mechanics and in the relationships of systems found in chaos theory, humanity as we know it could not exist. Perhaps life could not exist. Pain is the price the universe pays for existing. In the end, pain and suffering is a straw man to throw us off the scent or to provide an easy exit from the discussion.

The true difficulty with the problem of pain is to explain the problem of pleasure. Why should pleasure, joy, or even beauty be within the realm of experience?

Fascinans—Attraction

Life both attracts and conceals. A walk through the zoo will tell us so. We can see some animals whose coloration and form attract a mate. We can see other animals whose coloration and form conceal them from other animals that would eat them. Animals attract their own kind for reproduction, yet they conceal themselves from danger. Darwin's theory offers an explanation for this feature of life. The animals that adapted in such a way as to appear attractive or "beautiful" to another of their kind had greater success in reproduction. The animals that adapted in such a way as to conceal themselves within their environment had greater success in surviving ambush from a predator. The theory certainly makes good sense, but it does not provide a full explanation. Adaptation to appeal to the "beauty" impulse does not explain the origin of the "beauty" impulse. The presence of the "beauty" impulse implies preference in comparing the relative merits of potential suitors. Preference implies values. Values may be quite utilitarian and pragmatic, such as *better* as a protector, *worse* as a food provider, *better* as a reproducing mate.

Within nature we see the principle of attraction related to sexual reproduction. The features that operate in the "beauty" impulse may not have any correlation to the potential of the prospective mate to reproduce in the most favorable way. Human history is full of stories of people smitten by beauty who fail to produce an acceptable offspring. Henry VIII divorced his wife, suffered excommunication from the church he had defended against Martin Luther, risked war with the continental powers, risked civil war in his own country, and all to marry Anne Boleyn. He wanted a wife who would produce a suitable child, but he was attracted by beauty. One might argue that Henry's wives did produce three children. To this remark we observe that none of his children produced heirs. Physical features that animals find attractive may work to ensure that the attractive animal gets a mate, but this situation does not explain why physical features would make any difference at all for reproduction.

At the fundamental level of the atomic structures that compose the universe we find the principles of attraction and repulsion at work. Does this fact provide us with a natural explanation for these features at the level of complex organisms? No. It merely provides a description of the complete pervasiveness of the phenomenon. It offers no explanation. At every point in which God does something in nature we must necessarily see a physical cause because the action takes place in the observable physical world. To identify a physical cause does not preclude the action of God. A physical, describable event should not be confused with a naturalistic event.

Awe and wonder is a human response to nature. Not all people respond to nature in this way. Intelligent Design is an argument based on the analysis of what produced the awe and wonder in a person. It might most approximate an art or music appreciation course. Awe and wonder represent knowledge of the Creator without the cognitive content of knowing the Creator. Even the discovery of an awe and wonder gene, or the religion gene as some call it, would not prove that the appreciation of beauty or the apprehension of the personal mediated through creativity is merely a naturalistic event. It might describe the physical domain through which people experience such things, but Descartes's insistence upon the separation of the physical and the spiritual does not make it so. We in the West have drunk deeply of the dualistic wine.

Any action by God in the physical world can be described according to the laws of physics, otherwise it could not occur physically. To describe a phenomenon is quite different, however, from explaining a phenomenon. In the same way, any spiritual experience of a person related to the physical world will have a biological context through which the person had access to the physical world. It lies within the realm of science to describe the processes at work when a person responds to the physical world in a way often spoken of as "religious" experience. It is quite another thing, however, to explain the cause of the experience. The fact that drugs can produce similar experiences by no means suggests that the other experiences have no merit. Drugs can produce an experience to the tongue similar to tasting sugar. This does not suggest that sugar has no reality. It merely points out that all sources of knowledge are susceptible to distortion.

The ancient Hebrews described the interplay of the human body and spirit as the *nephish hayah* (living being). It was a concept quite different from Plato's view of the *psyche* (life principle). It is most unfortunate for Western civilization that centuries ago scholars translated both words as *soul*. For the Hebrew, the soul represented the unity of life that involved both a physical and a spiritual dimension. For Plato, the soul was the life principle of the universe that became embodied in flesh until it could cast off the physical shell. Physical life was a hindrance to the soul. Aristotle reacted to his teacher and suggested that the spirit had nothing to say to the body. Unfortunately, philosophers and theologians for over two thousand years have played off Plato and Aristotle while paying little heed to the ancient Hebrew understanding of the relationship between physical and spiritual reality. The Hebrew concept of the Creator and the Christian concept of the Incarnation of God in Jesus Christ affirm the dynamic relationship between the spiritual and physical realms.

THE EYE OF THE BEHOLDER

At the moment of perhaps the greatest triumph of science over the forces of nature, some involved in the effort expressed their own sense of awe and wonder at the experience. John Glenn was the first American to orbit the earth. On February 20, 1962, Glenn was launched into orbit around the earth. He orbited the earth three times in a flight that lasted almost five hours. Only two others, the Russians Yuri Gagarin and Gherman Titov, had orbited the earth. Some of Glenn's observations during his flight included:

> Oh, that view is tremendous. . . .

> Can see clear back, a big cloud pattern way back across toward the Cape. Beautiful sight. . . .

> The horizon now is a brilliant blue. . . .

> I have the Cape in sight. I can see the whole State of Florida just laid out like a map. Beautiful.[26]

After his historic flight, Glenn wrote about his experiences in light of his faith in God.[27] Glenn's comments were based on his studies about the nature of the universe as well as his observations during his space flight. Glenn was awed with the wonderful structure of the universe:

> It is the *orderliness* of the whole universe about us—from the smallest atomic structure to the most enormous thing we can imagine: galaxies millions of light-years across, all traveling in prescribed orbits in relation to one another. Could this have just happened? Was it an accident that a bunch of flotsam and jetsam suddenly started making these orbits of its own accord? I can't believe that. This was a definite Plan. This is one big thing in space that shows me

there is a God. Some Power put all this into orbit and keeps it there.[28]

Through a worldview shaped by his military experiences, Glenn saw design in terms of order and structure.

Apollo 8 was launched on December 21, 1968, and was the first manned mission to orbit the moon. The crew of *Apollo 8* included Frank Borman, James A. Lovell Jr., and William A. Anders. They arrived at the moon on December 24. The Apollo astronauts were the first humans to see directly the backside of the moon as well as see the earth rise over the moon's surface. They orbited the moon ten times before returning to earth. Their photographs of the earth are some of the most famous of the space age. One striking photograph shows the vibrant, blue jewel of the earth hovering over the barren moon against the blackness of space.

On Christmas Eve, as they approached a lunar sunrise, Anders began to read:

> In the beginning God created the heaven and the earth. And the earth was without form, and void; and darkness was upon the face of the deep. And the spirit of God moved upon the face of the waters. And God said, Let there be light: and there was light. And God saw the light, that it was good: and God divided the light from the darkness. And God called the light Day, and the darkness he called Night. And the evening and the morning were the first day (Gen. 1:1–5 KJV).

Lovell continuing the reading:

> And God said, Let there be a firmament in the midst of the waters, and let it divide the waters from the waters. And God made the firmament, and divided the waters which were under the firmament from the waters which were above the firmament: and it was so. And God called the firmament Heaven. And the evening and the morning were the second day (Gen. 1:6–8 KJV).

Borman concluded the reading:

And God said, Let the waters under the heaven be gathered together unto one place, and let the dry land appear: and it was so. And God called the dry land Earth; and the gathering together of the waters called he Seas: and God saw that it was good (Gen. 1:9–10 KJV).

Borman finished by saying: "And from the crew of Apollo 8 we close with good night, good luck, a Merry Christmas, and God bless all of you—all of you on the good earth.[29]

"As Anders said, 'The more I see of God's universe, the deeper will be my belief in God.'"[30]

EPILOGUE

WE HAVE SEEN that for over three thousand years in different places and cultures, the notion of the design of the universe has enjoyed remarkable resilience. This may not prove the thesis of design, but it certainly gives occasion for awe. Not only has this idea survived changes in religious context, but it has survived changes in philosophical and scientific worldview as well. It has survived the changes in worldview from Moses to Plato (via Augustine) to Aristotle (via Aquinas) to Copernicus and Newton to Einstein and Bohr.

Because of this resilience and the unending changes in science and philosophy, this book has no conclusion. We simply add this epilogue to a question that is easily settled for many but remains open for others.

We began the preface with a brief account of two conferences concerned with the design question. The sole bridge between the two meetings was Cliff Matthews, a prominent biologist and atheist who is inquisitive enough to be fascinated with the question of the existence of God. Matthews somehow violated the laws of physics—or at least managed to attend parts of both conferences. He gave a fair-minded report of the Concordia meeting that included the leaders of the Intelligent Design Movement during a general question-and-answer period. In his remarks, however, he reported that Ken Miller (professor of biology at Brown, author of *Finding Darwin's God,* and critic of Intelligent Design) took up Michael Behe's challenge of irreducible complexity. Behe gives the mousetrap as a mechanical example of Intelligent Design that requires all the pieces in place in order to work. The mousetrap is irreducibly complex: remove one element, and it will not function. According to Matthews, Miller produced a mousetrap and began removing pieces to show that it would still work! The brief report resembled a carnival show with Miller ready to pull a rabbit out of his hat for the next trick. As it turned out, Miller actually used conceptual drawings of mousetraps.

Michael Behe responded to Miller in an article posted on the Web site of the Discovery Institute. He defended the mousetrap analogy and critiqued Miller's slight-of-hand use of drawings of mousetraps of decreasing complexity. Behe demonstrated that even in Miller's drawings of conceptual traps rather than actual traps, multiple alterations must occur in the design of the traps at each stage of complexity for the traps to function.[1] Behe points out that a naturalistic explanation of the changes in complexity may have a satisfactory feel to it, but it collapses upon examination of the details. This explanatory power gave naturalism its charm as it provided science with what the postmodernists would call a "metanarrative."

Gayle Woloschak has pointed out the problem of the argument of irreducible complexity in terms of biology. As recently as the 1980s the immune system was considered irreducibly complex, but now it is not. Woloschak, a genetic biologist, observes that the human body has so much redundancy that we can live with a remarkable amount missing in each system. On the other hand, at lower levels of life, irreducible complexity becomes a greater issue because the redundancy is not present at those levels.

Irreducible complexity may be an example of the infinite regress so feared by the philosophers of old. Take the case of the steam engine. Steam power was one of the greatest achievements of the industrial revolution, but the first steam engine was nothing more complex than steam escaping from a boiling kettle: a one-cell system! The great airships of the 1930s with their rigid skeletons and massive gondolas that transported passengers in luxury across the Atlantic Ocean began as bits of ash sailing up a chimney in the late 1700s. The fact that such complex machines came from such simple origins, however, does not disprove the element of design that went into their formation over time. In fact, the analogy suggests the presence of intelligence that responds to the changing situation as it guides the development of complexity over time.

The argument of natural selection through the survival of the fittest in the competition for the resources of life makes sense at a certain level. As metanarrative it served to justify the imperialistic ambitions of Western Europe at the end of the nineteenth century. It provided Hitler with a scientifically based political philosophy with which he could rebuild Germany after the devastation of World War I. On a day-to-day basis we see animals and humans behaving according to an eat-or-be-eaten mentality. We see how it could be so at the functional level. The urge not only to survive but to prevail, as Faulkner would say, seems apparent at the cognitive level—so much so that it corresponds to our experience with other people. At lower levels of life, however, it appears that Darwin's natural selection actually operates as a metaphysical principle. He has not supplied a simpler explanation than the God hypothesis. He has merely camouflaged his metaphysics in the trappings of naturalism, as Hegel and Marx had done with their dialectics of history.

The desirability of pursuing design as either theology or science remains a heated topic of discussion. Controversy has surrounded the Intelligent Design Movement for reasons that often sound more emotional than intellectual. Some consider it a throwback to a time before the fragmentation of knowledge as specialization has engulfed the West. This fragmentation has occurred in theological and philosophical circles as much or more than within scientific circles. It has become the norm of academic culture, a culture in which the disciplines no longer speak to one another. The Intelligent Design Movement has made clear that it hopes to make design a recognized part of science. This hope has raised a specter of horror for many who fear the blur of interdisciplinary contact.

The Intelligent Design Movement has arisen at a time when the scientific community faces a major philosophical crisis related to the certainty of empirical observation resulting from advances in quantum theory during the twentieth century. In the context of postmodern views toward empiricism and rationalism, science faces a significant challenge in terms of what we can know of reality. Theology faces the same challenge after three hundred years of modernity as the mainstream of theological thought grew increasingly suspicious of objective revelation from God and subjective religious experience as well. Renewed interest in Intelligent Design creates an opportunity for a new discussion of the nature of human knowledge that could lead to an integration of ways of knowing, a discussion that has been largely absent from Western thought since Aristotle disagreed with Plato.

We have seen that both a more liberal branch of Christianity that is drawn toward naturalistic explanations of religious experience and a more conservative branch of Christianity that relies upon Scripture for all religious content view the design argument with suspicion. Has anyone ever actually come to faith by contemplating science and creation? As a matter of fact, this dynamic consideration led Augustine to faith. Ironically, the Reformed tradition's suspicion of natural theology originated with Augustine, who had failed to take note of God before his conversion. Augustine rejected natural theology as sufficient to arrive at an adequate knowledge of God on its own; Calvin would do the same after him. He did not, however, reject what truth can come through natural theology. Science and philosophy helped Augustine come to faith, but once he knew the Creator he realized that he had spent his life in ignorance of God. He thought that this could not be possible if our senses alone can give us knowledge of God unaided by the intervention of God. The problem lies in the interplay of the various ways of knowing and the human danger of giving priority to one way of knowing without recognizing that the other ways continue to operate whether we acknowledge them or not.

Many Christians fervently affirm that God created the world but just as fervently deny that people could come to this knowledge by observing the creation. Intelligent Design presents these Christians with a dilemma. They know as a matter of faith that life cannot be explained purely by appeal to naturalistic forces. Yet they refrain from endorsing the Intelligent Design Movement's attempt to establish an empirical method for demonstrating Intelligent Design. "The heavens may declare the glory of the Lord," but "we walk by faith and not by sight."

The Western tradition since Plato and Aristotle has taught us to choose between alternatives rather than to recognize how alternatives inform one another. This dilemma results from the fragmentation of reality and knowledge that occurred centuries ago and left its mark on all aspects of culture: religious, scientific, political, artistic, and philosophical alike. Satisfactory empirical evidence may be present to conclude that a Designer made the universe but that we receive this knowledge by faith.

Stephen Jay Gould explains this fragmentation of knowledge and experience by insisting that science and religion belong to Non-Overlapping Magesteria (NOMA): "East is East, and West is West, and never the twain shall meet." The discussion of design raises the possibility that spiritual reality and physical reality are intrinsically related. The old fragmentation may give way to an older integration. As the old West fades, the emerging postmodern culture has a thirst for spirituality and wholeness. Perhaps in this climate a new understanding of reality and the possibilities of human knowledge rooted in the ancient Hebrew understanding of the soul made in the image of God may emerge.

ENDNOTES

Preface
1. We explore this problem at length in our earlier book. See Harry L. Poe and Jimmy H. Davis, *Science and Faith: An Evangelical Dialogue* (Nashville: Broadman & Holman, 2000).

Chapter One
1. S. A. Nigosian, *World Religions: A Historical Approach*, 3rd edition (Boston: Bedford/St. Martin's, 2000), 37–42.
2. Ibid., 45.
3. Ibid., 31.
4. Ibid., 60.
5. Thomas Bulfinch, *Bulfinch's Mythology* (New York: Avenel Books, 1978), 12.
6. Ibid., 4.
7. Nigosian, 196.
8. Bulfinch, 329–30.
9. Ibid., 348–49.
10. Plato, *Timaeus* in *Plato: Selections,* ed. Raphael Demos (New York: Charles Scribner's Sons, 1955), 391.
11. Ibid., 394.
12. Ibid., 396.

Chapter Two
1. Tertullian, *Apology,* XLVI.
2. Tertullian, *The Prescription Against Heretics,* VII.
3. R. M. Wilson, "Mani and Manichaeism," *The Encyclopedia of Philosophy,* vol. 5 (New York: Macmillan Publishing Co., 1972), 149–50.
4. Augustine, *Confessions,* 3.4.7.
5. Ibid., 5.3.4.
6. Ibid., 5.14.25.
7. Ibid.
8. Ibid., 5.10.20.
9. Ibid., 4.7.12.
10. Ibid., 5.10.20.
11. Ibid., 7.12.18.
12. Ibid., 7.14.20–21.
13. Ibid., 5.10.20.

14. Ibid., 5.14.24; 6.3.4.
15. Ibid., 7.17.23.
16. Ibid., 8.11.27.
17. Ibid., 11.4.6.
18. Ibid., 2.5.10.
19. Ibid., 2.3.6.
20. Ibid., 2.6.14.
21. The five proofs of Thomas Aquinas may be found in his *Summa Theologica*, Part I, Question 2, Article 3.
22. Thomas Aquinas, *Aquinas on Creation: Writings on the "Sentences" of Peter Lombard*, trans. Steven E. Baldner and William E. Carroll, Medieval Sources in Translation 35 (Toronto: Pontifical Institute of Medieval Studies, 1997), 134–35.
23. Thomas Aquinas, *Summa Theologica*, 1.2.3.
24. Ibid.
25. Thomas Aquinas, *Aquinas on Creation*, 54.
26. Stephen W. Hawking, *A Brief History of Time* (New York: Bantam Books, 1988), 140–41.
27. John Calvin, *The Institutes of the Christian Religion*, trans. Henry Beveridge, vol. 2 (Grand Rapids: Eerdmans, 1957), 43.
28. Ibid., 51.
29. Ibid., 51–53.
30. Ibid., 53.
31. Ibid., 59.
32. Ibid., 62.
33. For a concise summary of Descartes' principal ideas, see Bernard Williams, "René Descartes," *Encyclopedia of Philosophy*, vol. 1 (New York: Macmillan Publishing Co., 1972), 344–54.
34. Matt. 11:27 "Neither knoweth any man the Father, save the Son, and he to whomsoever the Son will reveal him" (KJV).
35. Isa. 45:15 "Verily, thou art a God that hidest thyself" (KJV). Blaise Pascal, *Pensées*, trans. W. F. Trotter, Great Books of the World, vol. 33 (Chicago: Encyclopedia Britannica, 1955), 4.242. C. S. Lewis quotes from this section of the *Pensées* at the introduction of *The Problem of Pain*.
36. *Pensées*, 3.233.

Chapter Three

1. Amos Funkenstein, *Theology and the Scientific Imagination: from the Middle Ages to the Seventeenth Century* (Princeton: Princeton University Press, 1986), 3.
2. Ernest Campbell Mossner, "Deism," in *The Encyclopedia of Philosophy*, vol. 2 (New York: Macmillan, 1967), 330–31.
3. Bernard Ramm, *Varieties of Christian Apologetics* (Grand Rapids: Baker Book House, 1979), 113.

4. Isaac Newton, *Mathematical Principles of Natural Philosophy*, trans. Andrew Motte (1714; rev. and ed. Florian Cajori; Berkeley, California: University of California Press, 1934), 32 as quoted in John C. Hutchison, "Darwin's Evolutionary Theory and 19th Century Natural Theology," *Bibliotheca Sacra*, 152:335 (July–September 1995).

5. Though published in 1779 after Hume's death, the manuscript had been finished in rough draft since 1751. See J. C. A. Gaskin, ed., "Introduction," *Dialogues Concerning Natural Religion*, by David Hume, Oxford World's Classics (Oxford: Oxford University Press, 1998), xviii.

6. Hume, Part II.

7. Ibid., Part IV.

8. Ibid.

9. Ibid., Part V.

10. Ibid., Part VI.

11. Ibid., Part VII.

12. Ibid., Part VIII.

13. Ibid., Part IX.

14. Ibid., Part X.

15. Ibid.

16. Ibid.

17. William Paley, *Natural Theology: or Evidences of the Existence and Attributes of the Deity, Collected from the Appearances of Nature*, 2nd edition, vol. 1 (Oxford: J. Vincent, 1828), 1–4.

18. See John Hick, *Philosophy of Religion*, 2d ed. (Englewood Cliff, NJ: Prentice-Hall, 1973), 25; Hugh Ross, *The Creator and the Cosmos* (Colorado Springs, CO: NavPress, 1995), 106.

19. Paley, *Natural Theology*, 65.

20. The eight contributors were Thomas Chalmers, John Kidd, William Whewell, Sir Charles Bell, Peter Mark Roget, William Buckland, William Kirby, and William Prout.

21. William Buckland, *Geology and Mineralogy Considered with Reference to Natural Theology*, vol. 1 (London: William Pickering, 1836), viii.

22. Ibid., 130–31.

23. John Brooke and Geoffrey Cantor, *Reconstructing Nature: The Engagement of Science and Religion*, Glasgow Gifford Lectures (Edinburgh: T & T Clark, 1998), 147.

24. Morton O. Beckner, "Darwinism," *The Encyclopedia of Philosophy*, vol. 2 (New York: Macmillan, 1972), 300.

25. Ibid.

26. John Wisdom, *Philosophy and Psychoanalysis* (Oxford: Basil Blackwell, 1953), 154–55 as quoted in Hick, 86.

Chapter Four

1. For a more detailed discussion of this topic, please see Harry L. Poe and Jimmy H. Davis, *Science and Faith: An Evangelical Dialogue* (Nashville: Broadman & Holman, 2000), 65–69.

2. George Greenstein, *The Symbiotic Universe: Life and Mind in the Cosmos* (New York: William Morrow, 1988), 93.

3. In fusion reactions, nuclei are identified by the name of the atom followed by a number. The number represents the number of protons and neutrons present in that nucleus. For example, helium-4 is the name for a helium nucleus whose total number of protons plus neutrons is four.

4. Fred Hoyle, "The Universe: Past and Present Reflection," *Annual Reviews of Astronomy and Astrophysics* 20 (1982): 16.

5. Hugh Ross, *Beyond the Cosmos* (Colorado Springs: NavPress, 1996), 30.

6. Ibid.

7. Carl Sagan, *Cosmos* (New York: Random House, 1980), 298–302.

8. When NASA funding was cut off, SETI quickly raised more than $4 million dollars from technology leaders; such as, Hewlett-Packard cofounders William Hewlett and David Packard, Intel cofounder Gordon Moore, and Microsoft cofounder Paul Allen.

9. In August 2000, astronomers announced discovering a Jupiter-size planet orbiting the star Epsilon Eridani, 10.5 light-years from Earth and the home star of *Star Trek*'s Mr. Spock.

10. Greenstein, 27–28.

11. Martin Gardner, "WAP, SAP, PAP, & FAP" *The New York Times Review of Books* (May 8, 1986), 23.

12. John Archibald Wheeler, "Bohr, Einstein, and the Strange Lesson of the Quantum," in *Mind in Nature*, ed. Richard Q. Elvee (New York: Harper and Row, 1981), 18.

13. John D. Barrow and Frank J. Tipler, *The Anthropic Cosmological Principle* (New York: Oxford University Press, 1986), 677.

14. Ibid., 682.

15. Gardner, 25.

16. Quoted in Heinz R. Pagels, "A Cozy Cosmology," *The Sciences* (March/April 1985), 37.

17. Quoted in Marcus Chown, "Out in the Cold," *New Scientist* 166 (2000): 32.

18. Ibid.

19. Hugh Ross, "Big Bang Model Refined by Fire," in *Mere Creation: Science, Faith & Intelligent Design,* ed. William A. Dembski (Downers Grove, IL: InterVarsity Press, 1998), 372–80.

20. Peter D. Ward and Donald Brownlee, *Rare Earth: Why Complex Life Is Uncommon in the Universe* (New York: Copernicus, 2000). The

authors did an excellent job of presenting the scientific evidence of why the earth is a unique planet.

21. Quoted in Guillermo Gonzalez, "No Other Eden," *Touchstone* (June 2000), 37.

22. William A. Dembski, *Intelligent Design: The Bridge Between Science & Theology* (Downers Grove, IL: InterVarsity Press, 1999), 90–91.

23. Michael J. Behe, "Forward" in William A. Dembski, *Intelligent Design* (Downers Grove, IL: InterVarsity Press, 1999), 10.

24. Hugh Ross, *The Creator and the Cosmos* (Colorado Springs: NavPress, 1993), 125.

25. For a much more thorough and elegant discussion of these and other topics, please see Ross' book, *Beyond the Cosmos*. Ross has a Ph.D. in astronomy and is founder of Reasons to Believe.

26. Ibid., 44.

27. For a wonderful description of a two-dimensional world, please see Edwin A. Abbott, *Flatland* (New York: Dover Publications, 1952).

28. Ross, *Beyond the Cosmos*, 47.

29. Robert Kaita, "Design in Physics and Biology," in *Mere Creation: Science, Faith & Intelligent Design*, ed. William A. Dembski (Downers Grove, IL: InterVarsity Press, 1998), 386.

Chapter Five

1. A representation of the plaque can be seen on the NASA website: http://spaceprojects.arc.nasa.gov/Space_Projects/pioneer/PN10&11.html

2. Carl Sagan, *The Cosmic Connection: An Extraterrestrial Perspective* (New York: Anchor Press, 1973), 30.

3. NASA included a much more ambitious message on the *Voyager 1* and 2 spacecrafts. These spacecrafts carried a twelve-inch gold-plated copper phonograph record containing the sounds and images of earth. Instructions again include the "common mathematics."

4. It is interesting how current scholars deal with Newton's beliefs. In the Microsoft Encarta 98 Encyclopedia article entitled "Newton, Sir Issac," the author Richard S. Westfall states, "In addition to science, Newton also showed an interest in alchemy, mysticism, and theology. Many pages of his notes and writings—especially from the later years of his career—are devoted to these topics. However, historians have found little connection between these interests and Newton's scientific work."

5. All the atoms making up an element have the same number of protons but can have different numbers of neutrons.

6. The exception is helium that has only two electrons.

7. The arrangement is actually more complicated than this. The second shell is divided into two subshells or orbitals. The third shell is divided

into three subshells, and so forth. For the purpose of this book, the shell arrangement is adequate.

8. Whether a covalent molecule is nonpolar or polar also depends upon the three-dimensional structure of the molecule. Considering the three-dimensional structure though is beyond the scope of this book.

9. Samuel Taylor Coleridge, *The Rime of the Ancient Mariner,* st. 9.

10. An interesting discussion of the different ways to pack cannon balls (molecules) is given in the science fiction novel by Kurt Vonnegut Jr., *Cat's Cradle* (New York: Dell Publishing, 1963).

11. Philip J. Davis, Reuben Hersh, and Elena Anne Marchisotto, *The Mathematical Experience,* Study Edition (Boston: Birkhauser, 1995).

12. Ibid., 84.

13. Richard W. Hamming, "The Unreasonable Effectiveness of Mathematics," *American Mathematics Monthly* 87 (1980): 81–90. Eugene P. Wigner, "The Unreasonable Effectiveness of Mathematics in the Natural Sciences," in *Symmetries and Reflections: Scientific Essays of Eugene P. Wigner* (Bloomington, IN: Indiana University Press, 1967), 222–37.

14. Hamming, "The Unreasonable Effectiveness of Mathematics," 81.

15. Ibid., 82.

Chapter Six

1. Sylvia Mader, *Inquiry into Life,* 8th ed. (Dubuque, IA: Wm. C. Brown, 1997), 81.

2. Quoted in Maitland A. Edey and Donald C. Johanson, *Blueprints* (Boston: Little, Brown and Company, 1989), 235.

3. The two other RNA molecules, tRNA and rRNA, are synthesized in a similar manner.

4. If the codon on the mRNA is AUG, the anticodon on the tRNA would be UAC. This tRNA would be transporting the amino acid Met or methionine.

5. For a more thorough discussion of Darwin's theory of evolution, please see Harry L. Poe and Jimmy H. Davis, *Science and Faith: An Evangelical Dialogue* (Nashville, TN: Broadman & Holman, 2000), chapters 7–9.

6. Jacques Barzum, *Darwin, Marx, Wagner: Critique of a Heritage,* 2nd ed. (Chicago: University of Chicago Press, 1941, 1958, 1981), 11.

7. Charles Darwin, *The Origin of the Species,* The Harvard Classics, ed. Charles Eliot, vol. 11 (New York: P.F. Collins & Son, 1909), 511.

8. Ibid., 517.

9. Ibid., 210.

10. Ibid., 523.

11. *Teaching Science in a Climate of Controversy: A View from the American Scientific Affiliation* (Ipswich, MA: American Scientific Affiliation, 1986, 1987, 1989, 1993).

12. The Grants findings are discussed in the Pulitzer Prize winning book: Jonathan Weiner, *The Beak of the Finch: A Story of Evolution in Our Time* (New York: Knopf, 1994).

13. Michael J. Behe, *Darwin's Black Box: The Biochemical Challenge to Evolution* (New York: The Free Press, 1996), 4.

14. Ibid., 5.

15. Ibid., 39.

16. Robert T. Pennock, *Tower of Babel: The Evidence against the New Creationism* (Cambridge, MA: MIT Press, 1999), 271.

17. For a further discussion of this topic, please see Ian G. Barbour, *Religion and Science: Historical and Contemporary Issues* (New York: HarperSanFrancisco, 1997), 106–36.

18. Michael Polanyi, "Life Transcending Physics and Chemistry," *Chemical and Engineering News,* 45:35:54–66 (August 21, 1967).

19. Mader, 40.

20. H. H. Pattee quoted in Nancy R. Pearcey and Charles B Thaxton, *The Soul of Science: Christian Faith and Natural Philosophy* (Wheaton, IL: Crossway Books, 1994), 241.

21. David Hull, "The Limits of Cladism," *Systematic Zoology* 28 (1979), 419.

22. David Hume, "An Enquiry Concerning Human Understanding, Section XI," in *Principle Writings on Religion,* J. C. A. Gaskin, ed. (Oxford: Oxford University Press, 1988), 14.

Chapter Seven

1. Michael Shermer, "Why People Believe in God: An Empirical Study on a Deep Question," *The Humanist,* 59:6:20–26 (November/December 1999). This article comes from Shermer's book *How We Believe: The Search for God in an Age of Science* (New York: W. H. Freeman, 1999).

2. Ian G. Barbour, *Religion and Science: Historical and Contemporary Issues* (New York: HarperSanFrancisco, 1997), 59.

3. Francis Darwin, ed., *Life and Letters of Charles Darwin* (New York: D. Appleton, 1887), 2:273.

4. The scientific books reviewed were Darrell D. Ebbing, *General Chemistry,* 5th ed. (Boston: Houghton Mifflin, 1996), W. Thomas Griffith, *The Physics of Everyday Phenomena,* 2nd ed. (Dubuque, IA: Wm. C. Brown, 1998), Sylvia Mader, *Inquiry into Life,* 8th ed. (Dubuque, IA: Wm. C. Brown, 1997), and Michael A. Seeds, *Foundations of Astronomy* 2nd ed. (Belmont, CA: Wadsworth Publishing, 1988).

5. These texts did not have the words *awe, beauty,* or *wonder* in their indexes: Michael J. Behe, *Darwin's Black Box: The Biochemical Challenge to Evolution* (New York: The Free Press, 1996); Charles Colson and Nancy Pearcey, *How Now Shall We Live?* (Wheaton, IL: Tyndale House, 1999); William Dembski, ed., *Mere Creation: Science, Faith & Intelligent*

Design (Downers Grove, IL: InterVarsity Press, 1998); Hugh Ross, *The Creator and the Cosmos: How the Greatest Scientific Discoveries of the Century Reveal God* (Colorado Springs, CO: NavPress, 1993); and Robert T. Pennock, *Tower of Babel: The Evidence Against the New Creationism* (Cambridge, MA: The MIT Press, 1999). *Beauty* was mentioned in Kitty Ferguson, *The Fire in the Equations: Science, Religion & the Search for God* (Grand Rapids, MI: Eerdmans, 1994) and Ted Peters, ed., *Science & Theology: The New Consonance* (Boulder, CO: Westview Press, 1998).

6. John Brooke and Geoffrey Cantor, *Reconstructing Nature: The Engagement of Science and Religion* (Edinburgh: T&T Clark, 1998), 185–87.

7. William Buckland, *Geology and Mineralogy Considered with Reference to Natural Theology* (London: William Pickering, 1836), 341.

8. Adrian Desmond and James Moore, *Darwin* (New York: Warner Books, 1991), 122.

9. Paul Dirac, "The Evolution of the Physicist's Picture of Nature," *Scientific American* (May 1963), 47.

10. Steven Weinberg, *Dreams of a Final Theory: The Search for the Fundamental Laws of Nature* (New York: Pantheon Books, 1992).

11. Ibid., 133.

12. Michael Polanyi, *Personal Knowledge: Towards a Post-Critical Philosophy* (Chicago: University of Chicago Press, 1962), 133.

13. Weinberg, 98.

14. Charles H. Townes, "Logic and Uncertainties in Science and Religion," in *Science & Theology: The New Consonance*, ed. Ted Peters (Boulder, CO: Westview Press, 1998), 45.

15. Weinberg, 148.

16. A Platonic solid or regular solid is a three-dimensional body with identical faces. The five Platonic solids are the cube, tetrahedron, dodecahedron, icosahedron, and octahedron.

17. Albert Einstein, quoted in John Winokur, *Einstein: A Portrait* (California: Pomegranate Art Books, 1983).

18. Charles Misner, cited by Richard John Neuhaus in *First Things* 18 (Dec. 1991): 63.

19. Brook and Cantor, 226. They quoted Anon, "Is Nature perfect?" *Monthly Journal of Science* (London, 1879): 271–76.

20. Kenneth R. Miller, "Life's Grand Design," *Technology Review* (February/March 1994): 29–30.

21. Kenneth R. Miller, *Finding Darwin's God* (New York: Cliff Street Books, 1999), 101.

22. Michael J. Behe, *Darwin's Black Box: The Biochemical Challenge to Evolution* (New York: The Free Press, 1996), 223.

23. Steven Weinberg, "A Designer Universe?" http://www.physlink.com/essayweinberg.cfm. This Web article was based on a talk Weinberg gave in April 1999 at the "Conference on Cosmic Design" of the American Association for the Advancement of Science.

24. Kitty Ferguson, *The Fire in the Equations: Science, Religion & the Search for God* (Grand Rapids, MI: William B. Eerdmans Publishing Company, 1994), 274.

25. Harry L. Poe and Jimmy H. Davis, *Science and Faith: An Evangelical Dialogue* (Nashville: Broadman & Holman, 2000), 79–81.

26. John Glenn, quoted in "An American in Orbit Talks to His Planet," *U.S. News & World Report,* 52:10:42–44 (March 5, 1962).

27. John Glenn, "Why I Know There Is a God," *The Reader's Digest,* 81:483:37–39 (July 1962).

28. Ibid., 38.

29. "'Modern Magi' Put Moon Flight into Scriptural Perspective," *Christianity Today,* 13:8:36–37 (January 17, 1969).

30. Ibid.

Epilogue

1. Michael J. Behe, "A Mousetrap Defended: Response to Critics," http://www.discovery.org.

INDEX

Index 251